EVERYDAY
PSYCHIC
DEFENSE

About the Author

Cassandra Eason (London, England) is a best-selling author and a broadcaster on the paranormal. She has appeared many times on television and radio throughout the United States, Britain, Europe, and Australia. Cassandra originally trained as a teacher, and, while bringing up her five children, took a psychology honours degree with the intention of training as an educational psychologist.

A seemingly inexplicable psychic experience involving her two-year-old son Jack led to extensive research and the publication of a book on psychic children published by Random House in 1990. Since then, Cassandra has had more than 100 books published and translated into thirteen different languages. Cassandra also runs workshops in Australia and the United Kingdom and tours Australia each year.

Many of her books have been serialised around the world and she has consulted with and contributed to such publications as the UK *Daily Mail, Daily Mirror, Daily Express, People, The Sun, News of the World* magazine, *Spirit and Destiny, Fate and Fortune, Prediction, Best and Bella, Homes and Gardens,* and *Good Housekeeping* and in *Woman's Day* and *New Idea* magazines in Australia. Cassandra has long been acknowledged as a world expert on parent-child intuitive links and has appeared many times on television and radio, including shows such as *Sky News,* ITV's *Strange but True?,* BBC1's *Heaven and Earth,* and *Richard and Judy,* and she has also appeared in a series of mini films with Myleene Klass, and on Sky Living's *Jane Goldman Investigates.*

White Magic *for* Dark Moments

EVERYDAY PSYCHIC DEFENSE

CASSANDRA EASON

Llewellyn Publications
Woodbury, Minnesota

FIRST EDITION
Second Printing, 2018

Cover design: Kevin R. Brown
Interior art: Llewellyn Art Department

Llewellyn Publications is a registered trademark of Llewellyn Worldwide Ltd.

Library of Congress Cataloging-in-Publication Data

Names: Eason, Cassandra, author.
Title: Everyday psychic defense : white magic for dark moments / Cassandra
    Eason.
Description: First Edition. | Woodbury : Llewellyn Worldwide, Ltd, 2017.
Identifiers: LCCN 2017011247 (print) | LCCN 2017003456 (ebook) | ISBN
    9780738750453 (alk. paper) | ISBN 9780738752341 (ebook)
Subjects: LCSH: Magic.
Classification: LCC BF1611 .E185 2017 (ebook) | LCC BF1611 (print) | DDC
    133.4/3—dc23
LC record available at https://lccn.loc.gov/2017011247

Llewellyn Worldwide Ltd. does not participate in, endorse, or have any authority or responsibility concerning private business transactions between our authors and the public.
    All mail addressed to the author is forwarded but the publisher cannot, unless specifically instructed by the author, give out an address or phone number.
    Any Internet references contained in this work are current at publication time, but the publisher cannot guarantee that a specific location will continue to be maintained. Please refer to the publisher's website for links to authors' websites and other sources.

Llewellyn Publications
A Division of Llewellyn Worldwide Ltd.
2143 Wooddale Drive
Woodbury, MN 55125-2989
www.llewellyn.com

Printed in the United States of America

Other Books by Cassandra Eason

10 Steps to Psychic Power
1001 Spells
A Little Bit of Crystals
A Little Bit of Tarot
A Magical Guide to Love & Sex
A Spell a Day
A Year and a Day in Magick
Ancient Egyptian Magic
Angel Magic
Aura Reading
Becoming Clairvoyant
Candle Power
Complete Book of the Tarot
Complete Book of Women's Wisdom
Complete Crystal Handbook
Complete Guide to Faeries and Magical Beings
Complete Guide to Magic and Ritual
Complete Guide to Natural Magick
Complete Guide to Psychic Development
Contact Your Spirit Guides to Enrich Your Life
Crystal Divination for Today's Woman
Crystals for Love and Relationships
Discover Your Past Lives
Encyclopedia of Magic and Ancient Wisdom
Fabulous Creatures, Mythical Monsters: A Handbook
Fragrant Magic
Ghost Encounters: Finding Phantoms and Understanding Them
Illustrated Directory of Healing Crystals
Psychic Awareness
Psychic Power of Children
Smudging and Incense Burning
The Art of the Pendulum
The Magick of Faeries

Dedication

In this special year when I have been given back my life after so nearly dying from heart failure, I dedicate this book to my beloved children, Tom, Jade, Jack, Miranda, and Bill, and my dear grandchildren, Freya and Holly, all of whom kept me going when I was ready to give up. I also dedicate it to my literary editor, John Gold, and to Konnie Gold, my inspiration, dearest friend, and touchstone. This work has been a pure joy to write—and a return to life.

—Cassandra Eason, December 2015

Contents

Disclaimer

The contents of this book are not meant to replace legal protection or help from law enforcement. Readers are advised to contact the proper authorities if they experience harassment, extortion, mental health issues, abuse, or immediate danger. The publisher and the author assume no liability for any injuries caused to the reader that may result from the reader's use of content contained in this publication and recommend common sense when contemplating the practices described in the work.

Introduction:
Beginning Defensive Magic

Magic demands that we harm no one. To do bad magic even for an apparently justifiable purpose is to send out negative energies that come bouncing back on us three times as fiercely and may even give strength to the perpetrators of the harm.

But what if someone is trying to steal your partner quite ruthlessly and cynically out of pure jealousy, spreading lies and gossip about you at work, damaging your business with malpractice or illegal demands for protection money, hacking your computers, or bullying your teenagers or selling them drugs?

What if someone has abused your children and the law stands by wringing its hands while the evil continues to be perpetrated on other innocents? What if you are plagued by a stalker, have unpleasant neighbours, or have a vicious-tongued relative who is trying to split your family?

Suppose a neighbour or relative actually cursed you over a dispute, or you or your loved ones are convinced an unknown if suspected source filled with envy is jinxing you with the evil eye, a damaging form

1

of jealousy recognised from ancient Egyptian times onwards and in almost every culture. Things go wrong. You feel spooked. Illnesses, accidents, minor disasters, and ill fortune come one after the other far beyond the normal course of events. You feel, and probably are, under psychic attack.

You can and should powerfully and magically defend yourself and loved ones and indeed fight back psychically, without tipping your thoughts, words, and actions into the realms of cursing and black magic spellcasting or paying a negative practitioner to cast malice on your behalf. This book will teach you how to win against such adversaries without damaging your own karma.

Of course you also need, where possible, to seek legal or official redress for wrongdoing, as the more we do on the earthly plane the more effective magic is. Taking precautions for your physical safety and that of loved ones is essential. However, there will be times when no one will listen or believe us, and magic can in such cases stir the energies in your favour and make action in the everyday world more effective. Together the earthly efforts and magical input make the perfect team.

Ancient and Modern Evil

The Internet has made knowledge of and dabbling in demonology commonplace, especially among curious but vulnerable teenagers who may recite names of ancient devils out of sheer spite and unwittingly release powers that can seriously mess with their minds (more of this in chapter 11). Ouija boards can wreak havoc on the young who have unwittingly summoned low-life spirits in an apparently fun midnight séance during a sleepover, only to discover the dark presence haunts them day and night.

According to my own research over a number of years, there has also been a sharp rise in sexual demon attacks, which were first described in biblical times, particularly among women in their twenties and thirties, and this is such a taboo subject that many suffer in secret and dread going to bed. I have investigated many hundreds of cases over more than thirty years, beginning when I was an honourary research fellow at the Alister Hardy Religious Experience Research Centre, and many people talk to me as I travel the world giving consultations, perhaps having never spoken to anyone before about this problem.

All these issues and more will be dealt with in this book in order to explain what is happening and to suggest effective remedies you can practise yourself against psychic attacks at all levels, using ordinary household materials or those easily obtainable from supermarkets, from health stores, or online.

What Is Psychic Defense?

Psychic defense or protection is the natural human ability to detect and deflect free-floating negativity that can affect us in daily life and to send back deliberate malice to its source. For many of us, this protective power is never activated or even recognised. Yet we are our own best psychic defenders, and by the end of this book you will feel secure, confident, and able to direct your own life positively and powerfully without malicious interference or attack. You will also learn how to cast protection around homes, families, workspace, vehicles, and valuable possessions.

Understanding Psychic Defense

How can protection that stems from the mind and not physical weapons or barbed wire boundary fences be possible even against physical attack? Naturally, the process is partly psychological in that, if we feel safe, we unconsciously radiate confident "don't mess with me or mine" signals from our personal energy field that are picked up by would-be predators, mind-game players, and attackers who automatically back off.

As a bonus, psychic protection, though mainly defensive except in extreme cases where we need to psychically kick ass big style, has a springboard effect that opens our energy fields to new opportunities and positive relationships.

However, psychic protection is far more than pure psychology.

We know that everything is made of moving and changing energies and that the human mind has a natural ability to affect energies both in its immediate environment and across oceans in the case of technological attack via our electronic gadgets. Using the spells I suggest in this book or ones you devise yourself with the materials and methods I suggest in the appendices, you can push away with this spontaneous power of the mind what is potentially harmful to yourself and loved ones or what drains your energies, as well as draw to you what is advantageous.

The Origins of Psychic Protection

Formal protective techniques date back thousands of years to the ancient Babylonian and Egyptian worlds. In ancient Egypt, protection—often in the form of bone or crystal amulets, spoken defensive words, or written hieroglyph spells—was sought against the dangers of daily life, the crocodiles and hippopotami that threatened the Nile fishermen, the annual flood that brought life but also took it away, and restless tomb spirits and invaders. Crystal amulets were also placed on the body of the mummy to safely guide a deceased person's soul through the perils of the afterlife to everlasting happiness.

Modern psychic protection is still rooted in these old techniques, which have similarities in different ages and across cultures. For we still suffer from the envy and malice of others, though these may be expressed through cyberattack via social media sites or by the hacking into personal and business data on our computers, as well as the perils of long-distance travel, terrorism, and urban living.

Protecting Ourselves and Loved Ones from Psychic, Physical, or Psychological Attack

Each chapter of this book explains how a particular form of defensive magic works and suggests simple but powerful harm-repelling spells and daily defenses you can create yourself.

Indeed, many ordinary foods or household items, once we have endowed them with power, can be our most effective defensive weapons for attacks that frequently occur in our everyday world and workplace. For example, against a spiteful colleague or neighbour, take half a lemon and press it down in a deep bowl of salt, saying as you do so, "As your spite dries up, so you, (name), trouble me no more with your vicious gossip." When the lemon is dried, bury it, and with it dispose of the malice.

Throughout the book are numerous equally simple methods, and I describe how they helped people fight back against psychic attack. I use actual cases and spells I have created for clients, friends, and family, though of course I will change names and details to protect confidentiality. The book is divided into two parts: the first is the basic methods of defensive magic, and the second is specific kinds of negative magic and psychological and psychic attacks as well as special ways of repelling these. However, in practise you can mix and match most of the spells for any purpose.

How to Know if You Are Under Psychic Attack

If things are going wrong in your life, you have not necessarily been cursed or psychically attacked, though continuing misfortune may make you feel as though you have. Your distress may be caused by lack of sleep; being physically unwell; or anxiety about relationships, finances, or work, and as a result you may experience a constant free-floating jittery feeling and continually break or spill things, and everything you do seems to go wrong.

In such cases, first check any physical or earthly causes for your distress. If you still feel under attack or sense nasty vibes bombarding you, you may well be right that someone is thinking maliciously about you, gossiping behind your back, or even cursing you.

Almost always the person who has cursed or ill wished you will let you know, and malicious e-mails or social media attacks are the modern version of leaving a dead chicken at your door and are equally nasty.

If you get sudden stabbing pains around your heart or in your temples and you have no other physical symptoms (if these persist, get them checked medically), then a person may be thinking negatively of you and fuming over some imagined wrongdoing or injustice, sending out what are the equivalent of poison arrows. Equally, sudden and continuing pins and needles, again without any obvious cause, can also be a symptom of someone physically or emotionally sticking pins in an image of you or simply sending out needles of spite, unkind thoughts, or jealousy.

If computers or tablets malfunction without logical cause, smart phones won't connect, e-mails don't reach their destination (technology is remarkably sensitive to bad vibes), or you lose or break a number of items when normally you are very careful; if you, family members, or pets have a series of minor accidents and unexplained and persistent minor illnesses that do not respond to treatment; if you feel spooked and feel like you are being watched; or if you suddenly lose confidence and concentration, you may have been ill wished, cursed, or had the evil eye put on you or loved ones. (Read more on the evil eye and ill wishing in chapter 9.)

Equally, if you constantly feel exhausted, jittery, or unwell in the presence of particular people, it may be necessary to create psychic shields as described in chapters 2 or 3 to protect yourself from an emotional vampire or follow rituals to cut cords with them.

Can You Cast Spells on Behalf of Others?

Certainly you can on behalf of a young person or someone who is sick and vulnerable by adding "if and when this is right to be for (name)" to the spell. For adults you would ask permission unless they were too sick or perhaps in a dire emotional state.

While you should attack no one, it is permissible to act defensively against someone's destructive behaviour towards you or a loved one and to shield you against their words, actions, or indeed free-floating jealous thoughts from someone who you know wishes you ill.

Creating Your Own Defensive Spells

Throughout the book I give many examples of specific spells as well as describe the situations that prompted them to be cast in people's lives. However, most useful is to be able to cast your own spells for every defensive occasion and, even if you have never used magic before, spellcasting is remarkably easy. Just like a cooking recipe, all you need do is to add the right ingredients, and these I have listed throughout the book and in the appendices. Then you follow a set format, adding your own words as feels right. For speaking from the heart, especially when protecting those we love, is a hundred times more powerful than the most carefully crafted spell words of others.

Of course, with any negative situations it is important to attempt to resolve matters with legal or practical responses and physical protection. However, casting your own spells or following mine will strengthen both your determination and positive powers sent from your own energy field to overcome the threat and to achieve a positive result.

Below is a template from which you can create your own defensive spells that can be adapted to most needs and occasions. However, the main reason I am describing basic defensive spellcasting at this early stage is so that you can follow the spells as I describe them throughout the book. In this way you will understand why and how I am choosing the methods and particular format I suggest.

The following is an all-purpose spell to stop any negative attacks or forces, and if you only ever followed this, you could repel most psychic and psychological attacks. Read through the following section and then set the ingredients I suggest on a table, and you are ready to go.

All-Purpose Spell Template
Stage A: Define the Problem and the Ideal Outcome

This is called the "intention" of the spell. It might be to bind someone from bullying your partner at work, to stop a huge corrupt corporation from swallowing up your business, or to reduce the power of an addiction slowly destroying a loved one.

Defense can be against inner as well as outer demons, a phobia ruining your life, a manipulative person who claims to be your friend and fills you with guilt when you say no to their demands, or a relative who regularly drains your energies.

By naming or writing the intention and ideal outcome you are establishing your purpose for defense on the energy field of life and so giving it form and life. Some practitioners used the spoken or written word instead of a symbol.

Stage B: Represent the Intention of the Spell Symbolically

To represent the intention magically most people use a symbol as part of the spell.

Let's start with a cord or strong thread as an all-purpose symbol for the purpose of learning spellcasting. Indeed, for any psychic defense you can use an all-purpose thin red cord (red being the fiercely protective colour of Mars and the mighty Archangel Camael, who rides on a leopard) or a strong piece of red thread long enough to tie three knots in the centre to bind from harm.

You can of course use any appropriate symbol (for example, a key to prevent burglary); a crystal, whose meanings are listed in appendix C (for example, pink rose quartz for calling back love where someone has come between you); a bag of herbs as in appendix D, each of which has a different significance (such as tarragon, called the dragon's herb, to counteract threats); or a featureless clay figure with a stone where the mouth should be to stop gossip or lies.

You can tie the knotted thread round any symbol for the purpose of learning basic spellcasting, and when you adapt and understand spellcasting in more detail as you work through the book, you can omit the cord.

Stage C: Generate the Power

Generating power to transform your intention into effective action both on the psychic and the earthly plane is the essence of every spell.

Collect Your Ingredients and Tools

In appendix B I have listed specific colours to use in candle lighting, but in any defensive spell you can work with a single white candle. White represents the light of the Archangel Michael and the power of the sun to transform darkness into light and can be substituted for any other colour in protective spellcasting.

You will also need an incense stick, either a tree fragrance such as cedar, eucalyptus, or pine (which are very cleansing) or, if in a dire situation, a strong incense of the Archangel Camael, Angel of Mars, such as dragon's blood, tarragon, or any spice (such as ginger). Alternatively, use Archangel Michael's frankincense or copal.

You can add salt, representing the magical element or substance earth, as a cleanser and water to enable the spell energies to easily flow, but the aspects of air to stir action (the incense) and the fire to ignite the spell energies (the candle flame) are most important in defensive spells.

Indeed, a candle represents all four of the magical elements traditionally used in spellcasting to create the fifth magical element, aether or akasha, in which magical changes take place. The wax of the unlit candle represents the earth, the smoke and any fragrance represents the air, the flame is the fire, and the melting wax represents the water.

The words you use in any spell, often repetitive and/or rhyming and spoken progressively faster and louder to build up the power, also generate energy. The ancient Egyptians, the first true magicians, believed words were power, since the first sunrise was manifest when Thoth the wise god spoke the words that gave life to the creator Ptah's concept of the world. For this reason, you can also write words on paper as a spell symbol and burn them in the candle flame or speak the intention words and ideal outcome progressively louder and faster during the spell ending in step 3. This can be done in addition to cord tying.

STEP 1: BEGINNING THE SPELL

Light the candle and name first yourself to establish your identity and confidence. Name the perpetrator of the nastiness or "persons unknown." Then ask aloud for whatever you need to bind or stop a negative process, person, or behaviour.

Ask the blessings and protection of your personal guardian angels or the ultimate defensive archangels, Michael or Camael. I will introduce further archangels later in the book and in appendix A.

Step 2: Raising the Spell Energies

Take the cord and pass both ends in turn through the flame so they do not catch alight. As you do this, say what or who you need to be bound from harming you or loved ones and the desired timescale, remembering that, for example, you need to bind bullying in the workplace until you get a new job or justice through official channels. The words and actions increase the power within the symbol, in this case the red cord.

For binding or preventing someone or a situation from harm, tie three knots in the centre of the cord, saying, as you tie each one, words such as these:

> *Light is stronger than darkness,*
> *Blessings are stronger than curses.*
> *By the power of the light and the angels*
> (name any you asked for blessings at the start of the spell),
> *I bind and tie*
> (name the harmful person, people, or situation)
> *Three by three from*
> (name what you wish to stop happening)
> *To* (name yourself, any family members,
> or business colleagues who are adversely affected).

Do not join the ends of the cord.

When you use an additional symbol you can, after passing the cord through the flame, tie it round the symbol and continue the spell with the tied symbol.

You can of course create your own spell words, and often these will come spontaneously and from the heart, and because of that they will have great power.

From the candle, light your incense stick. In doing so you are joining the generative power of fire (the candle) with the transformative energies of air (the incense).

Holding the cord in the hand you do not write with, write this in the air round the cord using the incense stick like a smoke pen:

Bound be from troubling me and (add names of anyone else who
needs protection whom you are seeking to help).

Writing in smoke imprints the written form of the intention into
the aether, the magical space where magic takes place, adding to the
power of the spoken word. For additional power you can speak the
words as you write them in smoke. Again create your own binding
words.

STEP 3: RELEASING THE POWER

This is the most important part of any defensive spell, as the power
catapults into the cosmos to be transformed into results in the everyday world—the moment of release.

Set the cord in front of the candle. Blow out the candle so that the
light enters the cord and then say words such as these:

So shall it be that I/we are free,
in the time and manner that is for the highest good for all.

Blowing out the candle frees or releases the power of the spell to
ricochet into the cosmos, bounce back into the daily world, and bind
the target of the spell who is causing the angst. You would extinguish
or snuff out a candle if you want to shut down the energies.

Hang the empowered cord in a safe place until the spell timescale
you specified is over, and then cast it into running water or burn it, so
marking the end of the spell.

If you did use a symbol, keep that in a purse or bag until after the
specified timescale, and then bury it.

Repeat the spell with a new cord (and, if desired, symbol) before
getting rid of the old one if there are still issues or the cord is fraying
if an unspecified time limit.

The cord acts as an ongoing repository of power and a reminder
that the spellcaster is free. If there is doubt, the spellcaster can hold
the cord and repeat the words to reinforce the determination gener-
ated by the spell.

Virtually all spells follow the same stages, and I will describe suggested additions as you progress through different concepts.

This basic spell is called a binding spell because it ties up harm and is one of the most effective and common methods of defensive magic. In the next chapter I will describe in detail the techniques of binding magic and the way it works as well as specific case studies and spells to bind nasty words, thoughts, or actions coming your way.

Binding magic is a powerful form of psychic defense to block the effects of disturbing or threatening behaviour or influences from harming you or those you love and to tie up any destructive behaviours or fears that hold you back.

Part
I

Protecting Yourself
from Evil and Malice

Binding Magic

Binding magic is especially useful when banishing magic against danger, mind control, or threats. Though banishing magic is strong, because of circumstances, we may not be able to banish a person either by earthly means or magically from our life or personal space—for example, a vicious-tongued relative for whom we care, who is physically frail. They need us in their lives, but we do not need the dripping poison. However, we can bind the relative's hurtful remarks that may be upsetting our children.

Hand in hand with advice that may in the case of the angry relative fall on deaf ears, we can often, through binding what is disruptive and hurtful, bring harmony to a situation.

Though in later chapters I deal with issues surrounding paranormal evil, 95 percent of cases I help are caused by human issues that strike at the heart of the home and workplace fueled by jealousy, resentment, and a desire for domination.

Binding magic can offer time and breathing space to find a new job if we are in a bullying workplace or time to get debt collectors off our backs while we get practical help. It can offer advice or stop an ex-partner from harassing us until we get legal protection, which can take months if the attacker is very devious and makes sure no one else hears the threats. In addition, since binding can be continued indefinitely, the person being bound may, as often happens, soften their attitudes or move on as a result of the binding.

Let's start with an example of how a binding spell worked in practise. The spell I sent can be used by anyone who is facing intimidation or bullying, whether from unpleasant neighbours or in a work or domestic situation.

Binding Wrongdoers from Harming You or Loved Ones by Intimidation, Violent Actions, or Threats

I was asked to cast a binding spell for Lorraine and her sister Becky, who were living in an apartment block in a large industrial American city and were terrified of the drug dealers next door. Lorraine had informed the police, but because they were overwhelmed by problems in the area, they managed no more than a routine call and just logged the complaints on intimidation, saying Lorraine needed to provide evidence. The drug dealers were very clever and laughed at Lorraine after the police had gone, threatening to kill her dog if she complained again.

Lorraine asked me to carry out the spell on her behalf, and I sent her a copy of what I was doing. Then she also decided to do the spell herself, as it contains simple instructions and details. I have included this spell below, and it can be adapted to any purpose. You will recognise the format from the template given in the introduction.

Lorraine e-mailed me a week later to say that she was no longer afraid, and the drug dealers seemed less troublesome. This could have been because she was feeling more confident through the spell energies she was absorbing, and so her more powerful personal "back off" vibes made the drug dealers less unpleasant when they met her on the stairways and front entrance.

However, within three weeks the drug dealers unexpectedly moved out in the middle of the night, leaving almost everything, although they had been in their apartment for many months. I suspect that the drug dealers were revealed in their true light to other even nastier people or that the law had rumbled them, and they had to move on fast. Magic can work in all kinds of unexpected ways and, once you bind someone's behaviour from harming you, often karma kicks in, in unexpected ways.

. . . .
Spell to Bind Someone from Causing Intimidation, Violent Actions, or Threats

Ingredients and Tools

Two small, clay, featureless dolls
A dragon's blood incense stick, the fiercest fragrance
A purple candle for Cassiel, the archangel of protection of the
  vulnerable, who is said to ride on a dragon

Timing

Saturday, the day of Cassiel, who imposes boundaries and limitations, and also the planet Saturn

The Spell

Set the clay figures in front of the candle. Light the candle and say,

> *By this light your darkness is revealed,*
> *By this light this binding shall be sealed.*

From the candle, light the incense stick and, holding the incense like a smoke pen, weave a smoke incense curtain of knot shapes like very tight spirals in the air round the figures, saying,

> *You,* (name the perpetrator[s] of harm if known), *are bound from*
> *harassing and molesting or disturbing me/us.*
> *You are tied till you are revealed in your own true light.*
> *Gone are your victims, gone from your sight.*

Extinguish the candle, saying,

> *May your power to harm me/us be gone*
> *With the dimming of this light,*
> *Gone are your victims, gone from your sight.*

Leave the incense to burn. Once the incense is burned, scatter the cool ashes over the dolls and put the dolls in a dark cloth bag out of sight in a dark cupboard, saying,

May the mists remain,
You cannot harm again,
For bound you are,
Till you are revealed in your true light,
And wrong becomes right.

Once the matter is resolved, roll the dolls back into a clay ball and put the ball in the garbage.   · · · · · · ·

Binding Spite and Malice against Vulnerable Family Members

A very common dilemma I encounter professionally in my psychic counselling work in Australia, Sweden, and the United Kingdom is when an ex's new partner is hostile to the children of the earlier relationship. We cannot banish the new partner from our ex-partner's life, because our ex chose this person and is part of the children's life.

However, we can bind the ill effects of spite or unkindness on the children, as sadly sometimes a new person will resent the children as a reminder of the earlier relationship, and talking often just generates denials or even greater hostility.

For example, Bethany is the stepmother of Georgina's children and has lived up to the reputation of the wicked stepmother, blatantly favouring her own children and being extremely spiteful to eight-year-old Susan and six-year-old Billy. The courts insist there must be access, as Bethany is extremely devious and is publicly loving to the children, and the frequent pinch marks and small bruises are explained away to social workers as the children play fighting and the children making up stories to please their mother. Georgina wants the children to spend time with their father, but she needs to stop Bethany from making the children unhappy.

I sent details of the following binding to Georgina to restrain Bethany's unpleasant behaviour towards the children. After the spell, when they were with their father, Georgina kept the cord wrapped around a picture of the children, and over the following weeks Georgina said the children told her Bethany was out a lot and when home ignored all the children, even her own. Within six months she had moved out with her children, having cleared out her partner's bank account and credit cards and gone abroad with an old lover, leaving her own elderly parents to care for *her* children.

It is hard with magic to trace precisely the course of events, but the binding spell results were achieved and Georgina's ex is now with a nice woman who dotes on the children. Georgina neither asked nor cast a spell to break up the relationship as that was clearly happening in the background already. I gave a version of the following spell to Georgina.

. . . .
Spell to Bind Someone from Causing Physical or Emotional Harm

You can adapt this spell to protect yourself or those you care for who are vulnerable, especially if legal or official help is not forthcoming. I believe it is totally acceptable to cast protection around children and those who cannot protect themselves in the same way you would physically defend them with words or actions.

Ingredients and Tools

Three hairs from the hairbrush of each of the vulnerable people and
   three from your own, regardless of whether or not you are including yourself in the protection, to establish the psychic protection
   between yourself and those you are protecting. If you can't get
   hairs or don't want to use them, use red thread.
A long red cord and a red candle
A photo of yourself or whomever you are casting the spell for
A dish of soil

Timing

Tuesday after dark

The Spell

Light the candle, saying,

> *Still your tongue, (name perpetrator), soften your words.*
> *Your unkindness shall no more be heard.*
> *Do not harm them by word or deed.*
> *So do I bind you, this binding shall you heed.*

Knot each hair along the cord, saying for each,

> *I bind my strength, I wind my strength.*
> *Protect (name) when they are with you.*
> *So shall it be, (name perpetrator again).*
> *Your viciousness is through.*

Extinguish the candle by inverting it in soil (a good way of extinguishing candles and incense sticks in any form of binding, banishing, or limiting magic), saying,

> *Your power to hurt is ended,*
> *Gone and done. I have won.*

Wrap the cord and knot it three times round the picture, and if possible touch it before meeting with the perpetrator or potential confrontation.

· · · · · · ·

Binding Magic in Your Everyday World

Though binding magic is most frequently used against a known person or organisation that is doing damage to you or loved ones, you can also restrain in advance known or as-yet-unknown predators you fear may enter your home or area to attack you or loved ones or if you must undertake a dangerous journey.

Binding can also positively hold in check destructive habits, fears, or phobias or stabilise a rapidly deteriorating situation at work or an increasingly abusive or emotionally draining relationship until you feel strong enough to take practical steps to resolve the problem or move on. You can even bind the effects of an incurable illness from getting worse, and bind symptoms if you are suffering daily chronic pain. (More about this in the section on binding knot magic.)

However, it would be counterproductive to try to bind someone you love to stay with you if they are behaving badly or have become indifferent. Unwilling love is always destructive, and holding on to love gone wrong will stop you from finding someone new who would be devoted and good for you.

You can specify how long you wish the binding to be for. For example:

- Until this cord or clay figure decays
- For three months or until they learn the error of their ways or are shown in their true light
- Indefinitely

Repeating the binding weekly or monthly can build up the power if a situation is dire.

Magical Timings for Binding Spells

For a binding spell in which the hold of the wrongdoer is strong, use the night of the full moon when the sun opposes the moon in the sky. Afterwards, the slower energies of the following waning moon days will spontaneously bind into inaction the now much looser and less powerful grip the perpetrator has over the victim.

You can repeat the spell on subsequent full moon nights if necessary to further weaken the hold. This can be effective, for example, if you are trying to break free of a lover's manipulative hold over you, but you keep weakening. The minute the moon turns full is most effective to begin the spell. You can find this time online, in diaries, or in the weather section of a paper. Alternatively, use any or all of the three evenings at the end of any moon cycle.

I recommend Saturdays after dark for ongoing or emotionally charged bindings, the day of Saturn the planet as well as the protective Archangel Cassiel, and Tuesdays, for Archangel Camael and the planet and Roman god Mars, for powerful, urgent bindings.

You can combine these energies in any way you wish. These are also good times for banishing magic, which I describe in chapter 4.

Binding Knot Magic

Binding knot magic, which you met in the introduction when I was describing basic spellcasting, is remarkably simple, as power lies in the words you speak, in the knot tying, and in the intention or purpose that you bind into the knots. You can use absolutely any thread, piece of wool, thin curtain cord, or ribbon.

Plaiting and Knotting

Plaiting and knotting cords or wool triples the effect. For example, in an unstable situation like spiralling debt or an impossible workload, the first thread length of a double-plaited knot cord could symbolically represent holding the situation steady and prevent the problem from getting worse. The second thread plaited to it would signify magically building up your inner stamina and finding practical help to fight back effectively when the time is right.

Knot the double cord at the top and name what you are binding. Tie a second knot halfway down to bind yourself or loved ones from all harm, and tie the third at the bottom (with the option of tying it to the beginning of the cord in a loop) for the time for which you are making the binding.

Combining Colours

Use three strands of red, white, and black wool for making protective travel bracelets to bind all from attacking you or stealing your possessions while travelling and while on holiday or staying away for business. As you plait, say,

Bind and wind protection in,
Safe from malice,
Secure from danger,
From accident or threat of stranger.

Tie the ends together with nine knots, one after the other, saying,

Nine times the sacred knot I tie,
Be safe on earth, on sea and sky.

You can plait wool in three healing colours (such as green, white, and blue or purple) to bind an illness. As you plait, say,

Bind the sickness, bind the pain,
In the binding of these knots,
make me (or name the person for whom you are making the bracelet) *free/whole/well again.*

Tie the ends together with three knots, one after the other, saying,

Three times all illness do I tie,
Be healed by earth and sea and sky.

If the illness is progressive or debilitating, then adapt the words to ask for relief and peace, remembering that all kinds of medical spontaneous remissions and recoveries can occur even in seemingly hopeless situations.

Number of Knots

NINE

Nine is the traditional length measure of a knot cord or string, whether you tie three, seven, or nine knots, the customary number. Use any multiple of nine-centimetre cord or thread, as nine centimetres may be a little short for holding more than three knots, as used in the introduction.

SEVEN

Seven knots can be used for binding fears, phobias, illnesses, or an ongoing issue in which emotions run deep and may require time to resolve.

Use these tying formations or just tie the knots left to right:

6—2—4—1—5—3—7 or 6—4—2—1—3—5—7

FOUR

If you are being threatened and you need to bind debt or financial issues, tie a blue cord or ribbon with four knots to give yourself breathing space. Tie the first knot about a quarter of the way down the cord, saying,

> *Knot one I make,*
> *The flow I break,*
> *Outgoings bind,*
> *Money find,*
> *Within this knot.*

Tie a second knot about halfway down the cord, as you do so saying the same chant but changing the first words to "Knot two I make." Tie a third knot about three quarters of the way down the cord, as you do so repeating the chant but changing the words to "Knot three I make."

For knot four at the end of the cord, say,

> *Knot four, the last,*
> *Outgoings past,*
> *Money bound,*
> *Solvency found.*

Hang the knot cord inside the front door and touch it each morning to deter debt collectors and threatening letters. Four is the number of limitation and Saturn.

Personalisation

Personalise knot spells, as Georgina did, with your hair. For example, if you have long hair, you can knot seven or nine hairs from your hairbrush into the cord before you begin the spell. If you were protecting a partner or child, you could legitimately use their hairs, one to three from each person you are protecting, according to the intensity of the binding. If you cannot or prefer not to use hair, blow softly three times on each end of the cord and the centre before beginning the spell to endow it with your essence and power.

You can use the same binding empowerment for each knot, saying words such as these:

> *I bind, I wind protection in,*
> *As the knots are tied, binding begins.*

Placement of Knot Cord

Hang the empowered knot cord somewhere it is not easily noticed but where the air will circulate. For protecting land or property, you have the option of hanging it from a tree on the land and letting it decay naturally (using biodegradable cord, of course).

Whenever you have doubts or come under threat after the original binding, touch each of the knots in turn and say or think,

> *May* (name) *be bound from harm for the highest good*
> *and with the purest intent.*

Instead of hanging the cord up, if the perpetrator is persistent or particularly unpleasant, freeze the knotted cord in the coldest part of your freezer in a container. This is effective to hold things stable and bound, to keep a pressing debt or legal matter against you under control, to keep a chronic illness from getting worse, or to address a threat of anger, physical damage, or violence.

Alternatively, you can add the power of fire. Light a beeswax or fast-melting, pure wax candle secured on a flat tray, and press a blue cord tied in three knots into the melted wax to bind someone from lying about you in court or at work. Blue is the colour of justice. When the wax is cool, cut out a circle of wax with the cord in it and keep it in a blue cloth knotted three times.

Binding a Figure

Use knots to bind a person who is gossiping or making trouble, who is influencing your teenagers towards drugs or alcohol, or who will not leave you alone. Make a featureless figure out of self-hardening clay or children's play clay, or make a wax image. Melt a beeswax candle or soften a sheet of beeswax with a hair dryer to fashion a wax image.

Tie a piece of red cord or string just below the solar plexus (the seat of power) on the figure, secured with three, seven, or nine knots, according to the degree of threat, to prevent the named person represented by the image from doing harm. Say,

> (Name), *I bind you not with ill intent.*
> *No malice towards you is meant,*
> *But from* (name troublesome behaviour) *are you bound,*
> *Till good changes are in you found.*
> *May you discover the error of your ways,*
> *Until then binding stays.*

The advantage of clay and dough is that as the clay or dough figure naturally crumbles, so does the hold of the perpetrator. This will not harm the person, and you should keep the figure wrapped in soft pink fabric for the duration of the binding.

When the matter is resolved, free the created figure from any connection with the actual bound person by wafting the smoke of an incense stick over it counterclockwise. Bury the now magically empty figure beneath a fragrant plant, or if it has not crumbled, roll the clay back into a ball and replace it in a new binding spell with a new image if necessary.

Alternatively, you can cut out and sew a small, featureless, fabric poppet or doll from a piece of white cloth with red thread. Put inside the name of the perpetrator of the harm written on white paper crossed through in red, and say,

> *May s/he be bound from* (name negative behaviour)
> *until s/he learns the error of their ways.*

Add defensive herbs such as chopped nettles, dried sage, rosemary, thyme, and parsley. Sew up the head afterwards. I strongly disapprove of stabbing the figure with the needle or leaving the needle in the middle (just below the solar plexus).

When the matter is resolved, unpick the figure and dispose of the contents. There is no time limit.

You can also make a poppet to bind pain or a chronic illness from parts of the body by adding the source of the illness to the paper and naming it and not the person.

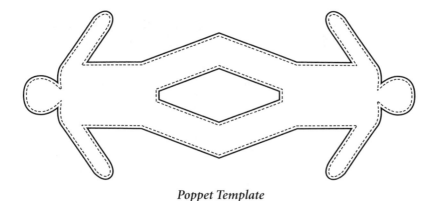

Poppet Template

Smoke Knots

If for any reason you cannot use physical knots, you can draw knot shapes, like spirals in incense smoke in the air, with your index finger of the hand you write with or with a pointed crystal.

For safe travel, weave nine lavender or rose incense smoke knot shapes in the air in a circle round a circle of luggage and travel documents, plus pictures of any small children and pets who will be travelling with you, saying,

I bind you to me totally,
From thief and vandal, loss, mislay.
Loved ones, I bind you not to stray.
May none harm or take you away.

Other Kinds of Binding Spells

Burying Items

Cast binding protection round your home by burying in the ground nine rusty iron or steel nails, each bent with pliers to form a knot shape, in a sealed container if animals dig there, saying as you bury each,

The iron of Mars, keep away
All harm from my home
And loved ones each day.

If you have weight issues or problems with smoking, drugs, or alcohol, it is often hard to go cold turkey by totally banishing the problem unless you are very strong willed. Bury the item or a dark-coloured stone on which you have scratched words or an image of what is to be bound (a cigarette, for example, to give up smoking) with a diagonal cross drawn through it. Bury it under a thriving bush or plant, saying,

Mother Earth,
Bind this, my craving,
Till I desire it no more.

Freeze the cigarette in a sealed container.

When tempted to light a cigarette, draw the above spell words over it in the air invisibly with the index finger of the hand you do not write with.

Paper and Red Ink

To bind an angry or abusive person from whom you cannot immediately walk away, or if you are waiting for an abuse or violence case to come to court and you fear the restraining orders will not be effective to keep them away, write the person's name on a small square of white paper over and over again in red ink. Then put a diagonal cross right through it and say,

> *So are you* (name) *bound from anger/abuse towards me*
> (or name loved one),
> *Until matters I/*(name) *can be free of you or the law be invoked.*

Fold the paper as small as possible. Put the paper in a small plastic container, half-filled with water, in the coldest part of the freezer.

Crystals

You can also place a tiny rose quartz in the mouth of a clay figure to bind a gossip, a spiteful person, a persistently barking dog, or noisy neighbours. Press a crystal or button into the mouth of each offending clay person or animal, saying for each,

> *Disruptive* (or list noisy, antisocial, or complaining behaviour as is
> appropriate) *can you no longer be.*
> *I bind you to be neighbourly.*

Wrap a layer of cotton wool around each figure and tie it with three wool knots, saying for each,

> *Disruptive* (or name behaviour) *dare you no longer be.*
> *I command you live in harmony.*
> *Bound are you indefinitely.*

Place the wrapped figure or figures inside a drawer. Once the problem is resolved, throw the crystals into running water and reroll the clay, if it has not crumbled, into a ball and bury it or the crumbled figures.

Empty Boxes

For someone who is threatening you physically or intimidating a member of your family, blow into a small empty box three times.

Take a padlock and chain and put the key from it in the box, saying,

> *I bind you thus from harming me*
> (or name person under threat).
> *I take away the key.*

Wrap the chain round the box, close the padlock, and take the box to the local garbage site, saying,

> *You are bound till the key be found.*

You can also adapt the words to protect your home if you are going away.

Creating Your Own Binding Spells

The ideas I have suggested in this chapter are templates for you to make your own binding spells that are exactly right for your unique situation. Read through the basic spell format in the introduction if you wish to remind yourself of how spellcasting works. This is a more specific and stronger spell format for binding and can be adapted for absolutely any form of defensive binding needed, including paranormal attack and curses.

Decide first who or what is to be bound and how you intend to symbolically represent the person to be bound, whether by knots, a clay figure, or their name written on paper or scratched on a stone.

The Spell

Start your binding spell by lighting a candle or visualising a sphere of light and stating who you are and whom or what you wish to bind, including your own fears or despair that may be making a bad situation even worse when you wake at 2:00 a.m. (called by some the Hour of the Wolves) worrying. If necessary, you can do the entire ritual in your mind, saying the words internally and visualising the actions, perhaps subtly moving your hands as if you are tying knots. For example, it is a family occasion and the perpetrator of harm has unexpectedly arrived, or you are at a meeting at work and know instinctively someone is going to try to humiliate you.

After lighting the candle in an external ritual, name the person to be bound aloud or say the name in your mind as you make the knots physically in a cord or in smoke or as you write the name of the perpetrator of harm on paper and draw a cross through it. State the different aspects of the situation or person you want to bind.

Create a four- or five-word rhythmic chant or a rhyme you recite continuously to endow the binding with growing power. Clap or stamp as you chant, if you wish, faster and faster to build up the power. Then for the climax, the moment when the binding is sealed, bring the spell to an end by extinguishing the candle, pressing it inverted into a bowl of sand or soil and saying aloud or in your mind,

> You (name) *are now bound with the dimming of this light*
> *from harming* (name those who are affected by the person)
> *for* (name timescale, which can be indefinitely)
> *or until you learn the error of your ways.*

If you prefer, leave the candle to burn through and end the spell with a loud clap over your head, bringing your arms down behind your back and then in front of your body at waist height. Hold the cord (if you made one) or the symbol high above your head with the hand you write with. End with a clap and stamp and these words:

> *Bound be from troubling me/my family.*

If the person is really nasty and you feel in spite of everything still angry and bitter, add calmly and quietly,

May you feel the pain/damage you have sent
because it comes from you, and so to you it must return.

As you speak in this case, extend the index finger of your writing hand. (This is no time to be polite.)

Decide what you will do with the symbol: hang the cord from a tree, freeze the name, or wrap the clay or cloth figure in a knotted scarf and put it away where it will not be disturbed.

While you are filled with power, plan your essential earthly strategies for dealing with the problem, and then sit with your hands on your solar plexus, your inner sun, the psychic energy centre that is in the centre of your upper stomach just below the ribs.

Picture the inner gold and yellow light of your willpower, determination, and strength to overcome anything or anyone rising upwards through your body to the top of your head and downwards through all your limbs to your feet.

Finally, picture your foe and say this in your mind or aloud using the golden power from your solar plexus:

You are bound from entering my thoughts.

Keep the spells you write and any information about the timings and colours or fragrances associated with particular kinds of magic in a special journal or computer folder.

A Stronger Version

For a particularly nasty bully—whether a neighbour, an ex, or someone at work—stand outside your home after the spell, facing the direction in which the person lives or works.

Pointing the index finger of your power hand (the hand you write with) towards the source of unpleasantness, or straight ahead if an unknown person, say,

You, you are henceforward restrained from spreading your
poison and nastiness to me/my family.
I bind your venom from this moment on.
You, you are restrained and shall not follow me
or my loved ones with thought, word, or deed or with unjust insinua-
tions, lies, and gossip by and from whatever source.

Turn and drop a trail of vinegar behind you as you walk back to the house. Do not look back.

Drip the remains of the vinegar under a cold running tap, repeating this till it is gone:

You, you are henceforward restrained, you who spread
your poison and nastiness against me/my family.
I bind your venom from this moment on,
and so I take away your power to harm.

Remember that any legal or official action you take will seem easier with your new magical determination to aid you.

Bind Runes

Finally, follow the Anglo-Saxons and Vikings who created bind runes, two or more runes combined to give an accumulation of power greater than the single rune.

Runes are consistent, distinctive angular symbols, marked on either round stones, wooden discs, or wooden staves, forming a set of anything from sixteen to thirty-six runes, depending on the particular region and time period in which they were used. They were used in the Scandinavian world as far north as Iceland, among the Anglo-Saxons on the plains of western Europe, and in lands the Germanic peoples conquered, including Northumberland in the northeast of England. Runes were created by the Germanic peoples, the English, German, and Scandinavian peoples who shared a common heritage and language, which gradually split into different languages. The earliest runic forms have been found in ancient rock carvings in Sweden in great quantity, dating from 1300 to 1200 BCE (the second Bronze Age) and 800 to 600 BCE, which formed the transition period to the Iron Age.

The runic systems that are used today date from the second or third centuries BCE, when the Germanic peoples of the Middle Danube, where the modern systems seem to have originated, came into contact with the Mediterranean Etruscan alphabet system and traded across Europe as far as the Baltic, famed for its amber. The runes followed the trade routes, spread by the traders themselves, who cast runes to discover propitious times for journeys and negotiations. The runes have slightly different names in the different systems, though they have similar meanings. The history and interactions between the different systems are open to debate and beyond the scope of this book.

Bind runes are very much an all-or-nothing protector, though they were also created for power and wealth, since each rune is not just a symbol but also releases the power of the rune itself when it is touched, cast into water, or burned when etched on a candle.

I have used the aptly named bind runes for many years primarily as binders of harm since, as you make or etch the joined runes, you are physically creating the psychic binding. These are ones I have created with advice from Scandinavian magical practitioners (I lived in Sweden for eleven years), who taught me to use bind runes for binding. However, you can of course go online and find magical runes and combine your own. In appendix I you will find more information on runic symbols.

Temporary Bind Runes

Create bind runes by etching them with a palette knife, paper knife, or small and sharp screwdriver on the side of a candle and letting the wax melt to release the power.

Alternatively, trace them on the inside of a beeswax candle with a palette knife before rolling the candle to release the power secretly as the candle burns. You could even trace them invisibly on the side of the candle with the index finger of the hand you write with (so no one knows), or on the side of your desk or your mug at work (retrace when you wash it).

These temporary spell bindings are a good way of giving a surge of power to a longer-lasting bind rune and also are imprinted on the aether, or spiritual plane, and so, though invisible, are also long-lasting.

Indeed "alerunes" were etched on the inside of drinking cups by Vikings who wished to protect themselves against evil people. The Vikings would drink from marked cups.

You could also, when unobserved, trace them with your finger on something belonging to someone nasty at work or on your own possessions as a good way of hanging on to your property. Bind it to return if it is always being borrowed without permission.

Draw bind runes in salt water on your side of a neighbour's fence or etch it on the side of a wooden stake you have put in the garden, facing the direction of the foe. The Vikings were a bit more ruthless and hung a horse skull on a *nyd* pole, which they set in the direction of their enemies, but the cursing aspect of this is not to be encouraged, as curses always rebound.

Permanent Bind Runes

If you wish to carry the binding with you or keep it at home or in your vehicle for protection, etch it with an awl (a pointed spike), or use a small screwdriver on a small rectangular piece of wood and colour the combined runic symbols with red paint and a thin brush when you have finished etching.

Note that permanent protective bind runes are usually made on Thursday, the day of the thunder god Thor. Though Odin the All Father is credited with creating runes, Thor is considered the mightiest and most protective of the gods. However, if you prefer, make them on Odin's day, Wednesday.

My Favourite Tried and Tested Bind Runes
Thor's Hammer Bind Rune for Bullying

A Viking Thor's hammer bind rune holds bullying or intimidation in check. Practise drawing *thurisaz* (Thor's hammer rune) and *uruz* (the strength of the wild cattle rune) separately and then as one bind rune, as shown. These are the names used in the Viking sets of runes, also known as the Elder Futhark.

Thurisaz, Uruz, and Thor's Hammer Bind Rine

Smooth a horizontal area in the wood and etch deep the combined runes to make the bind rune, saying this nine times:

> *By the hammer of Thor and the power of the wild beasts,*
> *Bind (name person or situation that is hurting you)*
> *that I may be free.*

Paint the bind rune symbols red, repeating the words nine more times. Keep the bind rune in a red bag, and each night and morning open the bag, trace the shape of the bind rune left to right nine times on the wood, and repeat the words nine times.

Bind Rune for Illness and Pain

This is an Anglo-Saxon bind rune to bind chronic illness and pain from getting worse and to bring relief. There is no reason why a binding cannot contain healing within it, and this bind rune from the Anglo-Saxon tradition (also known as the Futhorc) offers defense against pain and illness and offers relief.

Eh (*ehwaz* in the Viking runes), the rune of the horse, represents harmony and bringing healing.

Eh Rune

Aesc, the ash tree that does not have a Viking equivalent, is the tree of healing, endurance, and strength that holds in check pain and sickness. It is especially helpful with deteriorating or chronic conditions.

Aesc Rune

Ur (*uruz* in the Viking runes) represents primal strength, essential to prevent the body or mind deteriorating further.

Ur Rune

Eh, aesc, and ur can be combined like this:

Eh, Aesc, Ur, and Bind Rune for Illness and Pain

You could chant this as you create the bind rune:

Bind this my (or name person who needs healing) *infirmity.*
Take away pain,
That I may through the power of this binding
Be whole again.

Bind Rune to Protect the Home and Business

This is an Anglo-Saxon binding against persons known or unknown who threaten the home or business premises, potential muggers, and those who negatively influence vulnerable family members.

Odal (*othala* in the Viking runes) is the Anglo-Saxon tradition symbol of the home, domestic security, and the family, especially guarding vulnerable members.

Odal Rune

Beorc (berkano in the Viking runes) is the protective Mother Goddess and holds safe all within her arms.

Beorc Rune

Ger (*jera* in the Viking runes) is the rune of the harvest. It ensures prosperity remains with its rightful owners and is not stolen by those unworthy.

Ger Rune

Odal, beorc, and ger can be combined like this:

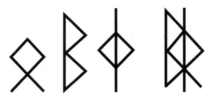

Odal, Beorc, Ger, and Bind Rune to Protect the Home and Business

Say as you create it,

> *May evil ones come not near*
> *Those I hold dear.*
> *May the walls*
> *Turn away in fear of this binding.*

Bind Rune for Malevolence and Psychic Attack

This is an Anglo-Saxon bind rune for strengthening your identity against all earthly malevolence and psychic attack from whatever source, normal or paranormal.

Ac, the oak tree, which does not have a Viking equivalent, is sacred to the Anglo-Saxon Father God Woden and the Viking Odin as well as Thunor, or Thor the thunder god, and is a tree associated with the power of the sky gods.

Ac Rune

Peorth (*perthro* in the Viking runes), the rune of destiny, represents the core essential person within us all.

Peorth Rune

Cen (*kenaz* in the Viking tradition) is a fire rune, the torch of pine that cleansed and illuminated the dark halls of the warriors.

Cen Rune

Ac, peorth, and cen can be combined like this:

Ac, Peorth, Cen, and Bind Rune for Malevolence and Psychic Attack

Chant as you make it,

> *Spectres all,*
> *At this binding fall.*
> *Earthly or spirit,*

Enter not here.
The light shines so clear.
Go back to the dark.
Leave not your mark.

Block Negative Forces from Emotional Energy Vampires

This is primarily a practical chapter using real-life case studies so you can learn to protect yourself from those who steal your energies and sometimes your resources and money by holding you in their power by a fascination you cannot break—and may not understand.

This form of mind control is all too common and explains why, at its extreme, a sensible, logical, and sometimes successful person is controlled or overshadowed by a partner, friend, or even employee who is clearly to the outside world a user, loser, or control freak, maybe all three. If a person is under the power of someone who is draining them, a protective ritual of the kind described in this chapter is a vital prelude and emergency brake on the situation before creating a more permanent psychic energy shield of the kind I describe in the next chapter to ensure the vampire's power does not return, for they are remarkably persistent once they have their emotional teeth in you.

By carrying out external actions and saying specific words in a spell or ritual, our inner innate protection against energy vampires is activated as the ritual actually changes the victim to victor energies within us, one of the true and most important functions of magic.

These inner energies are radiated quite spontaneously from our aura energy field, which surrounds us like an ellipse into the world as powerful "don't mess with me" vibes, so that we not only feel more confident, but others are unconsciously aware of this power emanating from us.

All the rituals and suggestions in this chapter can be used if you or loved ones encounter similar issues, whether to a mild or major degree.

Why Are Emotional Energy Vampires Such a Hazard?

Often called the "dreadful power of the weak over the strong," this insidious form of attack is one of the most lethal and destructive to an individual's power and confidence, yet it is often confused by the victim with love and friendship and a mistaken sense of responsibility for the vampire, who may in fact be as tough as old boots.

Many of us have encountered these emotional vampires, the lover whom we constantly try in vain to please and who even after parting is always there in the background actually or in our minds, preventing us moving forwards to new love. You may have encountered the friend or colleague who regularly offloads their problems rather than trying to fix them and is always sick when hard work rears its ugly head. You may have a seemingly vulnerable relative whose visits leave you totally drained with their moans, groans, and guilt trips and who sometimes demands for money with the latest hard-luck story even though we know logically they have more than us. And still we say yes.

People who are kind and gentle may find that one emotional energy vampire is replaced by another throughout their life, and so long-term psychic shields (chapter 3) are one of the most effective ways to actually protect yourself against this recurring over and over again.

Like the rituals and methods of protection suggested in this chapter, psychic shields, to which I have devoted a whole chapter, guard you not only from emotional vampires but from your own overeagerness to help the underdog at the expense of yourself and your unshakeable belief, especially in relationships, that the negative or absent love *will* change, given unconditional love and patience. Of course I am not suggesting you become hard-hearted and mean but rather recognise if you have been taken for one too many rides with users and losers, whether in love, in family, socially, or in your career.

In many cases where the vampire has their emotional fangs well embedded, perhaps over years (or, if the vampire is a parent, a lifetime), it is essential first to loosen the grip through maybe frequent ritual words and actions for there to be sufficient inner strength and determination by the victim to permanently overcome and eventually banish (see chapter 4) the predator.

For too often the victim is their own worst enemy who denies the harmful effects of the person emotionally or financially draining them and makes excuses for the vampire. People may be unable to let go of a destructive love, deep friendship, or overpossessive family bond and, even if the love and trust have been broken, to accept it is the end of the road and move on. In effect the victim keeps the vampire in their mind and heart and so in their energy field, just as powerfully as though the vampire were still physically present. Some emotional predators have even died but live on as voices in the head.

What is seen as psychological codependency may be in fact deeper and exist on a psychic karmic level. Often this negative love is a soul adversary who has appeared in past worlds and needs to be overcome once and for all in this lifetime.

Yet some people may then go and choose another equally bad lover, sometimes repeating a childhood pattern of the deserting abusive father or cold, neglectful mother. Along with conventional counselling and practical actions to remove the emotional predator from your life, repeating defensive rituals can actually break the self-destructive pattern.

Shielding against Obsessive Love

This first example is of people who love too much a hopeless cause who will never change.

So many spells and rituals (in practise the terms are interchange-able) as well as earthly attempts to find good new love fail because someone is still emotionally tied to a destructive former lover and is unconsciously or consciously not willing or able to banish them be-cause the psychic hold is too strong.

The following spells I used with Jenny, a thirty-year-old from Dublin, Ireland, with an excellent career in finance who had been in a relationship for ten years with Ted, whom she had supported while he stayed home playing his guitar. He had been serially unfaithful from the beginning, but Jenny had always believed he would change, though he showed no remorse or signs of staying in at night or even overnight. Three months ago he left Jenny for a young girl he had got-ten pregnant, taking several of Jenny's personal credit cards, which he was rapidly emptying and which Jenny did not have the heart to stop as she knew he had nothing.

Ted kept Jenny dangling with the vague promise he might return if things didn't work out for him. Yet she could not move on, in spite of friends and family telling her Ted was no good and never had been, and she was turning down other dates with really nice men. She still hoped at the eleventh hour Ted would change and come back to her as, in spite of his behaviour, she told me he was her "only true love."

However, eventually Jenny asked me for help because she knew deep down he was playing her for a fool, and she found out he was taking out loans in her name. We did the first spell described below many times, and gradually it built up protection around her so that she felt that she was no longer under Ted's destructive influence. It worked by blocking his hold on her.

Spells are often effective because we physically and symbolically in the spell process do something to resolve the problem and in doing so change the energies, in this case by creating a psychic roadblock for Ted to Jenny's loving heart. For the first time, she really wanted Ted out of her life for good, and that greatly increased the chances of spell success. Even the most powerful spell will not succeed if the person who is casting it or for whom it is cast does not deep down want the change being worked for.

Of course I suggested Jenny go to the police, as Ted was defrauding her, but she was so embarrassed and ashamed of her own weakness in not stopping the cards immediately that she felt it was all too hard to prove. While legal redress can go hand in hand with magic, nevertheless we have to respect that for some people, especially when friends, lovers, and family members are involved in fraud against us, taking the person to court would be too traumatic and would make public how they had been taken in.

We also added a second spell to the first to push away Ted's future manipulations and ways he played with her emotions, as in the past she would weaken when he invariably returned sorry and apparently helpless, so that she would be in effect protected from his soft talk. I also taught her the psychic shield technique I describe in the next chapter as extra defense since the relationship had been so long-standing.

Within a month Ted had returned, saying his pregnant girlfriend had thrown him out and gone back to her parents and he was broke and needed somewhere to stay temporarily. Jenny told him to go away—the first time she had ever denied her spoilt lover anything. She is now dating a kind, gentle man who is economically sound.

. . . .
Spell to Protect against Energy Vampires and Unwanted Intrusions in Your Life

This is a good all-purpose spell for redrawing your boundaries and making yourself resistant to specific emotional vampires in your life. It also works well if you are being stalked (especially if earthly help is not forthcoming, though you should persist) or if you are spooked by nasty spirits.

Ingredients and Tools

Five fragrant white roses
A white candle
Vase of water

Timing

After dark

The Spell

Light the candle. Take the rose. Hold it first in the light of the candle and then to your heart and say,

> *I surround myself with fragrance and with light*
> *To shield me at this hour, by day and night,*
> *That I may no longer be*
> *Entranced/threatened by* (name/your destructive power).
> *Go from me.*

Do this for the other four flowers and put them in a vase of water. Blow out the candle, repeating the words.

When the roses fade, take them outdoors and pluck each petal, dropping it on the ground. Say afterwards,

> *I am surrounded by fragrance and by light,*
> *By day and by night.*
> *You* (name) *may no longer enter my heart.*
> *Protected am I as I walk to my new start,*
> *Apart.*

Replace the flowers with fresh ones and repeat the ritual cycle till you feel the power around you.

Spell to Push Away the Return of the Emotional Vampire or Intrusion

This spell can be carried out immediately following the first if you have weakened in the past when a destructive and apparently contrite emotional vampire returns, promising changes.

Alternatively, you can cast it entirely independently of the first spell before you know you will be entering a situation where you will be taken advantage of or persuaded against your will. You can take a small makeup mirror or any small reflective steel surface with you to work or when visiting a guilt-provoking relative and look into it, while saying the words in your mind, immediately before the encounter. Alternatively, go to the bathroom and use the mirror there.

Ingredients and Tools
A hand mirror

Timing
After the first spell or if practising it as a separate spell, when the sun is shining or the brightest part of the day

The Spell
Look into the mirror, holding it in the hand you do not write with. With the index finger of the other hand, touch the centre of your hairline, sometimes called the crown chakra energy centre point (more on this in the next chapter), where light and power pour in from the cosmos. Say,

> *Immune may I be*
> *To all who would deceive me.*
> *Resistant to your machinations,*
> *I return unwanted your manipulation.*

Keep looking in the mirror as you speak.

Then touch the centre of your brow energy chakra, seat of the third or clairvoyant eye (in the centre of the forehead between and just above the eyes), where is activated your natural intuition to know that the person or situation you are barring is not worthy of you. While doing so, repeat the words.

Touch next the centre of your throat chakra energy at the base of the throat, where persuasive but unreliable words enter your soul and keep you dangling in vain hope, saying the same words.

Finally, between your breasts or the centre of your chest, where resides your heart chakra to guard your loving and overly forgiving heart, say the words once more.

Look into the mirror, smile, and say,

I am free,
Entirely me,
So shall it be.
• • • • • • •

Beware the False Guru

The emotional vampire may be an unscrupulous guru, often a clairvoyant, medium, or leader of a meditation or Reiki group who makes students totally dependent on him or her by encouraging them to confide their innermost secrets. By this unconditional sympathy, the guru makes the student feel that the other people are to blame for life going wrong and only the guru understands.

The student is regularly and gently criticised for mistakes in learning but always given new hope to keep paying and trying, and the guru tends to set one student against the other for his or her favour and attention. Frequent clairvoyant readings can make the student believe they cannot survive without the guru. This is a very grey area legally, and often extricating yourself, by using strengthening rituals, is the easiest solution. If you have lost a lot of money, you may wish to seek legal redress. Sadly, too many are understandably unwilling to tell others how they were duped, especially if, as in Patricia's case, sex becomes involved.

Patricia, who lives in the Far North of Australia, contacted me because she had been seeing her kinesiologist, Doug, for many years. He had helped her through marriage crises and a serious loss of confidence and always made her feel special, but recently he had started to make sexual and romantic advances. Patricia had also recently inherited a large sum of money upon her father's death, and Doug tried to persuade her that her husband was unfaithful and that Patricia should move in with him.

Doug promised he would teach her to become his assistant and, though the training course he offered was expensive, it would give her a career for life, and they could work and live as partners. But alarm bells were ringing as Patricia had heard from two, as Doug put it, "deranged" former female clients. They claimed to have given him money and had sex with him, only to be dumped when he had run through their money on his extortionate teaching fees and improvements on his premises. He had assured them the money for the business improvements was just a loan; however, he then said they had failed the course to become his assistant, and they had no paperwork to prove they had lent him money. And indeed he was chasing them for what he said were unpaid fees.

Patricia knew all this and trusted the disgruntled women, but when she did not see Doug, she felt unwell and could feel him calling her back in her mind each week. Yet she was not ready to remove Doug from her life, but knew she needed to be stronger. Binding or banishing Doug would not have worked because Patricia admitted she had fallen in love with him and, though she did not believe her husband was unfaithful, she was still under Doug's spell and unconsciously would not have bound or banished him effectively. Sex is sometimes the means a vampire will use to get their victim under their spell, especially if the victims are unhappily married.

Common sense, frequent rituals, and then a permanent psychic shield will often give a student or indeed long-standing client the strength to see the unscrupulous guru in his or her own true light and eventually walk away from this nasty form of vampirism; for the guru or consultant basks in his or her power, fuelled by the energies sucked emotionally or sexually from adoring students, as well as the financial gain from those who have been hooked. For even if the victim breaks away, unscrupulous gurus will continue to make contact and may turn nasty, as they do not like losing control.

I used the following spell with Patricia to set up a light shield between her and Doug so that she was not seduced at great financial cost, and I sent her home to perform this ritual. This is a method that can be used for urgent, powerful protection and to build up longer-lasting defense against a powerful manipulative force. Unlike the shields in the next chapter, it needs to be set up each time there is an encounter with this particularly unpleasant form of vampirism in order to build up the layers of protection, and it is intended to block a specific person.

After doing the first spell, Patricia made six more visits to Doug, though she felt herself starting to resist his hold (he started to appear to her in dreams), and so she carried out the ritual six times in total before the visits. Each time she realised more and more what he was actually doing.

Patricia cancelled the seventh visit and Doug tried everything from calling at her home to claiming she owed him money and telling people *she* was deranged. Each time Patricia did the ritual it strengthened her light shield, and eventually she heard Doug had moved in with another wealthy, unhappily married student who was buying him new premises so they could become partners.

Patricia is now studying with a very gifted female teacher who charges reasonable fees.

. . . .

Spell to Create a Protective Shield against Manipulation, Deception, and Pressure

This is the spell Patricia used, but it is suitable for any particularly nasty emotional vampire who is using sex and what amounts to fraud (and it can also give you the courage and clarity to consider legal redress if that is what you want). The spell uses light to create a protective shield against manipulation, deception, and undue pressure that is badly affecting your well-being and finances.

Ingredients and Tools

A white candle
A small bowl of salt

Timing

Every time before you are due to meet the false guru or powerful
emotional/sexual vampire

The Spell

Light the candle and say,

> *Light bright, from the sight of me,*
> *Take the intensity of* (name source of evil).
> *That I may shielded be*
> *From unwise action in his/her company.*

Put a pinch of cleansing salt in the flame, saying,

> (Name), *cease to sap your strength from me.*
> *No more shall you drain my energy.*
> *With salt I purify.*
> *Access to my mind and body I do deny.*

Circle your hands and arms round your body, saying faster and
faster,

> *I create this shield of light*
> *To guard me from your sight.*

When you can chant and move no faster, bring your hands over
your head, down either side of your body, and up again to clap in
front of your body. Blow out the candle and say,

> *Begone from my sight.*
> *I am guarded by light.*

· · · · · · ·

Taking Over Your Work or Social Life

Another form of psychic emotional vampirism is the man or woman who wants to *be* the person from whom they suck energy, and this is a deliberate and often preplanned psychic intrusion. Usually the energy vampire in this case is a person who plays helpless and makes you feel responsible for them, but in fact the vampire is deliberately manipulating you and, having sucked you dry, will move on to another fuel source.

At work they frequently operate as the boss's or manager's assistant. Watch out for the office dragon who guards and denies access to the boss, as he or she is often an energy vampire living and drawing his or her power through the energy field of his or her employer. At the worst, the emotional vampire can damage a business by denying others access to the boss's or manager's expertise and by alienating clients and employees.

Irreversible Business Damage

I encountered Izzy, possibly the worst energy vampire I have known, while I was acting as literary adviser in a small but successful advertising agency in France, a business that was based in Sarah's substantial three-storey home, where she and I had apartments on the upper floors. Sarah advertised for a live-in assistant to care for the apartments and office. Izzy arrived at the office, apparently homeless, having been thrown out by her parents "for no reason."

In spite of having no references, which made me question her suitability, Sarah took her on, for it seemed Izzy could do everything wanted and more.

Izzy, with the speed of light, made herself indispensable and before long became Sarah's lover. Sarah had recently got divorced and was feeling very insecure.

Thereafter, Izzy systematically picked off Sarah's valued employees and friends one by one by lying about them to the infatuated Sarah till she had totally isolated Sarah and taken over as manager and senior copywriter herself, though she had trouble spelling.

I offered practical advice and magical help but Sarah refused to listen and, therefore, I was unable to do anything.

Indeed, I was one of Izzy's victims, and it was made clear I was no longer welcome.

Izzy, in a short space of time, wrecked with her incompetence what was before her arrival a successful advertising firm. When things looked bad for the company, she ran off with all Sarah's money, having secretly drained the company funds, and left Sarah ill and exhausted. Sarah's company went bankrupt.

The moral of the tale? You can't win against an energy vampire unless the victim will listen and accept practical or magical help. Every story doesn't have a happy ending. Where competent adults are concerned, you can't go against their free will, even when disaster is staring them in the face, and sometimes the bad guy or gal does win.

A Vampiric Business Wrecker

Sarah had refused to listen to me, and the emotional vampire made sure a rift grew between Sarah and me. Shielding others from emotional vampirism is a tough one, as the victim is often unwittingly a coconspirator in maintaining the vampirism and may be very protective of the "helpless" vampire, whom it seems *you* are picking on.

But I *was* able to help Gaynor before damage to her company became irreversible. Gaynor, who lives in Manchester, United Kingdom, runs a psychic phone and webcam line that was just starting to get recognised.

Gaynor contacted me because she was experiencing constant blinding headaches and exhaustion at work and said business was rapidly dropping off, apparently without reason. She wondered if I could pick up psychically if the business had been cursed, because Gaynor was sure she was doing nothing differently.

I went into the phone line offices and there was the answer, an emotional vampire in takeover mode (and sadly most vampires are incompetent businesswise). Susan, Gaynor's office assistant, was sitting at Gaynor's desk, physically very close to Gaynor, and when I later enquired, Gaynor admitted that every morning Susan came in and sat right next to her through the day, even leaning across Gaynor to answer the phone. Susan had a perfectly good office of her own, but almost always emotional vampires will sit as close as possible to their victim, as if taking over their personal space.

Susan told me at once she and Gaynor were best friends and they made all the decisions for "their company" together, which Gaynor did not deny, though Gaynor looked uncomfortable. A psychic vampire invariably claims close friendship with the victim, and the victim, even if a good businessperson (which Gaynor was), doesn't want to embarrass the vampire. Gaynor had the fatal flaw that vampires spot: a kind heart and a desire to make others feel good.

Gaynor later admitted to me privately (we had quite a job to shake Susan off) that a number of mediums on the phone line were having issues with Susan criticising them and ordering them around, though Susan had little experience of the work. Indeed, Gaynor had only employed Susan because Susan was down on her luck. Gaynor agreed (in the end she had to come into the car park to talk privately) that she *was* deferring to Susan even though Gaynor knew the decisions Susan made were often wrong—"as if my mind is taken over and turns to jelly" was the way Gaynor put it.

The first thing I observed was that every time Susan moved away from Gaynor she touched Gaynor on the shoulder, though Gaynor insisted Susan was just an affectionate person. Almost all psychic vampires are touchy-feely people and use this contact as a way, consciously or otherwise, of drawing power from their victims.

As I observed, I could actually see the energy flowing from Gaynor's aura, which became lifeless as Susan's became brighter, like a neon sign, during the touch. Susan was invading Gaynor's physical as well as psychic space. Emotional vampires tend to drain someone more attractive or successful by physically overshadowing their aura. You could almost call this an earthly soul possession.

But Gaynor still would not listen to me when I explained the problem was not a curse but an emotional vampire, and I said I could help her no further until she was ready to work on the real problem. Then a few days later the mediums on duty at the offices refused to come in if Susan was there and started to move to other companies, taking clients with them.

Gaynor asked for my help as she realised she could lose her business and agreed the problem was Susan. Gaynor, however, still refused to dismiss Susan as "she has nothing else in her life, and it would be my fault if she couldn't get another job."

So as a first step we changed the seating arrangements, and to her annoyance Susan was banished to her own office and told that it was not her job to criticise the mediums or decide their pay. (Susan had stopped payment of two mediums she said were late, which they disputed.) That banishment resulted in tears and days off with unspecified illnesses during which Gaynor, in spite of a huge guilt complex, regained control of her own company.

Physical distancing from the vampire is a vital way of reestablishing your psychic boundaries. If the person deliberately touches you, push your hand in the air subtly at shoulder height to break the energy circuit.

Secondly and most importantly, I taught Gaynor how to block her aura energy field and chakra energy centres from this intrusion (see the Shield of Gold technique in chapter 3, which I also taught Gaynor to use after the daily rituals listed below).

Within six weeks of starting both the practical and magical work with me, Gaynor saved her company and got rid of Susan, but not easily.

Susan eventually found herself a new psychic energy source, having threatened Gaynor with constructive dismissal claims because Susan said Gaynor was being nasty to her. (Susan was probably feeling the effect of Gaynor's rituals, which were stopping her getting physically or emotionally close to Gaynor.)

Susan obtained a job with Gaynor's main rival, whom she contacted, offering information about Gaynor's business. (Susan had often harangued the mediums on their lack of loyalty.) The rival initially felt sorry for the dreadful way Gaynor had apparently treated Susan. In spite or perhaps because of the defection, Gaynor's business is going from strength to strength, her headaches and exhaustion have disappeared, and mediums and clients are coming from the rival firm because they hate having to deal with Susan, who has apparently taken over the boss, another kind, gentle woman.

Sealing Your Spirit against Emotional and Psychic Vampires

Emotional or psychic vampires come in many situations and guises, an overpossessive parent who blights an adult child's marriage and takes to their bed, if crossed; a child who constantly cries wolf well into adulthood to keep the parents' attention and stop them moving forward; an aging parent who becomes sick every time a dutiful son or daughter tries to go on holiday or break free; a friend who lurches from one crisis to another and gets distressed if you try to see other friends; a partner who frets if you are late home or want self-time or pay too much attention to the children at any age.

They are very common especially if you are soft-hearted and care for others. The following are the techniques I taught to Gaynor, but they can be used in absolutely any situation where you feel you are being taken over or on a constant guilt trip over others.

. . . .
Ritual for Daily Psychic Protection

This ritual aids daily psychic protection before going into the world in the morning and also peaceful sleep, if you carry it out at night.

This takes only a very short time and yet protects all day and night against emotional vampires as well as paranormal harm and those nasty people who would wish to hurt us psychologically and play mind games. It protects both our aura energy field surrounding us and our inner chakra energy centres.

In fact, you could carry out this ritual without the oil, as it works purely on an energy level, but the fragrance is a reminder of the protection if you waver or feel fear during the day and, as a bonus, rose and lavender have a high protective vibration.

Ingredients and Tools

A bottle of rose or lavender essential oil

Timing

Every morning and evening (optional)

The Ritual

Every morning, place a drop of fragrance in the centre of your brow, above and between your eyes, the site of your psychic third eye invisible energy centre through which most vampirism and psychic attacks enter the body and mind.

Rub it in counterclockwise, saying,

> *I shield the entrance to my spirit*
> *from all that is not harmonious and not from the light.*

Add if you wish,

> *And I shield my spirit against all* (or name a specific person) *taking my energies.*

Rub next counterclockwise a second drop into the base of your throat, the psychic energy point through which words enter to undermine your authority and confidence in your own decisions. Repeat the same words.

Finally, rub a drop, again counterclockwise, into each of your inner wrist points to protect your sensitive heart energy centre, through which emotional blackmail and guilt trips gain access.

Stronger Version of the Ritual

A stronger method of protection if your emotional vampire is potentially physically dangerous (perhaps a charismatic but violent partner or indeed any attacker that seriously messes with your mind) involves taking an eggcup full of salt and a slightly larger bowl of water.

First, hold the salt and using a small, silver-coloured paper knife, draw a cross on the surface, Christian or equal armed, and say,

I call the blessings of light and goodness
(or name your favourite angel or deity focus)
to enter this salt and shield me from
(name vampire or any potential harm and attack).

Do the same for the water and draw the cross on the surface.

Now add three pinches of the empowered salt to the water, swirl the water bowl nine times, and use the water for sealing your third eye, throat, and heart chakras as before.

Alternatively, carry it to your place of work in a little sealed glass bottle or socially, wherever the vampire is, to splash on brow, throat, and wrist points whenever you feel you are being taken over.

You can also use this salt mix on your energy points before an imminent visit to shield you from overpossessive family members or even neighbours who have no sense of your privacy and boundaries or try to make you feel guilty.

Either leave the rest of the salt in your home or workplace to absorb attack (dissolve it in running water at the end of the day) or dissolve it in white vinegar and leave it in your home, again washing away at the end of the day.

. . . .

Ongoing Daily Rituals

Perform these rituals at those moments when others start to take over and you find yourself weakening. You can use the following techniques, as Gaynor did, against any psychological or emotional intrusion of your personal space and privacy, and they are also effective against those who intrude on your private conversations and read your computer or your papers over your shoulder.

. . . .
Early-Morning Ritual against Negativity and Emotional or Psychic Intrusion

Ingredients and Tools

A glass of water

Timing

When you wake

The Ritual

First thing in the morning, hold a glass of water, put your hands round it, and say,

> *Be protection for me against negativity,*
> *malice, intrusion, and hostility.*

Filter the water into a small bottle with a lid and add five drops of lemon juice or lemongrass, the archangel Raphael's fragrance against human snakes. Put on the lid, shake the bottle five times (Raphael's number), and say again,

> *Be protection for me against negativity,*
> *malice, intrusion, and hostility.*

Carry the bottle with you and keep it, if necessary, in your bag between you and the intrusive or hostile person to absorb any negativity and interference from them and to stop them invading your personal space. At the end of the day, pour the water away.

. . . .
Ritual for Washing Away Intrusion

Sometimes it is not just one person but the general atmosphere, whether at work, at home, or socially that is draining you or making you feel that you are being swept along against your will or like your privacy and integrity are being intruded upon. Whether it be a particular person or the whole situation, make an excuse and go to the bathroom. Then try this washing ritual for clearing your mind and personal space against intrusion.

Ingredients and Tools

A bar of soap or hand wash

Timing

Whenever you feel stressed by a person or situation

The Ritual

Using hand wash or soap, wash your hands. As you do so, say this slowly in your mind over and over again (or softly aloud if you are alone):

> *Away from here, stay from here,*
> *Your attacks I do shield.*
> *To your false power and intrusion*
> *I no longer yield.*

Rinse your hands under running water, repeating the words. Splash the water on your face and hairline, saying,

> *This is my shield;*
> *I shall not yield.*

· · · · · · ·

Creating and Activating
Psychic Energy Fields

In the previous chapter we looked at overcoming the hazards of psychic vampires using rituals to resist the energy takeovers. Here we will learn how to create ongoing and long-lasting psychic energy shields, not only to prevent emotional vampires returning, but also to protect ourselves and loved ones against any and every kind of abuse, threat, or attack in the daily or paranormal worlds.

If you wish, you can create psychic energy shields against attack purely by thought. However, many people prefer to use a crystal, candle, mirror, or fragrance as a focus for the energy transfers in the initial creation. With practise you will be able to create them easily and almost instantly entirely by visualisation.

Later in the chapter I will describe creating an all-purpose Shield of Gold step by step to familiarise you with the basic technique of creating shields, and once the steps are clear you can apply them to other forms of shielding for specific purposes. First we will consider how shields can be helpful in averting hazards of all kinds.

Psychic Shields for Physical Protection

As well as guarding against specific psychic or psychological attacks, psychic shields can offer protection in physically hazardous places and situations.

When we encounter drunks, aggressive drug users, or potential thugs, we naturally give off fearful vibes, and these can attract the danger to us.

Psychic shields work hand in hand with and supplement, but are not a substitute for, normal earthly precautions, such as avoiding deserted car parks after dark or crowded city centres near nightclubs late at night on a weekend.

Yet we can all find ourselves, however careful, in potentially hazardous situations. In such instances psychic shields can lower your psychic as well as psychological profile in the face of danger to create a cloak of invisibility (the Shield of Grey) or, conversely, emit "don't mess with me" vibes (the Red Shield of Defense).

How Psychic Energy Fields Work

Everyone and everything has an energy field or aura surrounding it: rooms, buildings, animals, people, and even spirits (the spooky white light seen round ghosts led to the fun image of the ghost in a white sheet). Saints pictured with a halo of white or golden light round their heads in paintings are reflecting their pure aura.

An unprotected aura is the means through which psychic and psychological attack of all kinds from negative people, including energy suckers, reaches us. This is also true for physical hazards.

The aura is described in various ways but most usually as seven rainbow bands of colour, red closest to the body, then orange, yellow, green, blue, indigo, and finally violet merging into white and gold as the aura reaches the cosmos. The bands become less structured and more diffuse and the energies more aethereal the further they move from the body. If you have learned a different way of looking at auras then use that method, but the seven-aura-level system corresponds well to the main seven invisible chakra energy centres within the body.

Each aura level is fuelled by its own related bodily energy chakra centre. For example, the innermost red aura level by the red root energy chakra extends from the earth through the feet, knees, thighs, and reproductive organs. (I have explained this connection in detail at the end of the chapter if you are unfamiliar with the concept of auras and chakras, and if you wish, you can read this now.) Because of the close connection between aura and bodily energy centres, we may feel the effects of psychic attack physically if our aura is unprotected and inexplicably feel ill or exhausted.

Once created, aura or energy shields can be activated instantly in any setting or circumstance. Shields are powerful against bullying via social media, e-mail, and texts; against predators who slip through the net and try to groom your teenagers or con you on dating or financial websites; and against computer hacking. You can cast one round your own or a teenager's computer. They are also effective against those who try to manipulate you or play mind games.

How Absorbing Energies Can Harm Our Well-Being

Individuals can absorb negative energies from negatively charged atmospheres, such as the collective aura or energy field of an overcompetitive or emotionally toxic workplace. You can also be affected by a property into which you have recently moved, where there has been ill fortune, illness, or quarrels, perhaps extending through a number of owners. This sourness becomes stuck like a psychic cloud over all who live there. (I describe domestic and workplace protection in part 2 of the book as well as dealing with negative earth energies beneath your home or workplace.)

The more sensitive you are emotionally and spiritually, the more badly affected your aura is by a negative workplace or nasty neighbour. Some people become so ill in a psychologically toxic atmosphere they are unable to go to work. If you are a gentle or intuitive person, psychic shields are doubly important.

Equally, we can be adversely affected by places where negative power has accumulated over centuries, not only haunted houses but scenes of past sorrows, such as the sites of old mental hospitals, prisons, battle-fields, or land on which massacres or evil deeds have occurred. The effects of this negativity can stay with us long after we have left the place, especially if we visited the sites around the anniversary of a battle or mass destruction, when the imprinted pain and anger can be heard as voices or even seen as visions.

Indeed, old prisons and asylums have become very popular as trendy hotels, but often guests complain of disturbed sleep without knowing why.

Joanna, a senior businesswoman in the south of England, told me how during the Second World War when working for the war ministry in England, she became inexplicably terrified when using a subterranean corridor beneath what is now the Imperial War Museum in London. She later discovered she was walking on the site of the former Bedlam Lunatic Asylum, created in the 1200s. It lasted for 600 years as an early and very brutal psychiatric hospital, where, especially in the 1600s, people would pay to come and taunt patients. The energies from the aura of Bedlam were so strong that they had remained in the atmosphere over hundreds of years, indeed fuelled by the very real fears of invasion of the United Kingdom and the bad as well as good news flooding into the war ministry that were kept secret from the general public. Joanna is a very sensitive person and so would have absorbed into her energy field all these negative impressions.

I have devoted a chapter to paranormal nasties and how to deal with them in part 2, but sometimes it can be the *impressions* of the past that are imprinted on the aura of the place, and these are different from the actual nasty ghostly encounters I describe later in the book. If you have a psychic shield, you will be automatically protected from these negative aura imprints, so if you live or work in one of those places of historical sorrow, then you do need to create a Shield of Gold round yourself.

Creating the Psychic Energy Shield of Gold

A psychic energy Shield of Gold is a multipurpose shield against specific, personal, physical threats or against psychic or psychological attacks or imprints from past worlds. What is more, the Shield of Gold will maintain ongoing background defense throughout your daily life if you are subject to a lot of stress or have to deal with difficult people. You only need to renew its strength every three months unless you have been under heavy attack, in which case recreate it every week till the danger or nastiness passes.

Step by Step: Making Your Shield of Gold

Hard? Not at all.

STEP 1: BRING GOLD INTO YOUR BODY

First, connect with the colour gold. Stare at something gold-coloured, even a piece of gold foil or a lighted gold candle. Close your eyes and picture the gold flooding your mind. Keep opening your eyes, staring at the gold, and then closing them, until you cannot only see the gold in your mind but *feel* it entering your body like basking by a warm radiator or under the sun.

An alternative way of filling your body, mind, and spirit with gold energy is to create a body of light within yourself. Sit in sunlight or any natural light, however dull the day, or in the light of gold candles, with your feet touching the floor, either in a chair or on the floor with your palms flat and facing up.

With eyes open so you can see the source of gold, at the same time visualise this in your mind: the gold light pouring into your body through the crown of your head (some call this the Archangel Michael light) and at the same time rich gold rising through your feet from Mother Earth (the source of physical gold). Visualise both golden streams meeting in your solar plexus, your inner sun chakra energy centre, in the middle of your upper stomach just below where the ribcage ends.

Sit quietly and let the golden light flow within you and around you, and using either method, end this step by repeating three times,

I am pure gold.

STEP 2: MAKE AN ENERGY BALL

Now we are going use your body of gold as the source for a shield round your external aura energy field that can extend up to six feet beyond your body all round.

Sit comfortably, holding the fingers and palms of your hands vertically, facing and almost touching each other. Then move them apart quickly. Continue to move your hands together and apart slower and slower, and you will gradually find it more difficult to move your hands as the energies from the force field accumulate between your hands and start to feel denser and sticky. Continue to gently move your hands, palms facing, together and apart but not quite touching until you feel the energy as a ball of light and maybe *see* lights and sparks building up.

Using the power of psychic touch that enables us to move energy from one place to another (one name for this power is psychokinesis), form from this invisible sticky substance an energy ball in exactly the same way you would roll between your hands a ball of very sticky clay, making it any size from a tennis ball to a small football.

When you can fully feel its roundness and firmness, rest the invisible ball against your solar plexus, and you will start to see or feel the gold filling the ball.

Rotate the invisible ball psychically with your eyes closed or open—whichever feels right—until you realise it is complete and separate from you but now glowing golden.

STEP 3: CREATE THE ACTUAL SHIELD AROUND YOU

Still holding the energy ball, sit with your knees together, raise your arms above your head in an arch, and push the aura energies you have collected in your psychic ball into a sphere above you upwards as far as you can. Picture it extending down the sides, in front of you and behind, completely enclosing you and surrounding you about the distance of an extended arm, and clear enough so you can see right through it. It will feel like being bathed in a golden, warm, shimmering light waterfall.

See or feel the shell of the protective sphere hardening into an iridescent gold, mingling with a mother of pearl edge so that only loving thoughts from others may enter and any negative feelings from whatever source will be repelled.

Now clap above your head to complete the seal.

Allow the golden aura shield to fade, but know it is there in the background waiting to be activated.

You can also, using visualisation, place a protective shell of golden light around those you love at any time they seem vulnerable.

STEP 4: MAKE AN INSTANT LINK TO ACTIVATE YOUR SHIELD OF GOLD WHEN THREATENED

Decide on a simple action or phrase that will always instantly activate the protective golden shield, perhaps at a time of stress or crisis, such as beginning to unobtrusively move your hands as though you were creating the ball of energy between your fingers or slowly moving your hands together as if you were clapping. Alternatively, trace a clockwise sphere with the index finger of your writing hand on to your other hand.

You can simply say in your mind words such as these:

I call my golden shield of light to guard me from all harm.

And if you wish, ask Archangel Michael to protect your shield from fierce attack. You will not see the shield; just know it is there and feel quietly confident.

You can repeat this affirmation each night before you sleep so that you are safe from negative thoughts or attacks while you sleep.

If you know you will be encountering a hostile or confrontational day ahead, activate your golden shield before you leave home.

STEP 5: ADD A GOLDEN ELECTRICAL PSYCHIC FORCE FIELD (OPTIONAL)

Some people just rely on the golden shield to protect them quite effectively. However, I would recommend adding a golden electric psychic force field immediately after creating the Shield of Gold for the first time if you are in a very abrasive atmosphere or in a situation where your energies are being drained or you are being abused or threatened. This was another technique I taught Gaynor, whose energy field was being taken over by Susan to the detriment of Gaynor's business (see chapter 2).

To create the force field, once you have sealed your aura shield, vigorously shake your fingertips on both hands, until you can feel the energy flowing. Hold your hands about fifteen centimetres apart, with your fingers spread wide open and palms facing each other. Bring your hands together fast in a clap until they touch.

Keep bringing your hands together so that they nearly touch, move them apart, and then move them back together, continuing this for five or six cycles, faster and faster.

As you move your hands, you will see or sense the light becoming brighter and clearer and creating sparks or rays all around you like children's sparklers.

Push these psychic sparks from your left hand so that they move clockwise upwards in the shape of the golden sphere around your body and then downwards until they join with your right hand. The sparks from your right hand will continue to travel clockwise downwards around your body to your feet and then up the left side, tracing the edge of the sphere, and join with those rising from your left hand. You don't need to trace this physically; just let it happen.

Picture the sparks as a golden zigzag in yellows and orange, not in any way harmful but firmly repelling any negativity. As you gently breathe rhythmically, on the exhale blow the sparks to settle around the aura shield, and continue until you have bright sparks all round.

STEP 6: ACTIVATE WHEN UNDER ATTACK (OPTIONAL)

Try this after activating the basic shield and when you need your extra electric force field. If you feel afraid and perhaps if you are alone in a dangerous place or know there will be a nasty confrontation with an ex-partner who has come to the door, unobtrusively shake your hands and see or feel again the sparks emanating from your fingers.

For a nasty attack you may need to make the sparks brighter and sharper in your mind, not to harm but to strongly repel.

When you feel the attack lessening, let the sparks fade along with the shield, which they will do automatically as you relax.

Reflective Shield of Gold to Protect and Return the Harm to the Sender

This is an alternative way of making the Shield of Gold if you are under attack physically, psychologically, or psychically from normal or paranormal sources, known or unknown.

It is a fiercer form of the shield and will not need sparks to repel harm, as the mirror principle is to return any negativity.

I used this form of the shield when out of the blue I was cursed by a woman claiming to be a Romany. I was walking through the very upmarket Covent Garden in London where there were numerous expensive and rather lovely stalls, and a woman was rather forcefully trying to sell sprigs of tattered lucky rosemary to passersby. I politely declined, as the woman was asking an extortionate price for the luck.

I heard her mutter a curse under her breath. I carried on walking and suddenly felt as though a huge sheet of curved steel was hurtling towards me. I did not turn but said, "You can have that back," and instantly activated my Reflective Shield of Gold.

When I did turn round, the gypsy woman was sitting on the floor with her rosemary scattered round her, unhurt but very much brought to heel.

. . . .
Creating the Reflective Golden Shield

Ingredients and Tools

Eight small golden candles

A small handheld or makeup mirror

Timing

If possible, when natural light is shining to supplement the candlelight

The Ritual

Place the candles in a circle. Begin with the southernmost candle and
light your candles in turn, moving clockwise. You can use a compass
to align yourself to the actual directions or use approximations. Say as
you light the first candle,

> *Burn bright, gold candlelight.*
> *Drive away all danger.*
> *Protect me as I work and live/sleep*
> *From false friend and stranger.*

Repeat this as you light each candle.

Pass the mirror behind each of the candles in turn, beginning in
the south again so the flame reflects within the mirror. Say for each
candle,

> *So will my gold shield,*
> *To harm, threats, malice never yield,*
> *I reflect back only what you send,*
> *Your power to hurt is at an end.*

Now facing south again, press the mirror against your solar plexus
inner sun centre in the middle of your upper stomach.

Now move the mirror slowly and rhythmically in clockwise spirals around your head and body and picture the light as liquid gold

ascending through the energy pathways, or meridians, that spiral through your body from your feet and body upwards. Visualise the golden warmth swirling round as it continues to rise and flow up-wards through your hands and arms, heart, throat, and brow and into your head. Continue to say the second set of words softly and slowly until you feel filled with the golden light.

Now picture the golden light from the candles and mirror harden-ing as a translucent, spherical golden crystal that encloses your aura in shimmering light. You are now protected.

Let the light fade, knowing it is still there, and extinguish the can-dles counterclockwise, beginning with the one immediately to the right of your southernmost candle so that the last candle alight is the first one you ignited.

Carry the mirror in a small pouch or purse and, when you need the Reflective Golden Shield, take it out if you have time and press it against your solar plexus energy centre, repeating in your mind,

> *Burn bright, candle light.*
> *Drive away all danger,*
> *Protect me as I work and live/sleep*
> *From false friend and stranger.*

If you don't have time to get out the mirror (you could keep it un-obtrusively in your work space or near the front door at home), say,

> *My golden shield reflects back your negativity.*
> *Your bad intentions no more shall be*
> *Against me.*
> *Feel the pain;*
> *Send it not again.*

If you live in the southern hemisphere, you can work with north for the initial direction of your sun power if you prefer.

· · · · · · ·

Red Shield of Defense

This is not an everyday aura shield but one to be utilised at crisis times in your life or when dealing with folk who intend you harm. It is even more powerful than the Shield of Gold.

If you are suffering from particularly bullying spite, sarcasm, or malice at work; suffering from unpleasant relatives, vicious neighbours, or a malicious ex-partner; facing physical threats or dangers; being treated unjustly; or are subject to paranormal attack, ill wishing, curses, or the evil eye (see also chapter 6), the Red Shield of Defense will shield you from all harm. You can also activate it in dangerous places or where you suddenly see or feel an unpleasant earthly or paranormal presence—indeed, in any critical situation where survival on any level is in question.

You can create more than one kind of energy shield round yourself and in time of need or crisis activate the one that is most useful. Make the Shield of Gold first, and then if you wish, add this one. You can ask for a particular shield to be activated or say,

(Name angels) *protect me with the shield most I need.*

Step by Step: Creating the Red Shield of Defense

To create the Red Shield of Defense, you will need any one of these: a red tiger's eye (called a bull's eye in Scandinavia), a red jasper, or garnet of any quality.

The chakra body energy we are using to make this is drawn from the red root or base chakra that is located around the small of the back and the perineum but can be most easily located through the knees, the thighs, or the small but powerful chakras in the soles of the feet, as they also draw root energy from the earth. This fuels your innermost red aura level that is closest to your body and is the layer of survival under difficulty.

The best time and orientation for initial activation are just before sunset and facing the sunset, but in addition, light a single red candle.

STEP 1: MAKE THE ROOT CONNECTION

Kneel and place the crystal on the ground indoors or out to connect with Mother Earth, the source of red power.

Still kneeling, hold the crystal in your open cupped hands and breathe on it nine times to make the connection between your essential self and the crystal.

Close your hands around the crystal and at the same time close your eyes. Picture red light flowing from the crystal up your arms and the front of your body, from your knees into your head, and then down your back and legs right into the soles of your feet. At the same time picture rich red light from your feet, knees, back, and perineum flowing back into the crystal, being empowered by the crystalline energies and flowing upwards and round your whole body, again in continuing circuits as ruby-red light.

STEP 2: MAKING THE RED ENERGY SHIELD

When you feel filled with red light and totally charged with power, push the red colour into your aura by raising and using the hand you write with, still holding the crystal in the other hand, allowing the red light to flood your whole rainbow energy field with rich red. Of course, the rainbow is still there but shielded with red, and this will temporarily obscure the Shield of Gold.

Open your eyes. Now, using the hand you write with, press the crystal gently against the small of your back, the front of each thigh, and your knees or each sole of the foot to activate the root energy centre.

Hold it there for a minute or two and say just once,

Protect me with power, courage,
and strength to resist what I most fear.

Now, with your hands cupped and open, toss the crystal up and down nine times, and say as you do so nine times,

Fill me with power, courage,
and strength to overcome what I most fear.

Finally, touch the centre of your brow with the crystal still in both hands and say,

May only goodness and light enter me.
Blessings be on all of good intent.

STEP 3: ACTIVATE THE RED SHIELD

Carry your red crystal in a little purse or bag, and whenever you need to activate the Red Shield, hold the crystal and picture the Red Shield rising. Say in your mind,

Fill me with power, courage,
and strength to overcome what I most fear.

If you can't hold the red crystal, just say the words three times and touch your knees.

Reempower the red crystal monthly or more frequently if the Red Shield is getting a lot of use.

Creating a Shield of Grey

This is probably the method described in myth and fairy stories where the hero or heroine puts on a magical cloak and becomes invisible.

It is one you can set up in advance and activate instantly when the need for a low profile arises, like at a potentially confrontational meeting at work or when you know a relative picks on you at a necessary family gathering. It should be the last shield created.

You can also cast a Shield of Grey round a child who is picked on in the playground or on an older child or teenager who has to travel some distance to school to lower their profile from those who mean harm. This can be important if the child is carrying a mobile phone or indeed if you yourself are travelling and have a laptop or large amount of cash with you.

The greyness masks the normal aura signals we emit when we are afraid or anxious. It can also be reassuring to cast greyness and invisibility if you have a relative or friend in a dangerous job or place where it is important they move or patrol undetected.

If you look in a mirror after you have created a cloak of grey, your outline may seem blurred.

Walking Unscathed through Danger Using the Shield of Grey

Trudy, a young Australian living in the United Kingdom whom I had advised on psychic shielding during one of my courses, got totally lost alone in the backstreets of a holiday island in the Canaries renowned for attacks on tourists, after she had stormed off during an argument with her boyfriend. Remembering what she had learned in the course, she stopped panicking (essential, as fear vibes can be sensed by predators) and surrounded herself in what she described as a "grey mist bubble."

Though there were gangs of youths waving bottles and knives and shadowy figures in the doorways, she passed unnoticed until she found a main boulevard that she knew her hotel to be on. The next morning, she and her shocked boyfriend heard of two rapes and several muggings that had occurred the previous night in the area she had walked alone after midnight.

Step by Step: Creating the Shield of Grey

STEP 1: CAST INVISIBILITY ROUND YOURSELF

Work in the evening as it gets dark, or on a misty dull day, and light a grey candle. You do not need a crystal.

Sit in a comfortable position and close your eyes. You are going to use your inner psychic screen and picture the candle flame as if your eyes were open and you were directly looking at it.

Breathe slowly and evenly deep in your ribcage and sigh out any feelings of panic, doubt, or any specific worries. These worries can be for the person for whom you are creating the misty aura. Remember you can protect a vulnerable loved one, even if they are not present or able to give permission, using the power of love and acting in the power of love. (Why then could I not protect Sarah, who was so badly hurt by

Izzy, as I described in the previous chapter on psychic vampires? Because Sarah married Izzy and declared all who were not 100 percent for Izzy were also *her* enemy, so effectively blocking our former friendship. I knew Izzy was doing wrong from quite early on and earthly warnings had fallen on deaf ears. Helping others who resist help is a very grey area in magic, and all I can do is give you my beliefs and leave you as the reader to make up your own mind.) Continue this breathing until there is total calm on the exhale.

Now focus on the visualised candle and on the inner screen imagine the circle of swirling rainbow aura colours around your head and body entering the candle flame and flowing out as grey mist, so you can hardly see the candle flame in your mind. Because the shield takes the form of grey mist, it is not a sealed sphere like the other shields. Alternatively, visualise this mist around the loved one.

When you can no longer see the candle flame for mist in your mind, open your eyes and extinguish the actual candle flame. Light one or two white candles to restore light to your aura and burn them for as long as you wish.

Step 2: Activate the Shield of Grey in Situ

Deliberately quieten your thoughts or anxiety about yourself or the person you are shielding so that your aura is not fuelled by emotion, rather like putting a car in neutral gear.

Whenever you need to draw the cloak of invisibility round you or someone you care for, close your eyes and picture the candle flame and the mist descending. Then visualise the candle going out, leaving only the mist.

If there is no time, say in your mind,

I wear the cloak of invisibility, and so I pass unseen.

When the danger or potential intrusion has passed, picture the mist dispersing and your aura once more unfolding and getting bright.

You can recreate this aura of grey monthly or whenever needed if you are using it a lot.

Instant Psychic Shielding Using Colour Breathing

This method is good if you are being bugged at home or work or are uncertain about your physical safety. Some people use it instead of the shields I describe above and try to find the necessary colour focus (not always possible) in the environment they are in.

The breathing method also works well if you feel internally under attack from your own negative emotions, perhaps caused by a bad day at work or a difficult emotional encounter, and you just can't relax or let a grievance or quarrel go.

How to Practise Colour Breathing

Sit comfortably with your feet touching the floor. Take a deep breath through your nose and, as you do so, tense your body by placing your hands behind your head, with your elbows pointing forwards, then move your elbows out so they are parallel with the sides of your head and gently lean your head back.

Breathe out slowly though your mouth or nose, releasing your arms and extending them as wide as possible at shoulder height, stretching like a cat awaking from sleep.

Return your hands and arms to your lap or sides, whichever feels most comfortable.

Now breathe in slowly; hold this breath for a slow count of three (one—and—two—and—three) then exhale slowly through your mouth with a sigh. Do this five or six times.

Visualise the air you are inhaling as pure white or golden light, radiating through your body. Exhale slowly, seeing black mist being expelled, leaving your body lighter and more harmonious.

Slow your breathing patterns a little more, letting the golden or white light enter your lungs and spread throughout your body.

Repeat the pattern, each time visualising the dark mist leaving your body becoming paler as the negativity or anxiety is expelled, until your outwards breath is quite clear.

You can adapt this method for specific occasions or needs, using the colour combinations on the next page.

Use your exhaled breath as before to banish negativity or anxiety and your inhaled colour to introduce calm or focused energy. The warmer colours (red, yellow, and orange) are stimulating and energizing; the cooler colours (blue, green, and purple) soothe and gently uplift.

For psychic protection and shielding yourself internally or externally from unsettled feelings and uplifting the spirit, the following combinations seem to work well:

- *Instant energy or courage in times of danger:* Inhale red and exhale blue.
- *Banish anger or resentment:* Inhale blue and exhale red.
- *Confidence when you are being criticised or undermined:* Inhale orange and exhale indigo.
- *Still the mind and spirit after stress:* Inhale indigo and exhale orange.
- *Overcome emotional blackmail:* Inhale turquoise and exhale dull green.
- *Repel jealousy and fears:* Inhale violet and exhale yellow.
- *Power to repel malevolence:* Inhale yellow and exhale violet.
- *Positivity in any sphere and banishing depression and despair:* Inhale white or gold and exhale black.
- *Overcome sadness:* Inhale pink and exhale grey.
- *Relieve any negativity, especially if you feel surrounded by a dark cloud and fear psychic attack:* Use silver.

Experiment with different colour combinations and monitor mood changes.

When you feel totally balanced, harmonious, and either ready for action or sleep according to the colours you breathed, stretch once more. As you circle your hands around your head and shoulders, feel the renewed colours either moving slowly and in harmony or whirling with energy and optimism.

The Night Shield

The Night Shield helps you close your energies at night to enjoy quiet sleep and prevents attacks from whatever source while you are vulnerable in sleep. I have already suggested that you can activate the Shield of Gold before sleep, but this is a quiet, slower way that is especially potent if you find it hard to relax at night or suffer from insomnia or nightmares.

Close down and shield your main inner energy centres for the night by passing your hand, palm horizontal and facing inwards, first over the centre of your hairline a few centimetres away. Picture the swirling white, violet, and gold sphere of light slowing down and dark, velvet blue, the colour of the midnight sky, covering it.

Next pass your hand over the centre of your brow in the same way and picture the purple and indigo swirling sphere of light slowing and being covered by the velvet blue that becomes darker and more opaque as it passes down your energy centres, till by the root energy centre it is inky blue, almost black.

Continue to move your hand down your body, pausing over the main energy centres, visualising the bright blue sphere in the centre of your throat slowing and becoming covered by the darkening blue as your throat chakra closes for the night.

Now allow the emerald green whirling heart chakra in the centre of your chest or between your breasts to also be slowed and covered in the ever-darker blue as you place your palm in front of it.

Picture the light carrying the calmness down in the same way into the yellowy gold solar plexus sphere in the upper centre of your stomach, and slow and close this chakra with your palm with a blue that becomes more and more opaque and shadowy. Again touch or gently press your solar plexus.

Next, your hand moves downwards again and covers the whirling orange and silver sacral chakra, which is situated just below your navel in the centre, and finally down to your feet, left and right, and upwards to the small of your back to seal the red root chakra that is now covered with inky and totally opaque blue darkness.

Then push down with your feet, sitting or standing, and keep your fingers pointing downwards with your hands at your sides to allow any excess psychic energy to flow back into the earth or floor.

Basic Information on Auras and Chakras

Red Root Chakra

- Located around the perineum, the lower back, the thighs, knees, and the soles of the feet. All of these areas are also linked with grey, brown, and black.
- Associated with physical functioning, basic instincts, potency, survival, strength, and the five physical senses.
- Corresponds with the innermost red layer or the aura called the "aetheric layer," which rules precisely the same body and mind areas.
- Attacked through creating fear, anger, and violence.

Orange and Silver Sacral Chakra (Also Called the Hara)

- Situated on or just below the navel and includes the womb and male genitals.
- Associated with spontaneous feelings and urges, self-esteem, desires, fertility, and aspects of comfort or satisfaction, such as eating, drinking, and sexuality.
- Corresponds with the orange emotional layer of the aura moving outwards.
- Attacked through guilt, emotional vampirism, and addictions.

Yellow Solar Plexus Chakra

- Situated at the base of the sternum around the upper stomach area.
- Associated with mental abilities, willpower and self-control, confidence, logic, and the evolving personality.

- This corresponds to the yellow mental layer of the aura moving out from the body and becoming less dense and more diffuse in shape.

- Attacked through spite, gossip, the evil eye of envy, and cyberbullying.

Green and Pink Heart Chakra

- Situated in the centre of the chest, its energies radiating over heart, lungs, breasts, arms, and hands.

- Associated with harmony within the self as well as with others, love, relationships, altruism, healing, and a love of beauty and nature.

- Corresponds to the green astral layer of the aura.

- Attacked through controlling and destructive love, more powerful emotional vampirism, malign nature elementals and negative earth energies, and psychic attack from those emotionally close, including ex-partners.

Sky Blue Throat Chakra

- Situated close to the Adam's apple in the centre of the neck. It controls the neck and shoulders and the passages that run up to the ears as well as the throat and speech organs and thyroid gland.

- Associated with synthesis of emotion and thought, ideas and ideals, and clear communication, which includes listening as well as speaking and the expression of creativity.

- Corresponds to the blue aetheric template of the aura.

- Attacked through curses; verbal, written, and phone attacks; and ill wishing.

Indigo or Purple Brow Chakra

- Centred just above the bridge of the nose in the centre of the brow and controls the eyes, ears, and more instinctive functions of the brain.
- Associated with unconscious wisdom, psychic powers (especially clairvoyance), angelic communication, dreams, and imagination.
- This corresponds to the indigo aetheric template aura level, which now is almost without shape and extending outwards.
- Attacked through spirits, sexual demons (who also enter through the second, orange level), psychic attacks by professional practitioners, and thought forms.

Violet, White, and Gold Crown Chakra

- Situated at the top of the head at the fontanelle area, extending from the centre of the hairline to several centimetres above the head.
- Associated with the union of mind, body, and spirit; the divine spark in us all; higher brain functions; our connection with divinity; and integration with the universe.
- Corresponds to the white ketheric template, is associated with the divine or universal consciousness, and is related to the seventh (crown) chakra that merges with the cosmos and may extend an arm's span beyond the body.
- Attacked through the open connection with the personal energy fields of others and the energies of places from toxic workplaces to haunted houses. This is the aura layer round which the shields are placed.

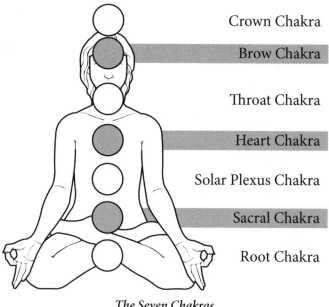

Crown Chakra

Brow Chakra

Throat Chakra

Heart Chakra

Solar Plexus Chakra

Sacral Chakra

Root Chakra

The Seven Chakras

Banishing Magic for Safety and Strength

In chapter 1 we worked with binding negative influences and people who cause problems in our lives and those of loved ones. Then we added psychic rituals and shields to block ongoing psychic attacks, emotional vampires, and deliberate acts of malice and in some cases to reflect back the harm or ill wishing to the sender.

In this chapter we will explore an even more powerful form of psychic defense, banishing magic, which nevertheless must involve no malice by the spellcaster. This can be hard when we are experiencing attacks against loved ones or ourselves, especially where official or legal routes seem to be leading nowhere. It is important in all magic, and especially in banishing magic, not to cast spells when you are angry or feeling vengeful (understandable human emotions if we feel under siege or on the receiving end of major injustice). Dig the garden, do some cleaning, or exercise until you feel calmer.

As a result of defensive spells, within a few weeks legal and official help, if sought, often seems to become more forthcoming as a bonus to the spellcasting. Again I cannot fully explain why except to say the energies are generally changed for the better in the everyday world in a number of ways, even if not specified in the spell, like ripples from a stone thrown into still water.

Banishing magic is the strongest and most empowering way of dealing with negativity, threats, and bad influences. As well as forcefully driving away external malice, banishing magic will help remove your inner demons of fear, unwarranted guilt that holds you back from happiness, debt, chronic pain, and problems such as overdependency on food, alcohol, or cigarettes. You can also banish on behalf of others you care for who may have lost their way.

You may need to bind the problem first until the hold has weakened and then carry out a banishing spell, especially in the case of bad habits, fears, or people who have deeply influenced you for years. Once you have banished external and internal bugbears, you can erect psychic shields to prevent their return. Indeed, by the time you have read the book you will have a whole psychic armoury to mix and match in your own unique forms of defensive magic.

Do banishing magic sparingly when you need a powerful and swift ending and—I will emphasise again, as it is so important not to tip over into bad magic—always when you are calm and without desire for revenge, just for rapid and permanent removal of the negativity. This often will mean banishing a negative person from your life and thoughts or from the life of someone being harmed who is dependent on you.

While banishing magic is best done after dark during the latter part of the waning moon cycle, you often don't have the luxury of waiting. Midnight (the turning of the old night into the new day) and sunset (the end of the day in some older calendars, like the Celtic and Nordic) are potent anytime of the month. Midnight on the last day of the week or month is also especially effective.

Banishments in the Ancient World

In physically hazardous life and death situations, magicians from around 4000 BCE in Sumeria, ancient Mesopotamia (modern Iraq and Syria between the Tigris and Euphrates rivers), and from about

3000 BCE in ancient Egypt did use curses as a form of defense and banishment of enemies.

In Egypt curse pottery would have a person's name etched into it before firing and then be smashed. It was believed in ancient Egypt that every part of the body, soul, and spirit was interdependent, and so to inscribe the name of an enemy on a pot or wax image and then destroy it had the power to destroy the living person.

Clearly, the concept of destroying anyone magically is abhorrent to us in the modern world, no matter how wrong their behaviour is.

Yet in our more sanitised world we can still take from those darker times sound defensive magical principles and give them a more positive but no less powerful spin.

Smashing the Negative Hold

Use this technique for ridding a bad habit or a person that is wrecking your life or that of a vulnerable loved one. You can write the name of a sorrow or fear or threat on an old pot and destroy that to banish what is holding you back.

However, when a person is being really unpleasant, you can also adapt the broken pot method to banish them and their malice from your life. Rivals who threaten our livelihood by dishonest means, drug pushers, gang members who try to influence our teenagers, those who hurt children, or those who use social media campaigns to make someone's life hell all need rapid and determined banishment; as long as you are not harming them magically you can work to get rid of them from your world or that of a loved one who cannot easily defend themselves. The desired result is to free someone in distress or danger. The rest is up to natural justice that sooner or later kicks in.

Overcoming a Bullying and Deceitful Colleague

John was in his late forties and was being badly bullied by his colleague Ned, who wanted John's job as an onscreen roving journalist in a talk show in Texas. Ned was deliberately sabotaging John's work and telling everyone John was unhinged and not safe to send out on camera shoots after Ned had bribed some local teenagers to provoke John on camera. John had no proof of Ned interfering with his broadcasts and destroying his material, as Ned was very clever, but Ned was taunting John daily that he would get him out.

Since things were coming to a head, we urgently needed something faster and stronger than a binding or shielding to banish Ned from any interference in John's work by word or action and to get him out of John's life.

I taught John a modern variation of the Egyptian pot smashing, and while this would not harm Ned or wreck his career, it would get him off John's case. A similar spell to banish the influence of someone who is wrecking your life or bullying or lying about you or a loved one follows this account. As part of the spell, since no one would believe John, we asked that Ned be shown in his true light.

Within a week of John doing the spell (and I also cast the spell on John's behalf with his permission, as he was becoming very distressed), Ned was caught red-handed by the producer erasing some special film John had recorded, and he was moved away from live broadcasting to a job in the archives. Ned was the instigator of his own downfall—the spell just revealed him in his true light—and necessarily fast, as John was at breaking point.

The following is the spell we carried out. If you do this spell to remove someone from your life who is harmful to you or your family, you have the option of smashing the bowl or simply burying it. Smashing is very empowering if matters are desperate, and then you can wrap and bury the pieces. The spell also works well if you are being slandered or someone is telling lies about you either in court or stirring up trouble in your marriage. It will banish a harmful influence, especially when dishonesty is involved.

· ·
Spell to Banish Harmful Influence

Ingredients and Tools

A purple or dark blue candle

A small, unglazed pot

A red pen to write on the pot, such as a permanent marker or glass
   paint pen
Growing basil (a fire herb, for fierce defense) and sage (brings wisdom and growth out of evil)

Timing

Saturday, the day of Saturn and of setting boundaries, or whenever
   urgent

The Spell

Light the candle, saying,

> *This interference and malice now must end,*
> *Though no harm to you I send.*
> (Name perpetrator), *you sabotage, make trouble about me*
> (or name victim), *and lie.*
> *To your disruption I say goodbye.*

Write round the centre of the pot the perpetrator's full name (or if
unknown, a descriptive phrase such as "the drug dealer who leads my
son astray"). Say,

> *You are barred from causing me* (or name victim) *distress;*
> *Your evil behaviour now shall cease.*
> *With the smashing/burial of this pot,*
> *I* (or name victim) *am released.*
> *Your power grows less and less and less.*

Hold the pot up to the candle and blow the candle out, saying,

> *Enter here light;*
> *There will be no more fight.*
> *You,* (name perpetrator), *are banished from my sight.*

Bury the pot in the garden or a very deep plant pot, or smash it, wrap the pieces in paper, and bury that. Plant the basil and sage on top.

• • • • • • •

Banishing Manipulators

Banishing magic helps against those who do harm or seek to control others by manipulation, threats of physical harm, or mind games. It will help to stop physical threats and the insidious mind games played by bullies who create in their victims a constant fear of attack against themselves or against children or vulnerable family members.

Lesley, who lives in Minnesota, was terrified because she was receiving constant threats from her ex-partner Trevor that he would break into her home at night and kill her and the children if she did not hand over all the money she had been awarded by the courts as settlement to her after their divorce. She had no proof, as Trevor only ever made verbal threats when not even the children were around. There were frequent middle-of-the-night disturbances (the nearest house was miles away), and she had seen Trevor prowling around testing doors and rattling downstairs windows. She had changed the locks but could not afford video surveillance.

No one would take Lesley seriously when she called the police, as Trevor always had an alibi from his girlfriend that he was at home at the time when disturbances occurred, and to the world her ex was a charming, kind man with a neurotic ex-wife.

Banishing spells have a dual function. They lessen the actual influence or power of the abuser or bully and at the same time increase your own confidence and activate your own self-defensive mechanisms to claim back your territory and sometimes bring an unexpected solution.

Lesley and I did a spell several times together on Skype, and she decided as part of the spell we should send the nastiness back to Trevor, an acceptable practise so that Trevor would know directly or indirectly the pain he had caused.

Regrettably, with unscrupulous people, love and light sent to the perpetrator of evil just brushes off the wrongdoer, who has consciously or unconsciously created a dark shield around himself or herself and can cause you inner turmoil because there are some things that cannot nor should be forgiven. Often immediately after banishing, negative activity can temporarily increase, a way you know that your banishing spells are hitting target and the target is unconsciously resisting the telepathic power.

Trevor took to watching the house at night but disappearing as soon as Lesley rang the police. Then after about two weeks the attacks and threats suddenly ceased and Trevor was not heard of again. He had never wanted to see the children nor contribute to their care. Lesley later discovered Trevor had been regularly beating up Toni, his girlfriend, who had been lying to her family about the cause of her injuries. But when Trevor attacked one of her children, Toni made a complaint to the police, and of course many of Lesley's complaints were still on file.

Before charges could be pressed, Trevor left the area with another young girl he had been seeing at the same time as Toni, and Lesley heard the girl was pregnant. Magic is very complex, like an intertwining web; while it could be argued Lesley had not directly caused Trevor's cessation of vileness by the spell, the results were those intended by the spell, and the threats stopped.

. . . .

Spell to Remove the Effects of Ongoing Threats, Physical Danger, and Mind Manipulation

These are the details of the spell I e-mailed to Lesley before the first Skype session, and we adapted it to her situation through detailed discussion before spellcasting. All the spells in this book are templates, and you should feel free to adapt the words and even actions to fit your need once you become confident.

This spell is one you can easily adapt against the nastiest neighbour, a vindictive ex-partner, bullying in the workplace, or threats from a big organisation or officialdom, or unscrupulous debt collectors.

Nothing is too small or too overwhelming if it is causing you distress. This spell is also good if you have a suspected paedophile in the family, and the rest of the family turns against you for daring to express concerns. These measures are no substitute for the law, but, while fighting for the truth, banishing spells offer some protection to those in danger and often expose the wrongdoer. As I travel around I meet many people whose families say they are crazy when they voice what are clearly real concerns about the inappropriateness of the behaviour of a particular family member towards the children, and this may have gone on for a generation or more as a conspiracy of silence.

Ingredients and Tools

Three dark blue (the colour of Sachiel, archangel of justice) candles of the same size

A jar of garlic salt or dried garlic granules, the kind you buy in supermarkets (Garlic has been traditionally used against vampires and evildoers for thousands of years.)

An eggcup-sized container for the garlic

Timing

Whenever you receive a new threat or feel anxious or upset about the situation

Thursday, the day of the Archangel Sachiel, is especially potent

The Spell

Place the candles in a row in holders and light them from left to right, one candle from the other. As the wax begins to melt, drop a few grains of garlic salt into each flame in turn. You may want to open the window, as burning garlic smells foul. Say for each candle,

> *Three times your viciousness I return,*
> *Three times sent back as candles burn.*
> *Take back the pain you cause me.*
> *From harming my life/our lives* (or name victim), *banished be.*

Extinguish each candle, right to left. As you do so, say for each candle,

Be gone from threatening me/my family (or name victim).
From wrong shall now come right.
No more trouble me,
With the dimming of this light.

Throw away any garlic salt you do not use, and wash out the bowl in hot water.

When casting this spell, I have found it effective not to name the perpetrator of harm, but this is a personal choice that seems to work with some spells and not others. Experiment, for each of us has our own way of creating magic that is right for us.

Sometimes magic seems to use existing but unknown circumstances round the perpetrator of evil to achieve the desired results. Indeed, under the returning nasty energies threefold principle, banishing spells will very frequently rebound the energy on the perpetrator by seemingly accelerating events in their lives caused by their own wrongdoing that can have the positive effect of banishing the perpetrator from your life.

. . . .

Banishing Spells and Relationships

Everyone has free will, and, as I said in the introduction, we cannot and should not use magic to bind a partner in love against their will. But sometimes the behaviour of a partner goes against their own loving nature, and they can be set to sabotage twenty or more years of happy partnership and family life on a seeming whim or an obsession for another person.

If a partner is determined to stray or is a serial betrayer, we cannot hold them by magical force, for such a relationship would never work and ultimately they are not worthy of our trust. However, a normally loving partner and parent may become secretive, especially if they hit a midlife crisis or, sometimes, a crisis of confidence in their career if younger people seem to be racing ahead. You may discover that a colleague, neighbour, or even the family au pair is pursuing your partner. In such instances you are entitled to banish the obsession or lust and deliberate attempts of seduction that would ultimately destroy lasting family happiness for a short thrill. For too often these lust liaisons do not last, and the instigator of the temptation will move on to wreck another marriage going through a difficult or mundane patch. This is another major issue where I am frequently asked to help, often but not always by the woman who is being abandoned for a newer model, especially if her husband travels away from home a lot.

Having seen as well as experienced much heartbreak due to infidelity, I believe that banishing is justified in order to bring a swift end to the misery, breaking the sexual hold of the vamp or lothario without harming them. Then the relationship has a fighting chance of being mended, or at least there is hope of a peaceful parting. I respect those who say this is going against the will of the straying partner, but I have seen many happy results in which the abandoned partner does a spell to remind the absent partner of the love still between them, and the love becomes richer than before. So, your call. You can't do defensive magic without picking your way through the minefield of ethics, and in every instance you must decide according to your conscience; but, especially where children are involved, I would say magic is permissible if it harms no one. If the marriage is truly finished, then it won't work, but at least you tried.

An example of a successful attempt to use banishing magic to help a relationship involves Paula, who lives in northern Australia, and her husband, Pete. They had been through so much together in their fifteen years of marriage, and Pete had often joked about Trixie, the glamorous older woman in the office who had made her rounds of the married men before moving on to her next conquest. Recently, Pete, who was worried about being passed over for promotion and was depressed and snappy with the family, had started working late. He kept his phone switched off on his frequent overnight stays at seminars, to which Trixie went along as his personal assistant.

When Paula went to a company dinner, Trixie was draped all over Pete, and he looked embarrassed but made no attempt to move away. Paula knew they were going on a weeklong conference together and was worried.

On the week of the conference, Paula did the spell that follows, which I taught her when I met her at a festival where I was lecturing and doing consultations in Australia's Northern Territory. Every night Pete was away at the conference, she continued to banish the undue influence Trixie had over him, which Paula knew was not love but just another notch on Trixie's belt.

To Paula's surprise, Pete phoned every night and sounded miserable. When he came home, he apologised for his behaviour and admitted that in the car on the way to the venue, Trixie had suggested they share a room, and he had agreed. But after dinner the first evening (after the first spell) Trixie had gone cold, switched rooms, and made it obvious to Pete he was not rich enough. Seemingly instantly, she transferred her attentions to a new colleague whose father had major shares in the company. Magic or coincidence, the spell had the desired effect. Paula accepted Pete back into the fold, and soon afterwards Pete left the company to start his own business.

Because magic does change energies, not only did Pete become less attractive to Trixie, but the new colleague she had known before and seemingly was not interested in became the new centre of Trixie's radar also during the period of the daily spellcasting.

This is the spell I taught Paula. You can use it to banish a destructive influence who is trying to wreck a relationship or your partner, who you know has a tendency to flirt but is otherwise a good person. You could adapt the spell words, inserting the name of *your* partner, if you yourself are tempted to have an affair but love your partner and know it would be disastrous.

· ·

A Spell to Banish a Love Obsession Wrecking a Happy Relationship

Ingredients and Tools

A red and a blue candle, the blue candle to the right
A thin paper knife or sharp small screwdriver
An eggcup-sized container of salt
An eggcup-sized container of pepper

Timing

Whenever you know temptation is going to occur

The Spell

Place the blue candle to the right of the red candle. Using the paper knife, lightly scratch "Be faithful only to me" on one side of the blue candle and "Temptation banished be" on one side of the red candle.

Light the blue candle and say,

As this wax melts, so the hold of (name the person; if unknown, say he or she who would come between your happiness)
shall likewise burn away.

Let none come between us, (name your partner),
or tempt you to stray.

Sprinkle a pinch of salt into the blue candle flame and say,

The love between us, (name partner), *is true, long-lasting,*
And in fire I call you.

Light the red candle from the blue one, sprinkle a pinch of pepper in the flame, and say,

False passion burn,
Away may false love turn,
Temptation banished be,
Grow cold like this flame I can no longer see.

Extinguish the red candle. Leave the blue candle to burn through and say,

Be only for me,
Look only on me with love and fidelity,
(Name source of temptation), *your power is broken,*

Banished, never to return.
No longer yearn for (name your partner),
But your eyes elsewhere turn.

Replace the blue candle if doing the spell more than once, and etch on it as before, "Be faithful only to me."

Etch over the writing on the red candle (don't worry if the writing is not clear in later spells as the candle burns down), "Temptation banished be."

Tip away any remaining salt and pepper under a running tap after each spell and replace for subsequent spells.

. . . .

Alternative, Stronger Spell at a Make-or-Break Time in a Relationship

Just as damaging to a relationship as infidelity can be a partner's bad habit or addictions to gambling, alcohol, or extravagance, and often a really good person can have this fatal flaw that is killing the love and causing harm to the partner and family financially, emotionally, and by causing the addict to behave in unloving ways. Many people who seek my help magically do want to stick with their addicted partner who just won't seek help, and sometimes I have found that spellcasting can change the energies to admit outside positive intervention as well as strengthen the suffering partner to take decisive earthly action. The following spell is not attacking the addicted person but rather their bad behaviour and those who are actively encouraging the bad habit. As the pins attached to the burning candle fall as the wax loosens its hold, so the addiction may become less entrenched. This is not an easy area to deal with practically and magically, and the drug ice is especially gripping people in its thrall. It may be necessary to do the spell many times.

Ingredients and Tools

A soft wax candle
Two long, strong pins

Timing

Every Saturday evening after dark until the problem improves

The Spell

Light the candle and say,

As this candle burns, so shall melt away (name the problem, bad habit, or destructive person causing problems between you—for example, one who is encouraging your partner to take drugs).

> *Melt and burn,*
> *Candle, turn*
> *Away this sorrow*
> *That on the morrow*
> *(Name) may be free*
> *His/her own true self*
> *Once more to be.*

As the wax begins to soften, insert the two pins, pushing gently but firmly through the centre of the wick halfway down the candle to form a cross. As you do so, say,

> *'Tis not these pins I wish to burn,*
> *But my lover's heart to turn.*
> *As this wax melts,*
> *So I do call*
> *All that/who mar/s our life*
> *Like these pins to fall.*

When the pins fall, extinguish the candle, disposing of candle and pins.

. . . .

Banishment through Drawing Boundaries

This is an excellent method of banishment since you not only remove the harmful person or force but set up a psychic boundary beyond which the perpetrator of harm cannot venture. This works especially well against a stalker, antisocial neighbours, an unscrupulous debt collector, or an ex who harasses you.

I helped Donald, who is in his seventies and has lived all his adult life in community housing in the suburbs of London, with drawing boundaries. Over the last ten years, families with unruly children, and some with vicious dogs, have moved in, and at night the street is overrun with teenagers who bang on his window, kick footballs against his car, and drop garbage and worse in his tiny front garden. If he goes out to complain, they abuse and threaten him—and their parents look on laughing.

The overworked police and housing department do their best, but it is a problem endemic in the area. Donald came to see me when I was working in London, as he had tried everything, and he said magic was his last resort.

I suggested he carry out the following spell early in the morning at a time when his street was deserted, and because he was anxious I talked him through on the phone before he actually did the spell. I checked up on Donald a week later and thereafter weekly, as he had no relatives and I was worried how he was coping.

Donald told me he had smiled as he wheeled his shopping trolley past the sneering matriarch of the ringleaders, carrying the ball of clay he had used as part of the spell, ready to be dumped after the banishing. Within a few days, he noticed the ringleaders were coming out less, though they still made a huge noise with their music and quarrelling through the party wall, and the other teenagers in the street drifted off, no doubt to wreak mayhem elsewhere.

About three weeks later the eldest son of the family next door (the chief troublemaker) and his brother were taken into custody and charged with a vicious attack on a local shopkeeper (perhaps why they had been lying low). The following week, the family, amid great protests, was evicted by official bailiffs for huge rent arrears.

Donald had not *caused* these misfortunes—maybe magic just sped up the natural processes of justice—though previous earthly attempts by the authorities to remove the troublemakers had failed. A peaceful family moved in and, with other neighbours, started a neighbourhood watch Donald had not been previously able to get off the ground. There are still no miracles, as there are still issues in the neighbourhood, but Donald feels much safer. The number of positive results that do follow spells would suggest, not to the satisfaction of scientists but relief to the victims, that magic does work in its own mysterious ways.

. . . .
Spell to Banish Those Who Come to Your Home to Threaten or Harass

Use this spell to banish antisocial neighbours or anyone who comes to your home to threaten, harass, or intimidate you and to keep away thieves or vandals if you live in an unsafe area. This also works well against cyberbullies and unpleasant or scam telephone or Internet callers.

Ingredients and Tools
A small jug of water
A small container of soil
A small bowl of salt
A piece of children's play clay
Paper
Red pen

Timing
Sunrise on a Sunday, the hour and day of the Archangel Michael,
    who defends the vulnerable with his mighty sword

The Spell
Sprinkle nine pinches of salt on top of the soil and add nine drops of water so the soil is still crumbly, then say,

By salt, earth, and water, three by three,
You who make my life misery,
Banished shall you be

From my home, garden, car,
And all that is dear to me.

Outside your home, facing the sunrise, scatter a straight line of soil, salt, and water mixture in front of you. Take a step backwards in the direction of your home, making a second line, and then step back again, making a third line.

Stand behind the three lines, facing the rising sun, and say,

By salt, earth, and water,
You can no longer reach me.
Banished shall you be.

Go indoors, close the door, and form a small, clay, featureless figure to represent any of the worst known perpetrators and one figure for any unknown predators. You can add a clay dog if you or your pets suffer from a vicious animal living close by.

Where the mouth should be, insert a lump of clay, saying for each figure,

Stopped are your obscenities,
Banished your abuse.
For your persecution,
I have no further use.

Write the same words on paper, draw a cross through the words, and fold it very small. Reroll the clay figures to make a ball of clay to enclose the paper, and throw the lot in a garbage bin away from your home.

· · · · · · ·

Creating Your Own Banishing Spells

Once you have tried one or two of the banishing spells in this chapter, you may want to create your own. Here are some suggestions that work on exactly the same principles.

Candle Power in Banishing

Fire is a very potent banishing tool. As the energy generates rapidly, it consumes malice. And, especially when a candle is engraved with the names of who or what you want to banish from your life and then burned, it takes with it the imprinted energies.

Extinguishing a deep purple or blue candle with a snuffer or a small cup is a very visual, tangible expression of banishing, with such words as these:

> *May all harm be gone with the dimming of this light.*
> *You,* (insert your own words of what/who is to be banished),
> *can be gone with the dimming of this light.*

Then, dispose of the candle. In banishing, candles are extinguished rather than blown out (blowing spreads the light), to remove what is harmful. Blue is the colour of Sachiel, the justice archangel, and purple is one of the colours of Cassiel, who imposes limitations and boundaries.

In a slower-acting banishing spell in which the banishment involves emotional pain that has built up over the years, the candle is burned right through and any remaining wax thrown away, thus marking an end to the negativity. Candles, especially beeswax ones, are excellent for melting away anything from bullying or sexual temptation (as with Paula's antivamp spell) to removing an addiction. Red, the colour of Camael, archangel of Mars, is potent for banishment, as are dark purple and indigo for Archangel Cassiel and blue for Sachiel and justice.

Etching words on a candle or tracing them invisibly on the unlit candle with the index finger of the hand you write with are equally effective ways of imprinting the power of the banishment on the candle. As the candle burns, the power of the written words becomes doubly powerful if spoken while etching or tracing, so the banishment is released. If a daily spell, you can retrace or redraw the words; it does not matter if they overlap the original words or are hard to fit on as the candle shrinks. The power is in the etching or tracing. For example, if you want to banish excess social drinking or overeating from your life or that of a loved one, etch with a thin-bladed knife on the side of the candle the word "alcohol" or "binging" just before you go out or you are tempted by a craving. Let the candle burn away. Dispose of the wax. You may need to repeat this many times if the habit is ingrained, but each time write the word fainter till you are just tracing it invisibly on the side of the candle. This method also works well for overdependency on prescription drugs.

Using Two Candles for Banishing

Using matching deep purple or blue candles, trace with the index finger of the hand you write with the name of the perpetrator of harm along one side of each of the unlit candles and on the other side trace "Banished be." Put the candles in their holders and light them. As the wax melts so will the threat.

Alternatively, a defensive white candle for Michael, archangel of the sun, is lit from a purple or blue one before the purple or blue candle is extinguished to transfer what was good from the past to the future and to replace negative energies with positive ones through transformation of negativity into light.

Burning Messages

Burning a banishing message written on white paper in red or blue ink for justice in the candle flame or in a fire is another potent way of using raw fire energy to instantly dissolve a threat or, indeed, a fear. Writing it faintly or even with a white pencil on white paper reduces the power you attribute to the wrongdoer. Traditionally, all the vowels are removed, and then the consonants are written together as one word, sometimes in capitals to emphasise the power of the banishing. For example, alcohol becomes LCHL and bullying becomes BLLNG.

Cutting Cords

Cord cutting in a candle flame, also described in the introduction, is one of the easiest and most tangible ways of breaking connections

and therefore is psychologically as well as psychically potent and satis-
fying if things seem hopeless.

You can also just use a white Michael candle to ask the archangel
to cut the cords that hold you in a destructive relationship or an old
bad love whose memories hold you back from new romance. It can
also help against an emotional vampire or a phobia or addiction in
your or a loved one's life, even in a situation where you are limited by
circumstances such as crushing debt, pain, or depression.

Having lit the Michael candle, hold a knotted white cord with the
knot in the centre of the flame till it breaks, saying,

Michael with your fiery sword,
Banish this (name), *hear my words.*

Catch the burning cord in a pot of soil and bury it in the garden or a
deep plant pot. In this case, blow out the candle to surround you or a
loved one with the Michael light.

For help against stalking, against anyone who threatens you or
loved ones or plays mind games, or if a loved one is involved in a cult,
name the stalker or threat as you tie a knot in a purple, dark blue, or
indigo cord or strong thread, saying,

I banish you from approaching me (or name loved one)
menacingly or needlessly.

Burn the knot in the candle, throw soil on top of the cord as you drop
the burning ends in a heatproof pot of soil, and extinguish the candle
in the same soil, flame downwards.

Banishing with Water

For banishing something or someone that has been in your life for
years or when there is a strong emotional attachment (for example,
a secret love you know will never work or if you love too much and
find it hard to let go of a love that is over and which in your heart you
know will never return) water is much gentler, and the banishment

can be more gradual. Water is also potent for banishing grief and un-warranted guilt if a relative died with bad feelings towards you.

Use a miniature tablet of soap. Before taking a bath or shower in the evening, etch invisibly on the soap with the index finger of the hand you write with the name of who or what you must let go of. Or use your index fingernail to scratch the words into the soap. Use the soap in your bath or shower to wash, saying words such as these:

Flow from me, go from me,
It must be so.
Banished must you be,
That I may walk free.

After using the soap to wash yourself, take out the plug to symbolise the release of energy. If you're in the shower, visualise the release of energy as the water escapes down the drain. Next time you use the soap, re-draw or trace the words. Repeat for each use until the soap is gone.

Water can be used for immediate banishment as well as the more gradual method suggested in the soap spell. Dying petals or leaves thrown off a bridge into fast-flowing water or cleansing salt (mixed with pepper for something really hard or horrible) washed away under a fast-running tap are immediate releasers of negative forces or fears.

If you live near to the ocean or a tidal river, the outgoing tide will carry sadness or bad memories away if you throw an appropriate crystal (such as smoky quartz) or dark stone into the water, naming what you are consigning to the waters.

Banishing with Earth

If you have deep-seated links, whether to a destructive person or situation or if you would like to bury old feelings causing rifts in a family or relationship, bury in earth what you wish to remove from your life, and scratch the symbol on a stone or a bone (the origin of the expression "burying the bone").

If the matter is one you wish to totally end, bury the symbol in earth in which nothing has been planted rather than beneath a flourishing plant. For transforming what was bad into good, bury a stoned or seeded fruit that will decay but form the basis of new growth. You can bury a related item and not just a symbol. For example, you might bury a cigarette or tobacco beneath a fragrant plant so when you smell the plant you are reminded of your good intentions.

Banishing with Air

Air in the form of the winds can also be used in banishing, and for a fast result, scattering dead leaves or dead flower petals to the wind from a hilltop will allow the winds to swiftly carry away what is symbolically dead in your life and carry you forwards to the next stage.

However, if it were a banishment, that would need longer to take effect. For example, if you were using nicotine patches or electronic cigarette substitutes to reduce a smoking addiction, hang a knotted biodegradable cord from a tree and wait for the cord to break naturally as the winds blow it. Alternatively, use a twig or branch on which there are dying or dead leaves and plant it either at the top of a hill or in a sheltered place for even slower action, touching each leaf and naming the inner demon over and over. Gradually, one by one the dead leaves will die off, leaving you free.

Defensive Bottles, Bags, Amulets, and Symbols

Defensive or witch bottles, bags, amulets, and symbols have a two-fold purpose. They can absorb or reflect harm or both. In addition, they act as a tangible background shield against earthly or paranormal malice against your home, you, and loved ones or while you are at work or travelling.

They are an added defense for those times when you are so busy or distracted you forget or do not have time to activate your psychic shield or domestic or workplace protection, which I will describe in detail in the next two chapters.

Symbols, according to the twentieth-century occultist Dion Fortune, are believed to contain the energies, power, protection, and experiences of all the people who had used them or seen the actual manifestation of the symbol in real life, and the same is true of protective amulets or charms.

Witch or Defensive Magic Bottles

Defensive magic bottles filled with protective items, such as iron, date from before Roman times.

The witch bottle tradition itself was popularised in the 1500s when the witch persecutions made ordinary people terrified evil witches might enter their homes through the chimney and doors and curse them. Therefore, they created countercurse bottles to harm witches as well as repel them.

The stoneware Bellarmine was the most popular kind of witch bottle, invented in the 1600s in Germany and also made in the Netherlands and exported to the United Kingdom and Scandinavia as well as parts of Eastern Europe. They are also made of coloured glass, often in deeper shades, and glass ones reflect harm whereas stoneware bottles absorb it. Either is effective.

Witch bottles continued to be used as protective devices right till the beginning of the twentieth century among the general population, often made by some old relative and given to a young person setting up home. There are fine examples of traditional witch bottles in the small and eccentric but fabulous Pitt Rivers Museum in Oxford, United Kingdom.

Witch bottles, or, as I prefer to call them, wise man or woman bottles, work by acting in the stead of the maker, people, or place they are meant to protect. They create an exclusion zone against deliberate ill intent and deflect unfocused negativity, without in any way amplifying the malice (karma does that).

A witch bottle is especially potent because the contents, each psychically protective in nature, mix within the bottle in the making, thus creating a defensive energy greater than the individual properties of each ingredient. Once buried, it forms a long-lasting defense. You can make more active temporary ones for protection against specific threats or malice.

As you learn different defensive techniques, you will notice methods from previous chapters (such as binding, shielding, and banishing) are often the basis of many kinds of protection, including bottles, and the more you see the interconnections, the easier it will be to create your own defensive spells.

. . . .
Spell to Create a Long-Lasting Witch Bottle

Ingredients and Tools

A red candle

A deep-coloured glass or stoneware bottle with a cork or tight lid
(You can often buy stoneware ones containing cider or dark glass
ones containing beer.)

Two or three sprigs of fresh rosemary or two or three teaspoons of
dried cooking rosemary

A quantity of old rusty nails and pins (Look in the bottom of a tool
box.)

Enough cheap or sour red wine or vinegar to almost fill the bottle
(The original protective fluid, urine, is not often used in modern
witch bottles.)

Sealing wax to put round the top or melting wax from a red candle

Pliers

Timing

Around 10:00 p.m. at the end of the waning cycle when the moon is
not visible in the sky

The Spell

Work by the light of the red candle and have all your ingredients
ready. Rinse the bottle under a cold tap before starting, even if new.

Add sufficient rosemary to line the bottom. Add the rusty nails and
pins to the bottle, bending them with pliers to form horseshoe shapes,
so the bottle is about half full. Then add enough wine to cover the nails
and rosemary and almost fill the bottle.

Put in the cork, seal the bottle with candle wax or sealing wax, and
shake it nine times, saying nine times,

Keep away harm, keep away danger.
Keep from my life/door, false friend and stranger.
Drive away malice, drive away spite.
Guard me/my home by day and by night.

Extinguish the candle.

The bottle is traditionally buried under the doorstep or behind the hearth to seal psychic or actual entrances of harm, but this is no longer always possible in modern times unless you are doing major renovations. However, you can bury your bottle anywhere in the garden, best close to a tree.

Alternatively, you can make a smaller witch bottle using a dark glass medicine bottle, ideally not plastic, and bury it in a deep plant pot of soil. As long as the bottle is underground, you will be protected from harm. If you really are cramped for space, you could bury an essential oil bottle, washed well, with crystal chippings, dried supermarket rosemary, and sacred water. It is the bottle's purpose and not the physical size that determines its effectiveness.

Put the witch bottle in sacking if burying it, so it will not harm burrowing creatures. As you leave the place you have buried your bottle, say,

Be for me the boundary
Against all negativity.
Bring only positivity.
Absorb/send back all harmful power.
Keep me/my home/family safe each hour.

If you cannot bury the bottle, keep it in a dark part of a basement or behind a pile of objects that will not be moved. Conversely, you can store it as near to the front of the house as you can, perhaps in the front eaves of an attic. In an apartment, you could erect a very high shelf near the entrance that can only be reached by a stepladder. But burying is always best.

Spell to Create a More Active Witch Bottle

A more active witch bottle is helpful if you live in a potentially dangerous area, if you live alone and feel nervous of intruders, or if you are threatened by a malicious ex-partner, aggressive neighbours, or unscrupulous money lenders.

Ingredients and Tools

A small, dark green or brown glass or stoneware bottle with a lid or cork

A deep shade of beeswax or candle with colouring that goes all the way through the candle (i.e., not dipped candles with white inside)

Sharp, shiny needles and pins in about equal numbers

Three tablespoons dried thyme, parsley, cayenne pepper, or cinnamon

Three average-sized cups boiling water

Sprigs of fresh rosemary

A heatproof jug, minimum size one litre

Timing

Midnight as near to the end of the moon cycle as possible

The Spell

Collect all the ingredients and make sure the bottle is well rinsed. Light the candle.

Line the bottom of the bottle with a layer of rosemary. Add the pins and needles alternately to the bottle, leaving both pins and needles straight. Continue until about a third of the bottle is packed with them.

Into a jug, spoon the dried thyme, parsley, cayenne pepper, or cinnamon.

Add the water. Stir three times clockwise, then three times counterclockwise, and three times clockwise again. Cover the jug and, after ten minutes, strain off the herbs, retaining the liquid. If you use pepper or cinnamon, they will have dissolved.

Pour the liquid into the bottle while it is warm but not hot. You need just to cover the pins and needles. Finish off with three or four more sprigs of fresh rosemary pressed down so they absorb liquid or add more infusion if necessary.

Carefully shake the uncorked bottle so the liquid does not spill, saying,

Needles and pins, your fierce defense shines.
Guard me/this home/this family of mine,
Not to injure, but drive far away
All who would harm by night or by day.

Put in the cork or screw on the lid. Drip wax from the candle to seal the lid, taking care not to burn yourself.

When the wax is set, hide the bottle secretly, preferably buried outside near your front door or at the end of your garden or, if you live in an apartment, store at the top of a cupboard or in any loft or basement space.

Leave the candle to burn.

. . . .
A Spell to Create Temporary Witch Bottles

Make these temporary witch bottles against specific harm, spite, or venom. If you are suffering from viciousness in your home life; from neighbours, local gossips, or cliques; or from bullying at work, a temporary witch bottle made weekly or monthly, depending on the intensity of attack, will offer quick-acting relief and protection.

Version 1: Ingredients and Tools

A small lidded bottle
Sour milk
Dried ginger powder or allspice
Eucalyptus essential oil or a bath foam or shampoo containing eucalyptus
A red candle (optional)

Timing

Any Saturday after dark by the light of a dim lamp or single red
candle

The Spell

Half fill the bottle with sour milk, saying,

> *Venom and viciousness,*
> *Sourness and spite,*
> *Be gone from my life*
> *And bring no more strife.*

Add a few pinches of ginger or allspice, repeating the words. Add
eucalyptus, saying the same, until the bottle is almost full. Put on the
lid, shaking the bottle vigorously, and repeat the words ten times.

Turn the bottle ten times counterclockwise, saying,

> *Turn away malevolence, mischievous utterings;*
> *Your unkind mutterings shall be undone,*
> *And so your power to hurt is gone,*
> (name the perpetrator if you wish).

Tip the contents away under a running tap, saying,

> *Transformed be negativity,*
> *As the river flows to the sea.*

Wash out the bottle with hot water and eucalyptus. Extinguish the
light or candle, saying,

> *May malice be gone with the dimming of this light.*

Repeat with a new bottle and ingredients as necessary, weekly or
monthly depending on the intensity of the threat.

Version 2

This is an even stronger version of the temporary bottle, created to help with human snakes and viciousness by a specific person or group against you or a vulnerable loved one.

Ingredients and Tools

A wide-necked, screw-top, dark glass bottle or jar with a lid
Vinegar or cheap red wine
Dried or fresh lemongrass
Dried garlic granules
A red candle

Timing

After dark on a Tuesday

The Spell

Light the red candle, working only by its light. Open the bottle and hold it between your hands, saying,

> *You who attack me*
> *Are not worthy to name,*
> *Yet you do I shame.*
> *You shall no longer spit your spite at me*
> (or name person you are protecting);
> *It is not right and ends this night.*

Add the garlic granules to the bottle a quarter of the way up, repeating the spell words three times. Add lemongrass, saying the words six times. Almost fill the bottle with vinegar or wine, secure the lid. Shake it nine times, saying nine times,

> *Hide your face in shame,*
> *You I do not name.*
> *You can no longer spit your spite at me*
> (or name person you are protecting).

I am free.
Banished be.

Extinguish the candle and take the bottle to the garbage bin as soon as possible. Repeat weekly or monthly as necessary.

• • • • • • •

Magical Word and Number Amulets

The ancient Egyptians believed that words contained and released power, and we will explore the concept of the power of words in chapter 8. In the sixth century BCE, ancient Greek philosopher and mathematician Pythagoras regarded numbers as not just having mathematical significance but as being central to all religious and philosophical wisdom. He believed that each of the primary numbers, one through nine, had different vibrations, and that these vibrations echoed throughout heaven and earth, including humankind. Therefore, both number and letter formations were used as defense, whether worn, carried, or hidden in the home, almost always concealed from sight.

The repeated creation of the same protective amulet over centuries endows it with the accumulated psychic energies of all who have created or used that form in times past, just as our usage will empower future generations when they use the same symbols. We do not know the significance of some of the letter squares, but they still are effective because of their antiquity.

Word squares were often created by mediaeval magicians, or sometimes their apprentices, using corruptions of mediaeval Latin words from ceremonial magic. The words are written forwards, backwards, upwards, and downwards.

The Sator Amulet

A traditional and effective form of protection called the Sator word charm dates from the Middle Ages and involves writing a magical word square. Some researchers have dated this square back to Pompeii.

The Sator amulet is especially defensive for travellers and all who are in dangerous or lonely places. The Sator Square was either written on parchment or wax and worn round the neck in a red flax bag, a colour and fabric associated with an ancient Greek warrior god, Ares, and a Roman god of war, Mars.

S	A	T	O	R
A	R	E	P	O
T	E	N	E	T
O	P	E	R	A
R	O	T	A	S

In Latin, *sator* means "the sower." *Tenet* means he, she, or it "turns" or "holds." *Rotas* are "the wheels," and *opera* are "works" or "tasks." "The sower turns the wheels with care" is a widely accepted translation, though the meaning of *arepo* (perhaps a sort of "plough" or "Arepo," a name created for the anagram) is unknown. You can make the square for yourself or someone close to you.

. . . .
Spell to Make a Protective Sator Square

Ingredients and Tools

A small square of high-quality paper

Red knitting wool or strong red thread

A red fabric bag or a metal tube in which to roll the word square, to
    wear round your neck (Write small if using the latter.)

A pen (if possible a nib pen and black ink)

Timing

In natural light on a Saturday

The Spell

Write the letters in silence and unobserved, even by the person for whom you are making the charm. In accordance with tradition, you should make all the letters the same size, work from left to right and top to bottom, and do not let your shadow fall on what you have written as you work. Otherwise, you must start again.

When your amulet is finished, roll it into a scroll and secure it with three knots of red knitting wool or strong red thread, still in silence.

Place it either in the bag or metal tube, and either carry it or wear it round your neck in the tube on a chain when you travel or whenever you know you will be facing physical or psychological hazards. If the square is for someone else, tell them not to open the bag or tube.

Replace it every Midsummer Eve just before sunset, burning the rolled scroll and writing a new one. Midsummer Eve has from Christian times been counted as June 23, the eve of the feast of St. John the Baptist, but if you prefer you can use the eve of the summer solstice (June 20 or 21 in the Northern Hemisphere and December 20 or 21 in the Southern Hemisphere, depending on the astronomical calendar).

Alternatively, if you want to protect your home while you are away or need general defense of your home against intruders, known or unknown, affix it to a wall behind furniture where it will not be seen, above a door frame, in a box in a drawer, or hidden behind a picture.

Number Charms

Numbers were also used to create talismans and amulets by applying basic numerology. Using the basic number-letter correspondences, you can make your own personalised (and secret) amulets that endow you with your own unique magical protection and power. The following table is based on the Pythagorean system of numbering letters and is most often used in numerology.

1	2	3	4	5	6	7	8	9
A	B	C	D	E	F	G	H	I
J	K	L	M	N	O	P	Q	R
S	T	U	V	W	X	Y	Z	

Numerology Table

First, you need to work out the number values of the individual letters of your name. You should use the name with which you feel most comfortable, perhaps the name and surname that friends would use if sending you a birthday card or message on the Internet. This you will use to create a special shape on your protective number square.

Mine is generally this:

C	A	S	S	E	A	S	O	N
3	1	1	1	5	1	1	6	5

Alternatively, you can use a secret power name that will both protect and inspire you. Many magical practitioners, shamans, and Druids and Druidesses already possess one. If you don't have a secret power name, this might be a good chance to create one that describes the person you would most like to be, and you can etch or draw it invisibly over any amulets you make or buy.

Using Magical Number Squares

Magic squares have been found in ancient Chinese, Jewish, Indian, and Arabian magic and are often ascribed sacred significance.

The set of numbers on the tambourine on the next page forms a basis for marking out the numbers that correspond to the name letters. You then trace your name on the number square to give you a personalised talismanic shape.

There are variations of this square, which is called the Saturn number square, and you can find alternatives online if you wish. I use the tambourine version, which was taught to me many years ago by a very old witch in the New Forest area of southern England, and I have found it particularly effective. By drawing your number square on a tambourine or drum you can bang out the shape and so release the magic in a powerful way. However, of course you can use any material from paper to clay to etch it if you wish. At different times I tap out not only my name but also a protective mantra or a power word, having written down the numerological values of the defensive words in advance.

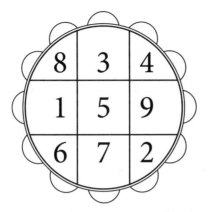

Saturn Number Square on Tambourine

Why is the Saturn square considered magical? Because the rows, columns, and diagonals all add up to fifteen, a mystical number especially in Hebrew numerology. Again, however, its true power, apart from the fact that the god Saturn was the god of boundaries, protection, and good fortune, lies mainly in its antiquity. In 1531 the occultist Cornelius Agrippa gave in his *De occulta philosophia* (first published in 1510) details of seven magic squares relating the seven traditional planets including the Saturn square, but he claims these magic squares are linked with the much older Western Hermetic tradition that owes much to the ancient Greeks. Though Saturn was an early Roman god, he was associated with the Greek Cronus.

Making Your Saturn Square

You can draw a magic square on absolutely anything.

First note the shape of the glyph formed by the number order or the represented letters. Then etch the shape formed by the numbers of the letters you have marked out (see the next page for an example) in your candle wax talisman, on parchment or paper, on a protective crystal or metal, on clay, and even in icing or pastry on a cake—eat it quickly to absorb the protection. Again, the shape can be transferred to a thin scroll of paper and worn in a small silver tube or locket.

If you feel under threat, you can draw your talismanic shape on a notepad at a meeting, covering it with circles or designs to keep it secret, or trace it on your hand.

Making Your Lucky Talismanic Shape Based on the Saturn Square

Let us return to my name as an example: CASSEASON becomes 311151165.

Traced out on a magic square (zigging and zagging where we have the three number ones) it looks like this:

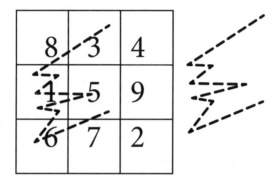

Saturn Square with Author's Talismanic Shape

If you have a specific need for protection (e.g., a trip to an overseas city and you are worried about a terrorist attack) write out the numbers of a word or phrase that sums up your need. For example, if you were nervous of flying you might write this:

S	A	F	E	P	L	A	N	E
1	1	6	5	7	3	1	5	5

You would then trace out the design and etch or draw it on an amulet. Use it for the particular event, remembering to zigzag back if a letter is repeated.

Defensive Symbols

Solomon's Seal

The Seal of Solomon or Ring of Solomon was originally the symbol on the signet ring attributed to King Solomon in mediaeval Jewish tradition, also referred to in Islamic and later in Western mysticism. The hexagram is also known as the Shield of David or Star of David in the Jewish tradition.

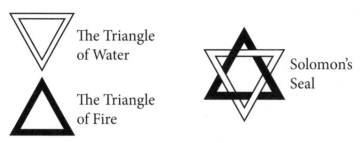

The Triangle of Water

The Triangle of Fire

Solomon's Seal

Solomon's Seal

This magic ring, it was claimed, gave Solomon the power to command demons and genies or djinn as well as good spirits because the ring was said to have been given to Solomon directly from heaven. The two parts of the seal on the ring, made of brass and iron, were used to seal written commands to good and evil spirits.

From this mystical beginning the symbol has passed into defensive magic, but the actual elemental correspondences also contribute to its power. Gradually Solomon's Seal has become a symbol of protection in the home, in the workplace, or personally. It is particularly very defensive against evil spirits, poltergeists, and curses.

You can buy pendants engraved with the Seal of Solomon that you can empower. You can also draw it in melted wax, on soft clay, or on paper (see different ways of creating amulets later in the chapter).

. . . .
Spell to Protect Using the Seal of Solomon

Use this spell to protect yourself, your loved ones, your home, or your workplace from malice or danger using the Seal of Solomon.

Ingredients and Tools

A piece of white paper folded into six equal squares
A blue pen
Adhesive
A red candle
A small bowl of water left outdoors from dawn to noon

Timing

Noon

The Spell

Hold the paper in front of the candle (not too near) so you can see light through it, saying,

> *Mystical Seal,*
> *Your power reveal;*
> *Guard all,*
> *I call,*
> *Against danger and harm.*
> *Seal, stand firm.*

Place the paper in front of the candle and draw a Solomon's Seal in each square, left to right, bottom to top, saying once for each,

> *Water descending, fire ascending,*
> *In these elements protection blending.*

When finished, sprinkle water clockwise round the paper. Cut the seals out and hide them round the home and workplace.

The Pentacle

A pentacle is a pentagram contained within a protective circle, and so it is ideal as an amulet since it adds the security of the enclosing circle.

Pentacle

You can often buy these on a chain or make one on wax (later in this chapter), etch one into a disc of self-hardening clay or into wood with a special engraving power tool (useful for making wooden amulets), or draw one on paper and hide it in your home or workplace. Amulets are not for the eyes of the curious.

You can in addition create a private one by drawing the pentacle with incense stick smoke or the index finger of your dominant hand over jewellery, on doors, on windows, in front of your computer (to guard against cyberattack and malicious mail or social media bullying), over objects that are precious to you, over your wallet or purse (for protection against theft, mugging, or loss), or in front of yourself if you are in a confrontational situation or are being bullied. Draw one daily over your child's picture to stop bullying outside the home. You will draw the pentagram part first as a banishing or protective pentagram and then again as an invoking or power one.

Whenever you trace over the pentagram image or just touch it, you are drawing energy from your own inner chakra or energy system and also from the cosmos, the earth, and nature. Think of your pentagram as a magnet that you can programme according to your current needs, whether to attract power to be protected or repel harm.

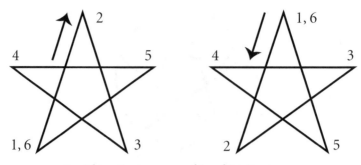

Banishing Pentagram and Invoking Pentagram

Once you have programmed both invoking or attracting and banishing energies into a single pentagram, you can in the morning trace or touch the pentagram in the invoking or attracting direction to welcome the energies of your new day, to bring good luck and opportunity, and to activate your own "go and get it" powers. Then at night before bed, the banishing pentagram direction brings quiet sleep and protection through the night while you are asleep, enfolded in the wings of the angels.

Equally, if you feel threatened during the day, touch your pentagram round your neck or trace or simply picture the banishing direction being drawn in light on your skin to shut out malice and danger. Trace three circles round your visualised or actual pentagram clockwise (counterclockwise in the Southern Hemisphere) to draw to yourself the extra protection of the circle.

. . . .
Making a Dual-Focus Clay Pentacle Amulet
Ingredients and Tools
Self-hardening clay

Tracing paper

Scissors

A broad-tipped pencil

Timing
Saturday as it gets light

The Spell

Roll out a circle of soft clay, the size you need for your pentacle, on a wooden board using a rolling pin or bottle. Cut a piece of tracing paper to precisely the same size as your clay.

Draw a banishing pentagram on the tracing paper and then, over the top of it, draw an invoking or attracting pentagram, saying continuously,

> *Bring stability,*
> *Restore security,*
> *Protection bring,*
> *Within this ring.*

Let the five points touch the edges of the paper circle.

Place the tracing paper over the clay and press down hard with the pencil, following the banishing direction.

Then redraw the invoking direction over the outline so that the pentagram presses through and appears on the clay, saying continuously,

> *Let security and strength slowly grow,*
> *By the power of the pentacle,*
> *Shall it be so.*

Remove the paper circle. Loosen the clay pentacle with a palette knife or spatula and leave it to harden.

Keep the amulet wrapped in white silk and in a small bag in your home or workspace. Touch it through the bag each morning, tracing the two pentagram directions followed by the enclosing circle on top of the bag.

For many people, the basic invoking and banishing pentagrams are sufficient for every purpose. However, if you are more advanced in your magic, you can adapt your pentagram to invoke or give you the protection of the four different elements (see appendix H).

• • • • • • •

Magical Wax Protection Amulet

Wax amulets are especially potent because they have been created from the four ancient elements: earth, the candle itself; air, as the smoke rises; fire, the flame; and water, the melting wax. The union is said to create a fifth element, "ether" or "akasha," that is captured in the wax.

Wax protective amulets and talismans sometimes were used to confer invisibility on the wearer. This was not meant literally but was casting a mistiness around the aura or, in modern terms, lowering the profile so that those who might do harm would not be aware of the presence.

Though we think of this ability primarily in terms of travel, it can also be very helpful to have a low profile at a meeting at work when someone is seeking to offload blame for a mistake or omission. In a new workplace, too, or a social situation where there are many potential conflicts or interrelations that are not immediately obvious, it can be advisable to initially observe the workplace before interacting.

However, you can make your wax amulet for absolutely any defensive purpose according to the symbol you draw on or over it and the powers you endow it with in its creation.

. . . .
Making Your Wax Amulets

You can create wax amulets for different purposes or make an all-purpose one using a single word such as "protect" or "defend" or an archangel name or archangel glyph (see appendix A for protective archangels and their glyphs).

You can also engrave it with a symbol such as a banishing pentagram, the Seal of Solomon, or one of the letter and number squares I describe in this chapter. You can also use your own or another zodiacal sign to draw to you necessary defensive powers or to assert your essential self at a time when your identity or abilities may be under attack.

I also give a list of defensive symbols in appendices G and I, which include Viking runes and Egyptian hieroglyphs, both of which are very powerful on amulets.

Usually deeper colours are used for wax amulets: purple for wisdom and spirituality; brown for the Earth Mother; deep green, Venus's colour, to enfold yourself in love; or navy blue for the protection of the ancient Sky Fathers.

You can buy or make naturally dyed beeswax candles or wax candles where the colour goes all the way through. Beeswax candles come naturally in quite deep yellows and browns that are suitable for defensive amulets.

Ingredients and Tools

One or two candles in different colours if you wish

A fireproof tray; large, thick piece of slate; or cake trays with large individual cups in which to stand your candle, for circular amulets and to make several different amulets at once, perhaps one for each family member

An etching tool such as an awl, a long nail, a slender-bladed letter opener, or tiny screwdriver

A wooden kitchen spatula

A frankincense or sandalwood incense stick

Timing

One of the three or four days after the full moon at dusk or just after dusk

The Spell

Light the candle and drop melted wax onto the tray to secure it and a second candle if you are using two. Light the second and allow the candle wax to melt away from both, but keep them close enough together to share a pool of melted wax between them. As the candle or candles burn, recite nine times,

> *Wax fall,*
> *Wax hold all.*
> *Gentle flame*
> *Contain*
> *This secret name.*

Repeat in your mind nine times (or if you are alone, whisper) the secret word or words of power and protection with which you will endow your amulet plus your own secret magic name if you have one.

As the wax forms a pool, write in the air over it with your etching tool your secret words of protection and power or magic name.

When the wax is almost set, ease it from the tray with a wooden spatula or with a knife very gently onto greaseproof paper or a wooden board. You can now carve a glyph, a protective word square pattern, or a personal number charm into the cooling wax. If you prefer, do this before lifting.

You do of course have the option of creating your amulet with invisible writing so that you can endow it with a more complex affirmation of protection. Use the index finger of the hand you write with or a lighted frankincense or sandalwood incense stick to write in smoke letters, just above it.

Dedicating Your Wax Amulet

Mix a few grains of sea salt in a dish of pure water and sprinkle a few drops around the edges of the amulet. Spiral your incense stick of frankincense or sandalwood, if you used one (or light one now), three times counterclockwise round it, and, finally, circle it clockwise nine times with a freshly lighted white candle, which, as with the incense, you leave to burn.

Afterwards repeat the purpose of your amulet, the secret word or words of protection, and your power or magic name silently or in a whisper.

· · · · · · ·

Defensive Magical Spell Bags

The magical bag, found in many cultures, is created to protect an individual, a home, or a workplace from harm or to reverse a run of bad luck, accidents, minor illnesses, or financial losses.

As with the bottle, the combination of defensive ingredients creates a greater energy than that contained within the separate ingredients. Spell bags are made with three, five, seven, or nine items. However, you can use a single item such as an empowered crystal.

Protective spell bags are ideal for the workplace, for carrying with you during the working day, or for putting in a drawer, a locker, or the glove box of your vehicle. Domestic magical bags are traditionally hidden near the family hearth, or if you do not have one, near the heart of the home where the family relaxes. If you have family members of any age who are feeling anxious, are having a hard time in the world, or seem to suffer more than their fair share of illnesses, minor accidents, or bad luck, make a bag for each of their bedrooms.

You can make spell bags, tied with nine red knots for a binding purpose, to prevent someone being bullied, or to stop burglars entering your home. Another method for a longstanding ongoing protection or luck issue is to use only natural ingredients in your bag and hang it outdoors where the wind circulates. As the bag withers and the cord eventually snaps, then you know it is time to replace it.

The Magic Bag

The magic bag itself should be made of natural fabric, velvet, or satin, or you can substitute a small leather or fabric purse. Use biodegradable fabric outside, and indoors keep bags out of the reach of small children and animals.

The size of the bag will vary according to whether you are making a large, all-purpose, household-defensive bag; smaller, individual ones to be carried; or a tiny version to be worn round the waist or neck inside your clothes. The colour of the bag is also significant, though you can use white or an undyed fabric bag for any purpose (see appendix B for the defensive meaning of colours).

The Contents of a Defensive Magic Bag

Mix and match to select items that are precisely right for your needs. You can tie nuts or seeds in a knot of cloth to make them one item and salt or pepper in a twist of silver foil. Generally, keep to the rule of three, five, seven, or nine items, but if there is a personal item you want to add, do so.

The following (except for the personal item examples) are particularly useful examples of natural items (such as herbs, seeds, roots, crystals, and metals) commonly used in magic bags. In the appendices, I have given a full list of herbs and crystals and their defensive properties to guide you, so you can make exactly the bag you need for a specific purpose.

CRYSTALS AND METALS

Crystals, metals, and naturally occurring substances (such as lava) are frequently included in magic bags, since they contain healing, empowering, and defensive energies.

- Agates protect animals and property and are good antiaddiction symbols, as is amethyst.
- Brass and gold reflect back all nastiness, defeating bullies and preventing attack against people and animals.
- Iron repels all viciousness; attacks; and physical, psychological, and all forms of paranormal harm.
- Lava and pumice (lava with holes) protect the home from natural disasters and intruders and attracts good luck.
- Meteorites give the fierce power of fire.
- Red jasper, lapis lazuli, and turquoise offer courage and power to defeat negativity and injustice and guard against loss, vandalism, accidents, and harm to animals.
- Smoky quartz and Apache tear (obsidian that is semitransparent) symbolise protection against evil spirits and earthly harm.

FAUNA

- Small animal bones protect against curses and ill wishing and prevent manipulators attaching psychic hooks to your energy field.
- Dark-coloured feathers blow away all kinds of danger and change the winds of ill fortune.
- White feathers attract the protection of the angels against paranormal attack.

Herbs and Plants

Use dried herbs, the kind you find in culinary sections of supermarkets.

- Basil defends against intruders; accidents; and physical, psychological, and psychic attack. It conquers fear of flying and is good against road rage.
- Pine needles purify emotionally toxic atmospheres; are antitheft; help prevent unfair financial loss; deter gossip, rumours, deception, fraud, and lies (try lemongrass); and keep away nasty spirits.
- Tarragon is associated with the courage and fierceness of the dragon and repeals physical attack and threats.

Roots

- Adam and Eve roots are usually sold in pairs, the long and pointed one called the Adam root and the round one Eve. Use for unity against a jealous ex, love rival, or overpossessive relatives who try to split a relationship.
- Low John the Conqueror/galangal root protects against injustice, unfair legal threats, and those who blacken your name.

Seeds

- Caraway, cumin, and coriander seeds prevent theft and repel earthly and spirit malevolence, violence, and spite.
- A tiny acorn from which one day a huge oak tree grows gives you the strength to fight back against seemingly impossible odds or a powerful opponent.

Sharp Natural Items

- Hawthorn berries, whole spiky cloves, blackberry leaves, dried nettles, or thorns offer fierce defense against physical attack, mind games, and emotional attacks.

SWEET ITEMS

- Sugar, in lump form, overcomes unfair competition in any area of life, false friends, vicious tongues, and gossip.

FRAGRANT ITEMS

Try to have at least one fragrant item, as fragrance helps to keep the defensive energies flowing. When the fragrance is gone, you know that it is time to replace the bag unless the purpose has resolved itself.

- Dried rose petals and lavender are defensive against all who attack the vulnerable, especially children, babies, and pregnant women.
- Peppermint guards against sickness, financial loss, and dangers while travelling or away from home.

LIQUIDS

In the Afro-Caribbean and American folk tradition, a small quantity of liquid, traditionally alcohol, is added to the mojo bag, another version of the magic bag. You can find details online if you are interested. Some modern practitioners from other traditions add a drop or two of fragrant essential oil into the filled bag before closing it, but this is optional. Essential or fragrance oils are ideal.

- Frankincense and sandalwood offer fierce defense against all evil, earthly and paranormal, and injustice.
- Patchouli protects possessions and property of all kinds, is anti-debt, and prevents financial fraud.

PERSONAL ITEMS AND SYMBOLS

These can be small manufactured items of personal significance or miniature silver charms of the kind worn on bracelets. There are no limits to what you can use. Be as inventive as you wish. If you do not have a suitable symbol, make one from children's modelling clay or softened beeswax.

- A blue bead is a common addition to a defensive bag in several cultures because of its protective symbolism (blue beads are traditionally associated with repelling the evil eye).

- Out of date or no longer usable credit cards cut diagonally are helpful for resisting financial pressures or intimidation and overcoming debt.

- Broken chains and rings will remove and reverse bad luck and destructive emotional links over you.

- Tiny padlocks, the kind sold with small travel cases or padlock lucky charms, that are fastened represent safety in the home, for possessions, and for you personally as you travel. They also represent job security. Unlocked padlocks or those with keys inserted open the way out of restrictions.

Magical Timings for Your Magical Bags

Bags generally last a year and a day from creation, but you can replace sooner when any fragrance fades. For some matters you may wish to specify a time frame. For example, "till three moons have travelled through the skies," or more specifically, "until my abusive partner moves out."

Make and empower protective amulet bags on any one of the three or four days after the full moon at twilight or just afterwards.

Some people bury or release the contents of a long-lasting bag on Midsummer Eve (June 23) or the eve of the summer solstice (June 20 or 21 in the Northern Hemisphere and December 20 or 21 in the Southern Hemisphere) and on the following morning make and empower a new one.

The date when Midsummer is celebrated will depend on the part of the world you live, but is always a day between June 19 and 25, so follow your local custom. In the Southern Hemisphere there are two options: the June 23 Midsummer Eve feast of St. John the Baptist or Midsummer in December on the summer solstice eve.

· ·
Creating Your Amulet or Talisman Bag

Plan in advance the precise purpose of the bag and not only the components of the contents, but the proportions you will need. If you are working with herbs, dried flowers, roots, or seeds, it is the nature of the item and not the quantity of the ingredient that counts as a single item. So for example, if you were worried about burglary in your area, you might add a handful of coriander seeds. You can also vary the quantities: for example, proportions of two to one of particular herbs according to the purpose of the bag. You might decide to add three pinches of tarragon, the dragon's herb, to one pinch of the gently protective lavender if a threat was great but you did not personally want revenge, merely to be able to live peacefully. If you do not have any ingredients in the lists in appendix D, use an all-purpose substitute such as lavender or sandalwood.

Ingredients and Tools

A table or flat surface you can move all the way round

All the ingredients you will need together in small dishes, if appropriate, together with the chosen bag or purse on the flat surface

A white or beeswax candle

Two incense sticks of the same fragrance, such as pine, frankincense, dragon's blood, or sandalwood, which all offer protection and reverse bad luck. Place them in a double holder. These represent the air element and also are used to put extra power into the completed bag.

A small dish of salt to represent the earth element

A small bowl of water for the water element

A white cord or piece of knitting wool or strong thread in an appropriate colour to tie the bag (You could use a different colour from the bag if there is another strength or protective energy you wish to add.)

Arrange these in the way that feels right, with the bag and ingredients directly in front of the candle, which should be central.

Timing
See "Magical Timings for Your Magical Bags" on pages 133–134

Beginning the Empowerment
Light the candle and state aloud,

> *I create this bag for* (name yourself, your family,
> or a loved one) *to* (name purpose or purposes—
> for example, to protect your home from unfriendly
> spirits or your workspace from spiteful colleagues).

From the candle, light the two incense sticks and return each to the joint holder.

Add each ingredient to the bag separately in the order that feels right, naming each one and its purpose. For example:

> *I add ginger to overcome this period of unemployment*
> *and to stop my previous unpleasant boss*
> *giving me an undeserved negative reference.*

Finally, add a single drop of essential oil (optional) with an empowerment to seal the bag energies, again naming the purpose. For example:

> *I add lemon oil to purify the negative feelings that have built up in the*
> *workplace since the proposed takeover and to prevent untrue rumours,*
> *intrigues, and dishonest actions from damaging what was previously a*
> *friendly, open workplace.*

Increasing the Power
Close or tie the bag with a cord with three, six, or nine knots, according to the intensity you wish to add, and set it in front of the candle.

Take the dish of salt in the hand you do not write with, and with the other hand scatter three clockwise circles of salt round the bag, saying as you do so,

*Be filled with the power of earth and her stability in uncertain times
to bring safety to* (name all who need protection or the place you are
defending from harm).

Taking one of the incense sticks make three counterclockwise circles round the bag in the air over the circles of salt. Say,

*Be filled with the power of the air to
clear away all misfortune/evil* (or name problem).

Now pass the closed bag above the candle in three clockwise circles, taking care not to burn the bag or your hand. Say as you do so,

*Be filled with fierce fire against all
that is not filled with light and goodness.*

Finally, return the bag to the table and sprinkle three clockwise circles of water droplets just beyond the salt circles. Say,

*May all that is harmful, ugly,
and disharmonious be washed away by the power of the water.*

Light the second incense stick from the candle and renew the light of the first by holding it in the candle at the same time.

Swirl the incense sticks, one in each hand, round the bag, saying faster and faster as you move them faster and faster,

*Defend and protect; guard and repel all evil, malice,
and powers of darkness. Deliver me/us from evil
by the power of this bag.*

When you can chant or move the sticks no faster, join the sticks for a second in the candle flame and say,

Flame and flare as I count three.
One, two, three. Darkness is done; evil is gone.

Extinguish the candle by blowing it out on three. Return the incense to the holders, saying,

So power continue until righteousness has won.

Leave the incense to burn through.

. . . .

Keeping Your Bag

Once sealed, your bag should not be opened. If the bag is for someone else, give it to them as soon as possible after the spell or keep it with a photograph.

It will not spoil the magic if the bag is seen, but it is better if you or the owner can keep it where it will not be touched. You could put it with your personal things in your bedroom, in a private drawer or locker at work, or hidden in a high place in the home.

Protection of the Home, Loved Ones, and Pets

Because our home life is so important, the home and family feature in several chapters in the book. This chapter, however, focuses specifically on different ways of protecting your home and all therein from danger, harm, and sorrow and on clearing the energies within the home.

Regular psychic cleansing of the home is essential if we are to remove tensions, pressures, and negativity that can accumulate in the collective energy field in our home, like dust around a light.

This collective aura of the flotsam and jetsam of daily life can affect your sense of well-being and that of all who live in your home or visit. This can cause quarrels and irritability or, conversely, inertia and lack of energy and can even bring misfortune, as positive, luck-attracting energies cannot freely flow.

Overcoming Threats to Home, Family, and Land

Anonymous vicious threats were occurring against Christina's family because her husband, Mark, refused to sell some beautiful woodland that had been in Mark's family for generations. Local developers wanted it for part of a large housing scheme that had been rushed through the local planning department, it was rumoured, through hefty bribes to the planning committee. It would turn a tranquil part of the north of England into a commuter's corridor to the motorway.

Christina's husband was approached by the developer with an offer that was repeated weekly for both house, land, and woodland through a land agent, though Mark insisted they did not wish to sell.

The threats were partly written in what looked like blood and were pushed through the letterbox, warning harm would come to the children, Betsy (aged nine) and Tom (thirteen), when they were outside the home. Very recently, small, mutilated woodland animals were found on the doorstep, one with its throat cut and the words "You will be next" scrawled in blood on the doorstep.

Earthly protection, naturally the first resort, was not working. The police said they could not act because of a lack of evidence, and they believed the acts of violence were probably caused by some local travellers in the area, who in fact were peace-loving people. Other people who had agreed to sell to the developers had received no such threats.

Christina's own understandable fears made her panic at every unusual noise in the house or if the children were late home from school. The latest thing was that the family cat had been killed and hung from the beams in the barn.

When she contacted me, a binding spell seemed the best option to prevent the developers and their minions from attacking the family, their home, and their pets, as well as the family's possessions and vehicles.

Below is a spell I sent for Christina to carry out herself weekly, and I carried out a modified backup version, though we did not name the developers as such, rather calling them the "perpetrators of harm."

As this was a physically vicious attack, I called upon Archangel Cassiel, whom we have invoked before. You do not need to be conventionally religious to use angelic defense.

At first the threats continued, but these became more subtle and through their agent (who was not involved in the nastiness and refused to accept his clients would behave like that). Three weeks later, the owner of the development company was questioned, not for what happened to Christina but for fraud involving a big development in Spain. He conveniently disappeared, leaving masses of unpaid debts, and amid the backlash the local development was totally shelved.

Magic? Coincidence? A vicious conman who got the justice coming to him? A further benefit was that Mark and Christina were given a conservation grant to develop wildlife habitats and breeding grounds for wildlife on the woodland.

Spell to Defend Your Home, Property, and Loved Ones

This spell is helpful against unfair repossession of your home or if you live in a neighbourhood where there are gangs or particularly nasty neighbours who make threats. Use it to defend your home, property, and loved ones from any who would do physical harm, intimidate, or seek to unjustly take your home from you. It is also good if there have been a series of pet attacks on cats, dogs, or horses in your area or vandalism against vehicles or property. You can word the spell accordingly.

Ingredients and Tools

An indigo or dark purple candle (Cassiel's colour)

Four dark stones from the garden or immediate vicinity, of similar size and shape, to connect the spell with the land

A patchouli or mimosa incense stick (Cassiel's fragrance), in a holder (Incense symbolically creates psychic invisibility, so predators become confused when attacking, as though in a thick fog.)

A long, dark purple piece of curtain cord; single-stranded, thick knitting wool; or very strong sewing thread

Photos of the family, vehicles, pets, home, and any land attached to it

Timing

Saturday (Cassiel's day) just before darkness falls

Repeat weekly

The Spell

Set the candle in the middle of a table, set the circle of photos round it, and enclose the candle and photos with the four dark stones round it in a square formation as though you were marking out the four directions. Spiritually, the square represents a protected area in ritual. In some traditions, such as the Norse and the UK Midland Water (Canal) Witch, from which my family is descended, a square was used instead of a circle.

The incense goes to the left of the circle of photographs. Place the cord in front of the candle. Light your candle and from the candle light the incense. Say,

I light this candle and incense to call wise Cassiel,
to guard myself and my family (name all resident members, including pets) *from all, whether known or unknown,*
who wish harm to our family/home/pets/possessions/vehicles/land,
whether by threat, intimidation,
or actual physical harm or damage.

Using the incense stick like a smoke pen, in the air draw a complete square shape in incense smoke above the stones, beginning with the stone farthest from you and going round clockwise above each of the other three stones till you have joined the four with incense smoke. As you do this, say,

Wise Cassiel, keep safe myself and my family from all,
whether known or unknown, who wish harm to our family home/pets/
possessions/vehicles/land, whether by threat,
intimidation, or actual physical harm or damage.

Now draw four symbolic smoke knots (loop-the-loop or tight spirals) above each of the stones in the air, repeating the words, followed by a similar smoke loop-the-loop to symbolise a knot over each of the photos.

Take the wool or cord and tie nine knots in it, left to right, saying as you tie each knot,

Restrain all, whether known or unknown,
from harming myself and my family/home/pets/possessions/vehicles/
land, whether by threat,
intimidation, or actual physical harm or damage.

Use the ninth knot to join the two ends. Then hold the cord circle above the candle, making sure it does not catch fire, and say,

Be filled with the protection of fire
and the defensive power of Cassiel to keep us safe.
So I ask and so it shall be.

Return the knot circle to the table in front of the candle inside the square marked by the four stones.

Now take the candle in the hand you write with and the incense in the other hand and walk round the table in a circle, saying nine times,

Safe am I/are we within the ring of fire.
All who come with evil desire
Cannot come near,
Cannot bring fear.
Be gone;
Your power is done.

Leave the incense to burn through and the stones enclosing the photos for twenty-four hours. Extinguish the candle with a cup or candlesnuffer over the flame. Hang the knot circle from a tree or bush close to your home.

. . . .

Psychically Cleansing Your Home

Every home, from a one-room apartment to a grand mansion, needs regular psychic as much as physical cleaning, especially after a spate of illness, a number of minor accidents, misfortune, inexplicable quarrels and when you move into a new home, to clear the space of the energies of the previous residents, especially if people did not stay long in the house or apartment.

To keep things fresh and positive, clear your home psychically monthly or every three months depending on the background factors, as your home will then have natural defenses, a psychic shield to filter ongoing free-floating negativity that you may bring home from work or which may be introduced by unfriendly or unhappy visitors or family.

Space Clearing in Practise

Every culture has its own space-clearing methods, such as the Native North American smudge stick or tied herbal bundle that releases fragrant smoke when it is lit. Tibetan Buddhists use sound, such as a singing bowl or bells and also healing water in which fresh flowers have been soaked. Incense, candles, water, and salt have been common purifiers in almost every religion, land, and age.

Wherever you live in the world, aim for a major space clearing at each seasonal change point.

Use a heatproof tray to carry the required materials from room to room. If you wish, you can choose just one or two of the stages. For each stage you will follow the steps described in the first stage, "Light/ Fire."

Do all the different stages of cleansing in one room or area before moving on to the next.

If possible, do this on a Sunday morning, the day of Michael, archangel of the sun.

If you have a home with more than one storey, start upstairs in the room to the left and back of the building (viewed as though you were standing in it facing the front of the house). Go from left to right and back to front of the house, including passageways and bathrooms. When you have cleansed the top storey, move downstairs, again left to right, working from the back left to the front right of the house. Retrace your steps to end at the front door.

Stage 1: Light/Fire

The main tool of light and fire is a candle.

In the centre of the first room you cleanse light a white, lilac, or soft blue candle in a heatproof holder so you can carry the candle round each room.

If you prefer, use a tea light in a foil container, on a small heatproof plate (on top of the main tray), surrounding it with fresh flower heads and small, clear quartz or amethyst crystals to carry round the room on the plate.

Lift the candle in front of you as you stand in the middle of the room facing the main door of that room and then carry it into the four corners in turn, beginning with the one nearest the door and moving counterclockwise.

Stale and negative energies accumulate in corners. As you visit each corner, say,

May only goodness, light, and peace remain here.

You can say the same words for each method of cleansing. When you have visited all four corners, return to the centre of the room, raise the candle again, and revisit the four corners, this time in clockwise order. You can do this in silence or repeat the words.

Candlelight is a very good way of removing any unwanted paranormal energy.

Stage 2: Sound

Follow the light/fire work with sound. Sound was said to bring the world into being, according to the biblical book of Genesis. In the Hindu tradition, *om* or *aum* is the first sound, the primal or sacred sound that brought the whole universe into being. There are a number of choices for methods with sound. Choose one initially and try others on different occasions. These include a bell, a singing bowl, a rattle or small drum, or even clapping. I will describe using a bell, as for me a bell is the best method of cleansing with sound. Sound is especially defensive against evil spirits and will stir lethargic energies.

Ring a single brass-, gold-, or silver-coloured bell with a handle softly three times in the centre of the room so that you are facing the main door and then in the four corners, again moving counterclockwise, ringing it once in each corner.

Return to the centre, ring the bell three times (again facing the door), and then move clockwise, ringing the bell in each of the four corners.

Return the bell to the tray, ready to carry into the next room.

For ongoing sound cleansing in your home, wind chimes are very protective and empowering, especially in hallways or just inside the front door to prevent dark energies entering and keep away negative spirits.

STAGE 3: FRAGRANCE

The following are dual-function fragrances and will energise any area of the home as well as purify it. Sandalwood is the best space purifier of all, but lavender, pine, sagebrush (as a smudge stick), cedar (as a smudge stick), frankincense, juniper, lemon, lilac, lily of the valley, and myrrh are also effective.

Incense sticks, cones, or smudge sticks are the easiest and safest for carrying round a home. You can either carry a lighted incense cone on a small heatproof plate or hold an incense stick or smudge stick in the hand you write with, lighting your chosen incense from the candle.

Follow the same order of moving round each room as for the light and sound stages.

If using an incense stick, you can spiral it as you walk. If using a smudge stick (you only need a small one in a room), you can, instead of spiralling, waft the smoke with a large feather, a paper fan, or with the hand you do not write with.

STAGE 4: WATER

Water can be used by itself. You can also soak a clear crystal quartz in a bowl of water overnight to clear any of the effects of sickness, unhappiness, or misfortune from the home, or try amethyst to restore balance and calm after a major upset or setback. If there are dark, spooky energies, whether caused by a ghost or negative earth energies (subterranean energy lines that may be blocked or soured), add three pinches of sea salt to the bowl of water and swirl it three times: first three times counterclockwise, then three times clockwise, and finally three times counterclockwise.

Alternatively, substitute rose water you have bought from a pharmacy, or make your own: add a tablespoon of rose petals to a cup of boiling water, leave the water for fifteen minutes, and strain it. Rose water is helpful if the energies in the home are too harsh and there is a lot of sarcasm, criticism, or jealousy flying round or a particularly dominant family member.

Slowly carry the water from room to room whilst visualising each room being cleansed of negative energy. When you have finished, discard the water either in plant pots in your home or over plants in your garden.

Protective Crystals around the Home

Crystals are a powerful and probably the easiest method of ongoing protection around the home. While all crystals have protective properties, all-purpose effective crystals around the home that I would recommend are purple amethyst, deep red garnet, green jade, red jasper, black jet, black obsidian, pink rose quartz, grey smoky quartz, deep blue and white sodalite, and turquoise.

A small bowl of a mixture of these crystals in the place where you and the family relax will continuously radiate harmony and absorb irritable or negative feelings. You can also wear them in pendants or other jewellery or buy them in the form of crystal angels or power animals.

Wash household crystals under running water weekly and leave them to dry naturally. If they are delicate, set them on a plate on soil for twenty-four hours or spiral sage or pine incense over them.

Crystals as Ongoing Background Defense in Your Home

- Amethyst removes paranormal presences or sour earth energies and prevents overindulgence when worn or kept near tempting foods in the kitchen or near alcohol or cigarettes.

- Banded agates and black tourmaline cool hot-headed family members and drama kings and queens of any age.

- Blue lace agate softens unkind words and critical people at family gatherings; set small ones in dishes mixed with rose quartz round the room you will be using for the gathering.

- Garnet protects against emotional blackmail and emotional vampires if worn or kept near your front door. It also protects against psychic attacks at night if placed by your bed.

- Moss, dendritic, or tree agate or jet buried at the corners of your home (in plant pots if necessary) will keep all within and your possessions safe from harm.

- Rose quartz in the bedroom guards against nightmares and children's fears of the dark, especially in the form of a crystal angel. Keep rose quartz by the telephone and, holding it in the hand you do not write with, circle it counterclockwise to absorb negativity if a phone call turns unexpectedly unfriendly or confrontational.

- Dark, pointed smoky quartz and obsidian arrows, set with the point outwards on window ledges, guard the home from burglary or intruders.

- Smoky quartz will help lower your psychological profile as well as filter negativity if you wish to avoid an argument or being pestered when you are busy; keep by the phone to deter cold callers.

- Titanium or cobalt aura and turquoise are very protective of personal possessions you take with you or that are valuable and you leave at home. Keep one in your computer bag and in your jewellery box.

• Turquoise also defends animals from being stolen, straying, or being harmed. If attached to a birdcage or on a bridle, turquoise prevents stumbling.

Protection of the Home and Garden

Witch Balls

Witch balls act as a mirror, reflecting back all harm from whatever source. They got their name because originally they were hung outside the front door or in a front garden to repel bad witches from entering the home.

These resemble huge Christmas baubles and are traditionally silver but also come in red, blue, and green. Originally they were made from deep green- or blue-coloured glass fishing floats, and you can still obtain these in antique stores or old-fashioned sea fishing shops. I saw some for sale in green, blue, and deep red glass outside an old store in a small, remote Central Australian store just a few weeks ago. They were first recorded in the 1640s when they were decorated with swirling eye-like patterns and were also called watch balls.

In some places, such as East Anglia in the United Kingdom, they took the form of a clear glass ball filled with tangled threads. I have seen modern individual Christmas lights, either a globe on a stand or suspended and clear glass filled with golden-coloured filaments, and these would make ideal witch balls.

A witch ball is generally suspended from a tree in the garden to move gently in the wind and hold changing images of the greenery and flowers. As it turns it deflects curses, the evil eye, and all malice and evil intentions, whether ill wishers enter the land or think or speak against you, even if far away. Your witch ball can alternatively be suspended indoors if you live in an apartment, on a balcony, in a hallway, or near the back door or a window that looks out to the street, if possible ensuring a gentle breeze circulates around it.

You can make a witch ball from any ornamental glass ball, decorating it with silver, gold, or green metallic paint, or even paint a goldfish bowl and place it inverted on a stand on a tall rock, a tree stump, or a table so that air circulates all round from the four directions, thus offering protection from malice wherever it originates. Modern silver discotheque balls make excellent witch balls.

If you make your own, silently endow it with secret words of power and love. At Christmas hold a large decorative bauble as it is hanging on your Christmas tree and pass into it through your fingertips for protection of all the presents at the foot of the tree if you have to go away before Christmas or have to leave the house unattended in the day.

Witch Ball Spell to Keep Harm Away from Your Home, Garden, and All Therein

Ingredients and Tools

A witch ball (large silver, green, or blue Christmas bauble or a glass fishing float) or a large convex mirror (miniature if indoors)

A large citronella, cedar, or pine outdoor incense stick or a sagebrush or cedar smudge stick. If you do not have a garden, use a smaller incense stick in cedar, pine, or myrrh indoors.

Timing

In sunlight or at the brightest part of the day if dull

The Spell

Hang the witch ball on a tree branch near the centre of the garden or on an ornamental branch indoors, saying,

Protect all with your brightness,
Fill everything with lightness,
Turn away all harm from here,
That I/we may live in harmony without fear.

Light the incense or smudge stick, moving round the tree nine times clockwise and repeating the words.

Swirl the ball nine times clockwise, nine times counterclockwise, and nine more times clockwise, saying softly and continuously,

Nine by nine,
Make protection mine
And brilliance shine.

Every week, polish the ball, repeating the second chant. Each time you pass the ball, swirl it and say,

Drive back with radiance,
Dazzle with brilliance,
That all who speak or act with ill intent
Far from this place shall their malice be sent.

· · · · · · ·

Seed Protection

This is an old folk spell that I have heard from many different sources, from the United Kingdom to Scandinavia and even from Australia from a family whose ancestors came from Ireland. Its power lies entirely in its symbolism that says whoever entered a home with ill intent would be forced to count all the numerous seeds hanging over the door in a bag or net and get the answer correct before being able to enter.

The magic lies in the empowerment of the seeds that would create a psychic barrier. Like many folk rituals, suspending a bag of seeds to deter intruders has been carried out for many centuries and passed down in families. A number of people I have met in the magical community have a net of birdseed hanging from a big bush or tree in the front garden, topping it up and reempowering it regularly without ever enlightening their neighbours about its true purpose. Lots of old folk magic uses everyday items specially empowered, and this practise was probably quite common in earlier times when people feared bad witches. The words I have used are the traditional ones I have heard in different magical communities. Since literacy was not widespread till the nineteenth century, almost all folk spells are passed down orally from generation to generation.

. . . .
Spell Using Seeds to Guard Your Property and Possessions

This spell is one of my favourites. It guards your property and possessions from intruders and all who enter by day or night wishing harm.

Ingredients and Tools

A bird-feeding tube with a seal if you are hanging it outside your home on a tree or bush where birds can eat from it (alternative: a drawstring bag or net suspended from a hook in the ceiling inside your front door)

A dish containing enough seeds of any kind to fill the tube or net. If indoors, include caraway, cumin, coriander, sesame, sunflower, and pumpkin; if hanging outside, you may want to use an approved wild bird mix.

A small scoop

A brown candle

Timing

Friday before noon monthly

Always entirely replace and recast the spell on a Good Friday

The Spell

Light the candle and shake the dish of seeds nine times in front of the candle, saying nine times,

Count the seeds;
Never the same.
Count them right,
Or leave in shame.

Fill the tube, net, or bag with the seeds, saying the spell words continuously. Seal the tube or close the net or bag and repeat the words nine times in rapid succession.

Blow out the candle. Suspend the seeds over the door or outdoors on a bush or tree.

. . . .

Making a Protective Magical Garden

In the modern world, a garden can be planted in the manner of our ancestors to endow natural protective energies to act as an invisible boundary to those who would do harm. If you do not have a garden, you can use indoor window ledges to hold a row of defensive plants in pots.

Protective Plants

- Basil, cumin, wild garlic, parsley, rosemary, sage, thyme, or vetiver are especially protective herbs that can be planted in your garden or as indoor pots or even a protective window box outside your apartment.

- Indoors, garlic bulbs hung in kitchens on strings or ropes keep away all hostile influences and emotional leeches. The string formation is especially potent. In a new home, garlic will remove sadness lingering from previous owners. Don't use it for cooking, as it has absorbed bad vibes, but bury it still on the string when it starts to shrivel.

- Bamboo is both defensive and luck bringing. Insert nine bamboo canes into your perimeter fence, surrounding each with a clockwise circle drawn in the earth. Tie scarlet cord from each of them, knotted nine times. Replace this cord when it decays. Indoors use lucky bamboo plants, each tied with red thread.

- Bay, eucalyptus, palm, myrtle, juniper, and rowan trees all form protective boundaries, and you can often buy miniature bay trees and small palms in pots for an apartment and stand one either side of the front door.

- A cactus or spiky palm can in a warmer climate be planted outdoors at each of the four corners of the house to protect the home from negative influences. Thick sagebrush or small wattle trees serve a similar purpose. In a colder place or if you have an apartment, you can keep the cacti indoors at the four outermost corners of your home.

• A small area of hawthorn hedge, raspberry or blackberry bushes, or beds of nettles where children cannot fall into them are also natural psychic defenses.

Calling on the Protection of the Earth Guardians

In many lands from Scandinavia to the Celtic world and those places throughout the globe where people of Celtic origin have settled, the land on which homes, towns, and villages are built is said to be protected by land guardians or wights, who in places such as America and Australia will be indigenous keepers of the place or guardian spirits who travelled with the original settlers.

In the Celtic world it was believed that each land wight had its ward and after dark would gather at the corners of the area to protect it. Often what is thought of as a ghost seen outside the window at night may be one of these shadowy guardians, and if asked respectfully, they will keep your home safe.

. . . .
Spell to Call the Earth Guardians to Keep Away Harm

This spell is used to keep away all paranormal harm and earthly evil from your home, land, and loved ones.

Ingredients and Tools

Four brown candles, one set on a table near the corner of each internal wall in the room nearest the front door

A bowl of dried rose petals or rose potpourri near the centre of the room

Timing

Each evening at dusk or whenever you feel the need

The Spell

Light the first candle in the furthest left corner from the door of the room, saying,

Wise guardians of the earth,
Keep safe my home this night.
From every danger be a shield
That all may to your power yield,
Till the return of light.

Carry the bowl of potpourri to the lighted candle and briefly hold it close, repeating the words.

Return the potpourri to the centre of the room and light the next candle, moving counterclockwise, repeating the words and actions until all four candles are alight.

Carry and lift the potpourri in the doorway of the room and in front of windows, moving counterclockwise and at each repeating the words. Return the bowl to the centre.

Finally, go to the front door with the potpourri, lift it in the open doorway, say the words again, and close the door.

If safe to do so, put each candle at a different window throughout the home. If not, bring them to the centre of the home and set them in a square formation, leaving the candles to burn till bedtime.

Leave the potpourri in the centre of the home, and in the middle of it set four small, round, dark stones you have found outside the home from the four directions to represent the guardians.

Repeat the spell with new potpourri when the original potpourri loses its fragrance, and scatter the old potpourri outdoors in the four directions, thanking the guardians for their protection.

• • • • • • •

Protection for Pets, from Hamsters to Horses, and Working Animals

An integral part of many households is our pets, as well as larger animals such as horses, which may be stabled on our land or close by. Therefore, even if they do bring us income through perhaps horse shows or breeding, like our smaller pets we often consider them part of our family.

Our animals, especially those that go outdoors, face many hazards from predators, infections, hostile neighbours, and traffic. Animals can also stray, be stolen, or be lured away, and even microchips do not offer complete protection.

Making and Empowering Protective Amulets for Pets

Animals naturally have quite a strong sense of danger, but as they become domesticated and increasingly humanised by some owners, their protective senses diminish. Protective amulets that can be attached to a collar, bridle, tank, or cage are an effective way of putting a shield round our pets, and it is important for any protective amulet that animals make connection with the earth to reactivate their natural defensive instincts.

A traditional protective device was to tie a tiny turquoise to the animal's collar, and this is still effective. Equally potent is a shiny bell, like the horse brasses of old, to act as a reflective shield around the animal and to repel those with negative intent. This, like the turquoise, can be attached to a collar, suspended in a birdcage, or attached on a bridle and uses both light and sound to shield the creature.

. . . .
Spell to Shield Your Pet from Harm

This spell helps protect your pet from sickness, injury, and infection and helps prevent your pet from straying or being harmed by other animals.

Ingredients and Tools

A small, turquoise crystal or, alternatively, a gold- or silver-coloured bell

A plant pot in which is growing a herb that is very defensive for animals, such as eau de cologne mint, lavender, or rosemary

Water, from a natural outdoor source if possible

A green candle for Ariel, the archangel protector of animals

Timing

The day of any waxing moon or Friday, the day of Archangel Ariel

The Spell

In the evening place the crystal or bell on top of the soil of the plant. At dawn or when you wake the following day, sprinkle water drops over the bell or crystal or dip it in the water to cleanse it.

Suspend it with strong thread (use a wire cradle to attach the crystal) where the air will circulate round it, or set it near an open window till noon or when you have time in the early afternoon. Light the candle at noon or early afternoon to dedicate the amulet with fire.

Pass the amulet over the flame once and then circle the flame with it clockwise four more times.

Say as you pass it over the flame for the first time,

> *Fire of one, keep* (name pet) *safe from all sickness,*
> *injury, and infection.*

For the second pass, say,

> *Fire of two, drive away all thieves and predators,*
> *human and animal.*

For the third pass, say,

> *Fire of three, keep distant vehicles, machinery,*
> *and all perils of the modern world.*

For the fourth pass, say,

> *Fire of four, keep* (name) *from straying,*
> *and may this fire light the way home if* (name) *becomes lost.*

For the final pass, say,

Fire of five, let those with hate in their heart not come near,
and let (name) not roam where she/he is not welcomed with love.

Finally, with your amulet in the hand you do not write with, pass your other hand, palm flat and facing downwards, a few centimetres above the crystal or bell, saying,

Earth, water, fire, and air;
Six, seven, eight, and nine.
May Archangel Ariel for my pet/animal care
And keep safe and healthy
This pet/creature of mine.

Suspend the bell from the collar or bridle; in the case of birds, hang from a mirror in a cage or aviary.

As the animal moves, the bell will jingle, dispelling any hostile energies.

If you have a horse, bind the amulet with three hairs from the horse's mane before beginning the ritual.

. . . .
Spell to Prevent a Pet or Animal Getting Lost, Straying, or Being Stolen

Ingredients and Tools
Three hairs or feathers from the pet (nine hairs from a large animal).
   Use hairs from the grooming brush or small feathers that have
   fallen naturally.
A small fabric drawstring bag
Red thread

Timing
Tuesday, the day of fierce protection

The Spell

Bind the hairs or feather with the thread in nine knots, saying nine times,

> *Do not stray,*
> *Not be stolen away.*
> *Do not roam*
> *Nor unwillingly be led from home.*
> *By the power of this charm,*
> *You shall suffer no harm.*

Put the knotted feather or hairs in the bag and call your pet's name three times indoors, then go outdoors and do the same.

Hang the bag safely outdoors or just outside the stable or animal stall. When it fades or rips, replace it by repeating the spell.

• • • • • • •

Crystals and Animals

Because of their gentle, ongoing release of energies, crystals are probably the most effective protection for animals of all kinds, and they also have healing and empowering properties to keep your pets well and strong.

The following crystals are good for protecting animals of all kinds, and you can empower them by holding the crystal in closed cupped hands, naming the creature, and saying,

> *May she/he be blessed and enfolded from all harm*
> *by my love and the protection of the angels.*

Repeat the empowerment weekly or whenever the creature has been especially stressed or unwell, after first washing the crystal under running water or spiralling a lighted pine or cedar incense stick over it.

- Brown and fawn banded agate calms anxious, highly strung, or traumatised creatures and absorbs stress and sickness, especially in older or chronically ill animals. Place them under animal beds, one under each corner; set one close to the cage of neurotic or feather-ripping birds; and place one in each corner of a stable if a horse is bad-tempered or hard to train.

- Amethyst can be used for animals who have suffered previous abuse or neglect or come from a rescue home; soak an amethyst overnight in your pet's drinking bowl to calm hyperactivity and aggressiveness and to prevent destructive behaviour (for example, excessive barking in a dog or cats clawing furniture or spraying). It's effective against fleas, mites, and ticks. Be sure to remove the amethyst prior to your pet drinking from the bowl.

- Blue lace agate, the most peaceful of stones, will calm even the noisiest or most hyperactive animal and is good to have in the home if you have multiple pets who compete in the pecking order. It quietens yowling cats, howling dogs, and screeching birds. Attach it to a lead or bridle if animals are exposed to traffic or excessive noise when exercising.

- Green fluorite counteracts the pollution and stresses of urban life, helps connect the animal with its own protective natural instincts, and calms fears and phobias. It helps any creature settle out of their natural habitat (so good for exotic, delicate pets) and move home without trauma (attach one to the travel box or vehicle).

- Jade protects animals, especially young ones, against malice and cruelty from strangers. Attach a small one to the collar of an outdoor cat, particularly if you have nasty neighbours or if you live in a busy road, to prevent them getting run over. Jade is also good as a homing crystal if your pet is suddenly frightened and runs away, and it is used to prevent the animal taking poisons, whether maliciously given or accidentally eaten. Jade can be reassuring if you have to leave a pet at the vet or in kennels or a cattery (keep a twin piece of jade and hold it nightly to telepathically comfort the absent pet).

- Malachite is protective for creatures that live in the centre of towns or in homes near radio masts, power stations, or electricity pylons. It is defensive at dog or horse shows against jealous rivals. Do not put in your pet's drinking water, as some people believe the stone is slightly toxic if absorbed internally.

- Snowflake obsidian protects horses and donkeys from being attacked or stolen from stables and paddocks, reassures those who have suffered trauma or previous ill treatment, shields against viruses and injury while exercising, and guards all creatures against malice and bullying from other animals and humans.

- Tiger's eye gives timid animals courage and reduces the dominance of an animal that has become a domestic tyrant, either with humans or other pets. Keep one with pictures of endangered species, especially those threatened by poachers.

- Turquoise is the most protective of animal crystals, guarding against toxicity, pollution, malice, and danger, especially when travelling. It is traditionally worn on collars, on bridles, on the mirrors of birds, and in small animal cages to cast a barrier of security round the animal and to prevent it from straying, being taken, or getting lost. It's good for valuable pets who may be stolen.

Protection outside the Home

In this chapter we will look at protection outside the home, both at work and when travelling and commuting. Because for many people the workplace plays such an integral part of their lives, it can be a source of great strength but also sometimes of stress. Therefore, I have devoted a separate chapter to it here, though you will also find numerous references to workplace defense throughout the book.

Whether you work in a small or large organisation, your workplace will have an overall energy field or aura just like an individual human aura. This collective aura has built up over years and unconsciously reflects the dynamics of that particular workplace. We talked about the aura of the home in the previous chapter, but because there are usually more diffuse as well as numerous energies passing through the average workplace in a day, workplace energies can be far more powerful than domestic ones and affect us more for good or ill.

Bringing Harmony to Your Working Life

If you do work in a restrictive environment or regularly stay in impersonal chain hotels on business trips, try to imprint something of your own personality on the space. Use as a focus a small personal item you have had for years that makes you happy or laugh, a small framed photograph or two, and a few favourite crystals. On your work computer have a happy family photo, a beloved pet, or a place with joyful memories as your screen saver.

If there is a lot of electrical or technological equipment, jangling phones, and faxes, then the workplace aura will be highly charged and volatile. Atmospheres can also become charged if influential individuals are hyperactive and crisis driven. If you set a calm tone and refuse to be stampeded into panic, others will follow your example, and in a relatively short time you can reduce overall stress levels and improve the general aura.

Gentle sounds encourage the flow of the harmonious life force through the workspace. A small wind chime or bells as part of a hanging mobile over your workspace will disperse tension, stagnation, and lethargy; encourage creativity; and discourage people telling lies about you or gossiping maliciously.

Improving Workplace Energies with Plants and Fragrance

Plants and fragrance oils make excellent ongoing background defense. Workplace energy fields generally respond well to greenery, growing pots of flowers, and flowering herbs rather than cut ones. Plants also absorb harsh electrical impulses from computers, faxes, and other machinery, and if set on a window ledge, they will filter at least some pylon, traffic, or phone mast pollution from entering the room.

If possible, do not put sharp or spiky plants like cacti near your phone or computer, and if there is a paper shredder or cutter near where you sit, screen the shredder with soft **ferns**. People do seem to get unusually irritable around cacti or when shredding paper without a plant shield.

On your desk or in your workplace, set two or three small dishes of dried herbs; for example, **sage**, dried **chamomile** flowers, **thyme** or **fennel** are all both protective and energising. Place them near the front of the workspace where tension or intrusions enter or near your personal phone/fax. Replace the herbs every three or four days or more frequently if there has been a tense period or a lot of gossip. Cast the old herbs to the winds in any open space.

If there is room, substitute the traditional odourless green plants with miniature **orange** trees for increasing self-esteem and so lowering aggressive competition. Bring in also tiny **bay** trees for protection and loyalty between workers, and pots of **lavender** and miniature **roses** for healing rivalries and preventing factions and cliques. Pots of **sage** will help counteract frequent absenteeism due to stress or minor ailments.

Fragrant Oils in the Workplace

Essential oils can also restore the balance by acting as a background filter of free-floating irritation or anxiety-provoking energies. Add a couple of drops of oil to a cup of warm water and place it on your desk or workbench, replacing it regularly. Alternatively, a bowl of fragrance oil near a radiator or in a diffuser surrounds you with the protective aura inherent in the fragrance. Try these:

- Lavender, eucalyptus, lily, rose, and orange promote a sense of well-being.
- Lemon, rosemary, and pine lift lethargy.
- Orange, neroli, and lemon verbena oils are excellent for creating an atmosphere of optimism and silencing moaners and those who see only problems, not solutions.
- Pine oil sends back negative vibes and encourages happy interactions.
- Eucalyptus repels spite and improves general office health.
- Tea tree will cleanse malice and increase productivity (which is good if you are paid by results).

Crystal Remedies in the Workplace

In the modern competitive workplace with constant targets, deadlines, and pressure, you may need to protect yourself more powerfully, especially from spite, gossip, bullying, cliques, prejudice, theft of ideas or credit for your work, or even someone trying to take your job.

Crystals form an even stronger ongoing background defense than plants and oils, and if you are able to have a small bowl of some of the protective crystals I list in this chapter in your workspace, you can hold an appropriate one at times of stress or psychological attack. If you cannot display your crystals because of the nature of your work, keep a single, round, gently protective crystal such as a **purple amethyst** or **grey smoky quartz** in your left pocket or on your left side and a more active pointed **sparkling yellow citrine** on the right to balance the energies. Some people reverse them, so experiment.

. . . .
Morning Crystal Spell for All-Day Protection

This is a general morning crystal spell to protect you throughout the day from all workplace tension and stress as well as deliberate unpleasantness.

Ingredients and Tools

One of the following deep-coloured crystals to set on your desk or in your workspace: black jet, black onyx, black obsidian, volcanic glass, grey or brown semitransparent smoky quartz, or black tourmaline

Timing

Every morning before work or driving to or in connection with work

The Spell

Hold the crystal between your open cupped hands. You can say all the following words in your mind if other people are around.

Blow three times gently on to the crystal, after each breath saying,

Be a shield for me
Against negativity,
Malice, and hostility.
Allow only harmony

To reach me,
So I ask that it shall be.

Each day after saying this, you can name any particular stresses, potentially confrontational situations, or people in the workplace from which you wish to be shielded, as well as any special wishes or tasks to be fulfilled by the end of the day.

Set the crystal in your workspace. If you drive a lot in connection with your job, keep the crystal in a small bag or purse in the glove compartment of your vehicle.

Take it home weekly and smudge it by spiralling an incense stick over it.

. . . .

Crystals to Keep in the Workplace

Empower each crystal before use and then cleanse it weekly as in the previous spell. Keep smaller crystals in a dish and hold the whole dish to empower and cleanse the crystals.

- Deep-green and red bloodstone protects against psychological bullying at work, an increasing problem. Set it between you and the bullies. Put one near the phone or computer if you work for a call centre or have to regularly deal with difficult phone calls or complaining e-mails.

- Blue calcite deters cliques, factions, and workplace rivalries; protects equipment, possessions, and premises from theft; and protects the workplace from dishonesty.

- Blue goldstone, dark blue glass with golden glints like a starry sky, is especially potent for shift and night workers and will also attract success and recognition to you.

- A clear crystal quartz sphere or a glass paperweight in your workspace, especially if it is near natural light, will absorb negative energies and transform them into well-being. Crystal quartz spheres also fight off office infections, coughs, and sneezes and transform free-floating negative or hyperactive energies.

- A minimum of five of any combination of clear crystal quartz, sparkling yellow citrines, glowing orange carnelians, and Herkimer diamonds in a bowl near the centre of your workspace or therapy room offer active ongoing defense. Run your fingers through them occasionally to keep your defenses and self-confidence charged. When you know you have a difficult client or you have a potentially confrontational meeting or interview, set one of the sparkling crystals on your desk or table between you and where the person will sit. Wash the crystal afterwards.

- Blue- and gold-flecked lapis lazuli or deep or rich blue crystals such as blue quartz, turquoise, blue sapphire, and sodalite worn as jewellery or attached to a belt buckle repel ill wishing, workplace envy, unfair rivalry, favouritism, or an overcritical boss.

- Green and black malachite guards against adverse effects of modern technology. Have one at each of the four corners of your computer at home and one near any fax or copier close to your workspace. At home, malachite at each corner of your computer protects you from social media bullying and your children from undesirables posing as peers.

- Orange carnelian protects you against accidents if you operate machinery or are involved in utilities, building, or construction industries.

- Four-pointed crystals in a deep colour such as smoky quartz or deep purple amethyst can be directed points outwards in the four corners of your desk or workbench to repel potential spite or gossip. To work undisturbed, point them inwards to create a protective enclosed space. Protect yourself against clients who demand too much emotionally by setting four dark crystal points facing diagonally outwards, one next to each of the legs of a table, desk, or therapy couch or round the phone or computer if you work online.

- Purple or pink kunzite or purple sugilite, both recently discovered stones, should be kept in a vehicle you use in connection with work or commuting to keep you safe and prevent road rage.

• Yellow jasper counteracts spite, jealously, lies, and those who would damage your reputation. Place five of these in a small dish in your workspace or in a drawstring bag in your drawer to stop colleagues gossiping about you; leave them inside your desk or locker when you have a day off to extend this protection in your absence.

Metal Workplace Defense

For acute or really troublesome workplace problems, metals offer the strongest shield of all. At work or when travelling, wear **silver**-, **copper**-, or **gold**-coloured earrings, a pendant, a wristband, or a shiny buckle. If an approaching person is unfriendly or super critical, visualise a metal shield so that any negative words bounce back.

Stainless steel, a metal of the warrior Mars, protects you from attack or confrontation while out and about travelling or returning home late from work, such as when travelling on a late-night train with drunks or in a deserted work's car park. You can use a shiny steel pendant or another item such as a shiny letter opener to combine the power of steel with the ability to reflect back negativity. Regularly polish the reflective steel surface in counterclockwise circles and say (in your mind if you are not alone),

> *May any bad intentions be reflected back from me*
> *and be transformed with blessings.*

Overcoming a Stressful or Negative Atmosphere in the Workplace

At the beginning of the chapter I described how a workplace, like a home, accumulates energies from those who work or visit the establishment, and over time the atmosphere can affect newcomers with the overall mood of the place. Rumours of layoffs or redundancies or new management can cause uncertainties that stick in the air and amplify natural concerns.

If the atmosphere is not conducive to harmony, absences due to psychosomatic conditions and stress-related minor accidents because of loss of concentration can occur. The following ritual will neutralise any negativity caused by workplace tensions, unnecessary pressures, and even personality clashes by changing the aura or psychic energy field to one of calm and positivity.

Since it is not easy to cleanse an office with incense in situ without attracting curious or adverse comments or setting off smoke alarms, you can work on the principle of sympathetic or attracting magic, creating a plan at home of the key features of the workspace, to transfer new, clearer energies.

. . . .
Spell to Improve the Workplace Aura

Ingredients and Tools

A square of paper large enough to draw a detailed plan of the workplace

A marker pen

Four geranium, rose, or thyme incense sticks (for harmonious vibes)

A small blue crystal such as sodalite, blue lace agate, or blue glass nugget to represent each of the key workers with whom you work or liaise (Blue is naturally calming and integrating.)

A larger clear quartz crystal for yourself

A blue candle in a deep holder or small, round metal plate

A small green plant

Timing

Any time during the waxing moon period or Friday, the day of harmony

The Spell

Using the marker pens, draw a plan of the workplace on the paper. You can mark a second floor by drawing on a second rectangle or square for the upper storey and repeat the ritual for that. Mark with circles where the key people sit and with small squares any areas such as photocopiers or coffee machines where staff congregate.

Set a crystal or glass nugget on each of the circles representing people. At the four corners of the plan place your incense sticks in their holders, and right in the centre of the plan set the green plant. Put the candle next to the east corner incense stick.

Light the candle, saying,

Light of blue, aura of blue,
Send your peace on all we do.
Aura of light, aura of calm,
Keep all safe
From pressure and harm.

Breathe in the candlelight slowly and deeply through your nose, and visualise yourself filled with soft, blue light.

On each exhale, with a sigh through your mouth, gently blow the light all over the plan, picturing it extending over your actual workplace and those who share it with you. Visualise blue light from the candle also entering the green plant and mingling with its natural energies.

Now light the incense sticks from the candle, starting with the north corner one, saying for each,

Fragrance of peace,
Fragrance of calm,
Keep all safe
From pressure and harm.

Spiral first the north and south incense sticks and then the east and west, one in each hand, round the edges of the plan counterclockwise, six times (the number of harmony) for each pair, saying,

Take away all
That burns too fierce.
Let none pierce
This aura of calm.

Take away pressure,
Take away harm.

Spiral each pair of incense sticks just once round your own space on the plan map six times clockwise, saying six times for each pair,

Turn away spite,
Turn away jealousy.
Leave only harmony.
Nothing harm; peace, calm.
Make this a place of happiness and tranquillity.
Blessings be.

When you have smudged counterclockwise, repeat with clockwise smoke first round the edges of the workspace and then in circles round each marked workspace, including your own.

Leave the candle and incense to burn through.

The next day take the plant to work and set it in your workspace, circled by the blue crystals, and place your clear quartz next to the plant in the centre.

When things seem fraught or tensions are set to rise, breathe in the blue and green aura of the plant and gently blow it on the circle of crystals, naming each key person they represent in your mind and sending them blessings even if they are being difficult. You will feel the atmosphere lift. You can set your own crystal in the centre next to the plant.

Wash the crystals under a tap at work weekly to restore energies and remember to take great care of your hard-working plant.

• • • • • • •

Practical Steps to Reduce Tensions in the Workplace

Once you have smudged the plan of the workplace to improve the atmosphere of the aura, if you study the plan you drew, you may notice practical steps you can take to prevent some of the problems, especially to further reduce your personal stress.

Usually it is only one or two people who ruin the atmosphere of an otherwise happy workplace. They may be disappointed with their own lives or resent younger people or indeed older, more experienced colleagues, or they may be worried about the security of their own positions and abilities. The problem may lie with an employer or manager who is very insecure and can only feel important by constantly criticising others. If you are a newcomer, especially if you took the place of someone who had been with the firm for years, you can find yourself unfairly excluded or the source of gossip.

First, study the plan and note where the main troublemakers sit or work. You may notice that they are in your direct line, and nastiness, like spirits, moves in straight lines. If negativity is flying towards you in a straight line, this may explain why you are getting extra tired and stressed. Moving your desk slightly may help, as bad vibes can't travel round corners so easily. If you can't, use a feathery plant like a fern to break up the direct line or use your crystal arrows. If things are really bad, I recommend using black obsidian or flint arrows (which are easily available online from a crystal store) hidden in a plant pot if necessary, points facing the perpetrator or perpetrators as a deterrent. As you place each, say,

Not to harm, but to calm.

Smudge the arrows weekly.

Seemingly, someone facing your back and glaring at you can cause inexplicable back pains. A few strategic spiky plants can break up the line of attack. This may not be a conscious attack at all but rather caused by your adversary seething with jealousy and resentment against you while smiling sweetly. You can also leave a makeup mirror or a pair of spectacles facing outwards on your desk or workbench, in the direction from which your critical colleague or employer normally approaches. You may notice your assailant heading towards you but looking puzzled and going away without spitting venom.

Protection while Travelling

In the modern, ever more hazardous world, because of faster vehicles, road rage, muggings, and threats of terrorism, it is important to protect ourselves and loved ones while travelling for business, commuting regularly, or on holiday. With gap years and younger family members backpacking round the world and being exposed to temptations that can temporarily make them lose all caution, we need to enfold our loved ones in our care while they are far from us.

If you are flying overseas or using domestic flights within a large landmass, such as the United States or Australia, it is natural to fear a terrorist attack. Cities and sacred shrines that attract a lot of tourists are also natural targets. Even if we are not in direct danger—and attacks are mercifully rare—the fears can mar what should be a peaceful journey or happy holiday if we are always not just alert, which is sensible, but constantly looking over our shoulder or afraid to travel or visit those places we most want to see.

. . . .
Spell for Safe Travel

This spell is an all-purpose spell that will protect you and loved ones from fears of terrorism and indeed other physical attacks whether travelling daily into big cities or far from home and will enable you to relax and enjoy the experience of travel and holidays. It invokes Archangel Raphael, the angel of safe travel, to counteract fears and threats of terrorism and while travelling and on holiday. You can adapt the words if you are casting the spell on behalf of a vulnerable loved one.

Ingredients and Tools
A map with your departure location and destination marked with
    stars (can be sketched)
Five yellow candles (Raphael's number and colour) in a row behind
    the map
Five yellow ribbons
A bowl of salt

Timing
Wednesday around dawn, Raphael's day and special time

The Spell
Light the first candle on the left and say,

I ask you, loving Raphael, that I/we may travel/holiday without fear or danger of terrorist attack and return home in safety.

Repeat the words as you light the other four candles, left to right. Sprinkle salt into each flame and say for the first,

Protect.

For the second, say,

Guide.

For the third, say,

Guard.

For the fourth, say,

Take away all fear.

And for the fifth, say,

Keep away all danger.

Roll the map and tie it with the five ribbons, making five knots. Say for each,

Loving Raphael, as we travel and as we stay,
keep violence, destruction, and fears far away.

Return the map to its place and leave the candles to burn.

Include the map in your luggage (or keep it with the photo of a loved one while they are away), and whenever you feel afraid, touch your solar plexus, your inner sun psychic energy centre, situated in the middle of your upper stomach just below the rib cage, and repeat in your mind if necessary,

Protect. Guide. Guard. Take away all fear.
Keep away all danger.
. . . .

Protective Travel Amulets

St. Christopher, Patron Saint of Travellers

Most famous of all travel amulets is the St. Christopher medallion that is carried or worn for safe journeys of all kinds. Over the centuries the medallion has become endowed with magical as well as religious symbolism.

Before he died, St. Christopher is reputed to have said that none who looked upon his image any day would die that day. In 1969 his feast day (July 25) was reduced to the status of a local cult because his influence had moved far beyond the Catholic Church to secular life. But July 25 is still said to be a particularly fortunate day on which to travel or begin a journey and on which to endow your medallion with blessings.

St. Julian the Hospitaller

(A Hospitaller is a member of a charitable religious order.)

St. Julian is the patron saint of ferrymen, innkeepers, long-distance travellers, and all who travel or holiday on a budget, so he is a special friend to backpackers.

St. Julian's day, February 12, is said to be another lucky day to travel or stay away from home and an auspicious time to endow his medallion with power and protection.

. . . .

Spell to Endow a St. Christopher or St. Julian Medallion with Power and Protection

Ingredients and Tools

A strong peppermint (the traveller's herb) infusion made from two
   peppermint tea bags in a mug of boiling water (or use two or three
   sprigs of fresh mint)
A small bowl of salt

Timing

Early Wednesday morning
Re-empower on the saints' own days

The Spell

Stir the infusion five times clockwise, saying five times,

> *Good St. Christopher/Julian, protect and bless me*
> (or name person travelling), *guard and guide,*
> *Through every danger, be by my/his/her side.*

Leave the infusion to cool, and then drain off the herbs, saying,

> *Deliver me* (or name) *from all evil and danger,*
> *From accident, loss, and malicious stranger.*

Add to the infusion a pinch of salt, saying,

> *By road, by air, and by sea,*
> *Good St. Christopher/Julian, be always with me.*

Now around the medallion create a triple circle of protection of
peppermint infusion drops, making the circles outwards. Finally,
sprinkle a few drops on the medallion itself, saying,

Blessed may I be,
By road, by air, and by sea.

Tip the remaining infusion into the earth.

Keep your medallion always with you (or give it to the traveller), as this builds up its power, whether on a chain round your neck, on a key ring, or in a small bag you carry with you. Whenever you sense or fear danger, hold the medallion and say,

St. Christopher/Julian, blessed may I be
By road, by air, and by sea.

. . . .
Knot Amulet Spell for Safe Travel

Knots can be another form of amulet for safety while travelling. Nine knots are traditionally tied in a red thread and worn as a bracelet during travel. Protection lasts until the wool breaks. The following spell uses three different colours: red for the mighty Camael, defensive archangel of Mars; yellow for Raphael, the traveller archangel; and either blue for the Archangel Sachiel if the travel is long distance or long term or green for Ariel, the archangel of short trips and freedom from restrictions. This amulet spell can be used for long or short distances, whether for business or leisure.

You can also make one of these bracelets if you or a family member commutes regularly or has a daily difficult journey.

Ingredients and Tools

Three strands of thick wool, each large enough to comfortably fit
    round your wrist: one red, one yellow, and one blue or green
A red candle

Timing

Any night by candlelight before the trip or before the beginning of
    the commuting week

The Spell

Light the candle and hold the ends of each piece of wool in turn close to the flame so it slightly singes but does not catch fire, saying for each,

Flare and flame,
Flame and flare;
Protection I call,
And you are there.

Weave or plait together the three pieces of wool, saying continuously and softly,

Bind and wind protection in,
Safe from malice, secure from danger,
From accident, or threat by stranger.
Travel safe,
Wrapped in care.
Protection I call,
And it is there.

Tie the ends together with three knots, one after the other, saying,

Three times the sacred knot I tie,
Safe on earth, on sea, and in sky.

Leave the candle to burn.

Wear the bracelet until it breaks. If it breaks and you still need protection, retie the knots at the place where the cord has snapped, saying the second set of words as you make the three knots once more.

When it finally frays, make a new one if needed.

. . . .
Spell to Protect a Backpacking or Gap-Year Adult Child Away Overseas

As I mentioned at the beginning of the chapter, increasing numbers of older teenagers and twenty- and thirty-somethings are taking time out to travel the world or work on overseas projects before they settle to home loans, a settled career, or families of their own. While the vast majority encounter few problems, there are unscrupulous people as well as natural dangers. In addition to all the right advice, emergency numbers, and so on, magical protection rooted in our love and concern seems to act as a maternal or paternal automatic shield to strengthen the amulets we may also offer.

Ingredients and Tools

A large ball of red thread
The backpack or a favourite garment the child will be wearing on the trip
A green candle
A fruit-fragranced incense
A special box

Timing

Monday evening
Every Monday until the wanderer returns

The Spell

Pass the ball of thread seven times through the smoke of the lighted incense and seven times round the flame of the lighted candle, saying for each,

May your travels be filled with fun and laughter,
Adventure and so much more,
May you travel safe in my protection
Until, victorious, you return to this shore.

Sew a loop of red thread in the lining of the garment or the inner lining of the backpack, repeating the words softly as you sew.

Blow out the candle and leave the incense to burn.

Each Monday while your offspring is away, cut a piece of thread, again passing it through the incense smoke and round the lighted candle, repeating the spell words once.

Knot it seven times, saying,

May you travel safe in my protection
Until victorious you return to this shore.

Put the knotted thread in a special box. Continue each Monday until the wanderer returns. It will not matter if the garment gets lost or discarded after the spell has begun because the thread you knot every Monday continues the link.

• • • • • • •

Travel Crystals

The following are particularly good protective travel crystals to wear as jewellery or carry in a small drawstring bag. Buy a selection so that you can carry or give to a loved one the most appropriate one for the purpose.

If you have only one crystal, choose the all-purpose turquoise, called by some the traveller's friend. You need not buy a large crystal, but polished tumblestones are better than uncut ones, as they will not crumble or break so easily. Empower before use by holding the chosen crystal in your closed cupped hands and asking for the protection you need and stating the place and time it's needed. If you wish, ask the blessings of your guardian angel or Raphael, the archangel of travel of all kinds. After use, wash the crystal under running water. If the crystal is delicate, spiral a lighted pine or cedar incense stick over it or set it on a plate of soil for twenty-four hours, and ask Mother Earth to cleanse it.

• Aquamarine (clear blue) is for journeys by sea, fears of water, or any long-haul travel that involves flying or driving long distances.

- Aventurine (blue) protects against travel disruption and against the loss of luggage or personal items, and it is used for protection on holiday or weekends away.

- Coral (red, white, or the rare black) is for safety on water, while swimming, and against travel accidents or muggings.

- Falcon's or hawk's eye (blue tiger eye) or any cat's eye crystal (colours vary) stops you getting lost while driving, stops you being conned while travelling or on holiday, and keeps backpackers or gap-year students safe.

- Jade (green) prevents you falling ill while travelling on holiday; is for travelling alone, especially if you are older; and protects children and animals from straying or being hurt during travel or holidays.

- Kunzite (pink or purple) guards against road rage, accidents, and becoming stressed or overtired while driving in heavy traffic or on long journeys; it also calms difficult passengers. Keep one in a vehicle glove box. It reduces travel sickness.

- Onyx (black) and Apache tear (semitransparent black when held to the light) are for protection while travelling at night and against terrorism.

- Silver or gold can be used as jewellery or as a St. Christopher medallion worn or put on your car dashboard.

- When you travel alone late at night or are in a crowded, potentially dangerous area, carry a brown or grey (semitransparent) smoky quartz. Breathe in the misty grey and exhale your fear as dull red light to act as a shield and lower your profile so that you will be less visible to hostility.

- Tiger's eye (red) protects your money and credit cards while travelling and protects you against being threatened by drunks or drug addicts, especially on trains and late-night buses.

- Tree or dendritic agate (white with green tendrils on surface) is for car travel, especially on fast, heavily polluted, or crowded roads; is for daily train journeys; and helps to combat fatigue on long journeys.

- Turquoise or its less expensive cousin, dyed-blue howlite, guards you and your possessions against theft, loss, or attack while travelling; prevents accidents, especially falls; protects pets and small children straying or getting hurt while in transit; is defensive for adventurers and those taking part in extreme sports; guards against picking up bugs and infections; and helps avoid falling foul of local laws and customs.

Overcoming Fear of Flying

A number of logical people have a terror of flying and, in spite of desensitisation techniques or tranquilisers, simply cannot use planes or endure a terrifying experience, making it hard also on travelling companions.

We need to be safeguarded against fears that ruin aspects of our life just as much as from external dangers, and some believe the fear of flying reflects a trauma from a previous life, such as being trapped in a wartime burning plane. But whatever the cause, the following spell is one I recommend that I have adapted to fit in with new international travel regulations.

· ·

Spell to Overcome Fear of Flying

Ingredients and Tools

A small, wide-necked, recyclable, lidded bottle half-filled with water
Basil, the most helpful herb for fear of flying
A deep blue and white sodalite crystal (the very best crystal for overcoming fear of flying)

Timing

The night before flying

The Spell

Surround the bottle with a clockwise circle of basil and say,

On the wings of the angels of the sky,
Carry me high.
Angels, safe in your care,
I can fly anywhere,
Knowing I will be unharmed.
I am calm,
With no fear, no anxiety.
So I ask, and it shall be.

Leave the crystal in the water until the morning.

Remove the crystal from the water and put the lid on the bottle. Dry the crystal and keep it in your cabin baggage, along with the bottle of water.

Drink the water before going through security, repeating the words, and dispose of the bottle.

Just before take-off hold the crystal in the hand you write with while reciting the spell words continuously in your mind.

Repeat if you encounter any turbulence and before landing.

Empower some more water with the crystal in a new bottle and repeat the spell before the return trip.

• • • • • • •

Travelling Alone in an Unfamiliar or Unsafe Place

Protection may be needed when travelling alone late at night, returning to a dark car park or subway, passing through a crowded area where there are drunks, or waiting for a taxi in a lonely place.

While we take every precaution to keep safe, there can be occasions when we are stranded in an unfamiliar place and can't immediately get a taxicab. We already learned how to create a Shield of Grey for invisibility in chapter 3, but this is an alternative if aura shields aren't right for you or if you have to regularly patrol an unsafe area, perhaps as a member of the security forces, and would like additional protection.

. . . .

Spell to Protect Yourself in Hazardous Places or Situations

Ingredients and Tools

A small sagebrush or cedar smudge stick or an incense stick

Red candles

Timing

When you know you will be in a potentially hazardous situation the next day, or monthly if these situations are a necessary regular occurrence

The Spell

Arrange the candles in a circle large enough to safely stand in. Light each candle counterclockwise, saying,

> *I call around me this circle of fiery guardians*
> *to keep me unmolested, unharassed, neither threatened,*
> *intimidated, nor menaced in places dangerous,*
> *lonely, or unprotected.*

Hold the smudge stick in each candle in turn, blowing the tip so it glows. Draw a circle of smoke round yourself waist high as you turn counterclockwise, repeating the words.

Blow out the candles fast counterclockwise, saying,

> *None may harm me within this guardianship of fire.*

Go outdoors and smudge again, repeating the words, and leave the smudge to go out.

Carry with you a small bag of the unburned smudge leaves in uncertain places, or if you used incense, crumble two fresh sticks and put in a bag.

Part 2

Recognising and Overcoming forces of Evil

Overcoming Curses

Curses—deliberate ill wishing through words and actions against another person, creature, or place—are never justifiable. However, they can be understandable in situations where a victim feels helpless, is being held hostage, is imprisoned by an unfair regime, or is in a situation where the vulnerable are being abused and no one will listen.

In mediaeval times, and in some instances up to Victorian times, magic was the only recourse for the brutally treated and often sexually exploited servant girl turned out of doors for being raped by the squire's son and becoming pregnant, or the older woman who had her home taken away by a ruthless landlord because her husband, who worked the land in return for a cottage, had died. Even today in some parts of the world, minorities, and especially women, are suppressed and again may resort to magic as their only defense. Binding and banishing are strong and more positive substitutes, and cursing, however seemingly justifiable, rebounds sooner or later on the curser.

Yet we can all curse carelessly though not unconsciously; addressing someone with profanity is a curse. Every time we do it, we experience jealousy, fury, or resentment—however justified—and bounce those feelings back at the cause, who may or may not be guilty, and then we send out negativity. These malicious thoughts do not leave us but flood our aura, making us, after the initial euphoria has gone, feel bitter, soured, and often depressed.

Am I Cursed?

If things are going wrong in your life, you have not necessarily been cursed, though continuing misfortune may make you feel as though you have. Almost always the person who has cursed you will let you know; malicious e-mails or social media attacks are the modern version of leaving a dead chicken at your door and are equally nasty.

Unless you have several of the following factors in play, then most likely you are locked in a cycle of misfortune rather than being cursed. You can try binding or banishing magic to reverse the trend, followed by shielding against further bad luck.

If you get sudden stabbing pains around your heart or in your temples and you have no other physical symptoms (and if these persist, get them checked medically), then the ill-wishing person may be thinking of you and fuming over some imagined wrongdoing or injustice. Sudden pins and needles, again without any obvious cause, can also be a symptom of someone physically or emotionally sticking pins in an image of you or simply sending out psychological needles of spite.

When everything should be and has been going right, if computers or tablets suddenly malfunction; if mobile phones won't connect; if e-mails don't reach their destination (technology is remarkably sensitive to bad vibes); if you lose things when normally you are very careful; if you, family members, or pets have a series of minor accidents and unexplained and persistent illnesses; if you feel spooked and like you are being watched; or if you suddenly lose confidence and concentration, then you may have been ill wished, cursed, or had the evil eye put on you or loved ones. (Read more on the evil eye and ill wishing in chapter 9.)

Should you suspect you have been cursed, there is no harm in doing an anticurse spell. Even if you have not been cursed, then it will reverse the accumulated bad fortune you may be attracting because you are giving out jittery, anxious vibes, which make accidents or bad luck more likely.

Returning a Curse

Bernadette, who lives in Denmark, sent me an e-mail asking for help. Greta, her ex-husband's mistress, placed a curse on Bernadette that she would lose her good looks, that everyone would see her as ugly and unfeminine, and that no one would ever love her again. She asked for me to release her from this, as people now saw her as ugly and were making nasty remarks about her appearance.

I explained that Greta must already have doubts about her own beauty and her ability to keep Bernadette's ex-husband, or she would not feel threatened by Bernadette and need to attack her in this cruel and totally unfounded way. Therefore, we decided to return the curse to its source, which would rebound like all curses three times as powerfully upon the original sender. Bernadette would not cause Greta harm by sending back the spell because the curse belonged to her, and she was simply returning it like unwanted junk mail.

In fact the curse had not changed Bernadette's appearance in any way, but it had filled her energy field with doubts about her charisma and femininity. Greta was fuelling Bernadette's understandable doubts about herself when her husband left her to be with Greta. She unwittingly took on this negative self-image by accepting the curse, and it was what she was now unconsciously radiating to the world through her energy field: she was feeling ugly and so appeared ugly to others.

I suggested the following curse-returning spell to Bernadette, who cast the spell herself, though I did it as well as backup. We both did the spell weekly for three weeks, and Bernadette described to me how she actually felt the curse lifting the first time she did the spell. After the second spellcasting, she started going out again, wearing makeup, buying new clothes, and fixing her hair, all of which she had stopped doing because she had not thought it worthwhile after the curse. A good spell is a mixture of the psychic with a touch of psychology.

Six months later she met a new man who adores her and tells her every day she is beautiful. Her ex-husband also started to contact Bernadette again with a view to reconciliation, as he had left Greta, saying she was vicious when crossed and not even that attractive. Bernadette refused.

. . . .

Spell to Return a Curse to the Sender without Harming Them

Ingredients and Tools

A white candle
Salt

Timing

Saturday or Tuesday

The Spell

Stand facing a window at the front of the house as darkness falls, with the hand with which you write vertical in front of you, palm away from you facing the window.

Push your palm through the air with fingers close together towards the window, saying,

You, hear me, (name curser).

Or, if you aren't sure of the precise source, having been told of the curse by a third party, say instead,

You, hear me, you who has sent this curse.

Continue by saying,

I return your curse. I do not accept it. Send it not again.

Open the window and close it, repeating the three lines of spell words through first the open and then the closed window with your hand still in position.

Light a white candle in the centre of the room, face the direction of the chosen window, sprinkle a little salt in the flame for purification, and repeat the words just once.

Extinguish the candle with a snuffer or small cup, saying,

The curse is returned to source and no longer has power to trouble my life. The way is barred to future sending with the dimming of this light.

You may want to repeat the spell weekly if you have been deeply affected by the curse, and like Bernadette you will feel each time the power weakening and eventually disappearing.

After the Spell

Should you encounter the curser, do not meet his or her eyes. Subtly push your hand towards him or her, keep contact to the minimum, and then smile politely and go on your way.

Push your hand towards the phone if the person telephones, and put down the phone without replying once you know it is the curser.

Delete any e-mails unopened from the curser.

If, however, the message is sent from another e-mail address, as soon as you realise what it is, don't be tempted to read on. Click reply so that you can delete the message using backspace from end to beginning. Then permanently delete the message from your trash or deleted items folder. Deleting using backspace to "unwrite" an e-mail is a powerful defensive technique for any hostile e-mails you receive.

Mark any written correspondence from the curser "return to sender" and use the same envelope to repost it. If you recognise the handwriting, do not even open the mail.

• • • • • • •

Curses and Hexes

Hexing tends to refer to casting a formal magical curse spell, often by a professional spellcaster. A curse can be more spontaneous and cast by anyone, but in practise there is a lot of overlap.

Whether via the curser directly or a third party who usually takes great delight in telling you, discovering you have been cursed can create a huge amount of fear, and the psychological effects are almost worse than the psychic. In cultures in which people "point the bone" against a wrongdoer, usually after careful consideration of the elders (for example, in parts of Africa and among the Australian Aboriginals), the act often results in the cursed person stopping eating and fading away—and we do not know how far this is psychological and how far psychic.

Not only witches and sorcerers, but ordinary people and even priests have in all cultures and all times inflicted what might be termed deliberate psychic attack or cursing their enemies. This can be frightening, and even in the most logical person it can create a sense of foreboding in which he or she is just waiting for something bad to happen. That very jitteriness can actually make us clumsier and less open to normal signals of danger, and so in a sense the prophecy of doom is fulfilled.

The most common method of cursing a person in evil magic involves using an effigy. For example, a curser might create a representation of the victim from the melted wax of a black candle and stick pins in it or burn it on a fire. Curse images were used from early times in India, Persia, ancient Egypt, Africa, and Europe. This practise continues worldwide, especially in lands where magic is still part of everyday life, such as parts of Africa, India, the Middle East, the West Indies, and Central and South America.

Curse poppets or dolls were also made from clay, wood, or cloth. We used these less negatively in binding magic, not to injure the perpetrator of malice but to prevent them from doing harm. Poppets can also be used in healing magic, for it is the intention, not the tool, that determines whether magic is positive or destructive.

An effigy would be painted or embroidered to resemble the victim, and hair clippings, nail parings, and even pubic hair or blood from the victim were attached to the doll. The doll was then harmed or destroyed and, in the case of a faithless lover, the heart and genital area would be pierced with a pin. The intention was to transfer by a process of "contagious magic" the pain to the victim.

Throughout the centuries in ancient India, Persia, Egypt, Africa, and Europe, animal or human hearts or eggs were buried close to the victim's boundaries so that as they decayed, so would the cursed person.

In Iran and Iraq, inscribed earthenware bowls known as Babylonian demon bowls, dating back to as early as the sixth century, have been found buried face downwards or sometimes stuck together with pitch. Written around the rim were magical formulae and images of demons. Inside the bowls were inscribed eggshells or even human skull bones. They were placed in the corners of rooms and used to trap demons who might harm the family and home. But literature suggests that sometimes the bowls were used to trap demons that were then released against enemies.

Another form of protective magic that tipped over into active curse magic was lead wishing tablets. They were called *katadesmoi* in Greek and *defixiones* in Latin. From the Roman baths at Bath in Avon, United Kingdom, 130 curse tablets have been recovered dating from the second and fourth centuries CE, dedicated to the Celtic-Romano goddess Sulis Minerva. All except one concerned stolen property, and the curse and the evil deeds were inscribed on the lead. Sometimes a magical binding ritual guarded against further evil deeds, and the tablet was then cast into the waters. One example printed in *Magic in the Ancient Greek World* said, "so long as (someone), whether slave or free, keeps silent or knows anything about it, he may be accursed in (his) blood and eyes and every limb, and even have all (his) intestines quite eaten away if he has stolen the ring or been privy to (the theft)."

Curses were used in centuries past to protect tombs from grave robbers throughout Egypt and Asia who would have known of the curse mythology but in many cases ignored it. We do not know how many of those grave robbers met bad ends or how far their own fears after the deed perhaps contributed to their becoming sick, as with the principle of pointing the bone in other cultures.

What to Do if You Believe You Are Cursed

The previous spell described the basic technique of returning what you do not want, and you can also reflect back curses using mirrors, as described in chapter 3 when we were making psychic shields. You are *not* countercursing the perpetrator because all you are doing is returning what you do not wish to accept. Of course, like hitting a tennis ball against a wall, the curse will rebound pretty fast to the sender. But you are entitled magically and morally to return your unwanted "gift," and you can do so on behalf of any loved one who is vulnerable.

Indeed, jealous souls may curse, ill wish, or cast the evil eye on a whole family who seems fortunate, and you generally know from their attitude on meeting you that they wish you harm.

The following are some very basic ways of removing curses that are highly effective and need very little in the way of materials or special protection. However, you have already learned in earlier chapters very effective techniques for returning or blocking curses. In chapter 5, I described various methods of returning ill wishing and blocking future attacks, and many of the rituals and suggestions in chapters 1, 3, and 4 are also useful as anticurse devices.

. . . .
Anticurse or Anti-Ill Wishing Spell Using an Egg

This spell works whether or not you know who has cursed you and so is good if you are just feeling spooked and things are going wrong seemingly without reason. Eggs can also be used for removing the evil eye of envy, but this anticurse spell using eggs is one of the simplest and most effective I know. In fact, if the curse was motivated by jealousy or envy then it also blocks the cause of the curse, therefore removing both curse and background evil eye. This spell does not send the curse back but disposes of it by putting it in the egg and symbolically washing away the residue of the curse.

Ingredients and Tools
Seven fresh eggs, one for each day of the week
A tall glass of water
Salt

Timing
Seven days in the morning beginning on Saturday, the day of the Saturn archangel, Cassiel, who sets limitations and draws boundaries to exclude harm

The Spell
On Saturday hold the first egg so that it touches the centre of your brow. Then hold it at the base of your throat and, finally, against your heart, saying,

> *Take from me this ill wishing sent;*
> *Its powers I now give to you.*
> *Malice be gone, all bad intent;*
> *The curse is spent and through.*

Add four tablespoons of salt to the glass of water and stir well counterclockwise, saying,

> *Cleansed be of this negativity.*
> *Curse be carried from the rivers to the salt sea.*
> *No more to trouble me.*

Place the egg in the glass of water and, just before sunset, remove the egg from the water and throw it against a tree so that it breaks, saying,

> *Fair is foul and foul is fair;*
> *I toss this curse into the air.*

Wash out the glass well with hot water.

Repeat the spell for seven days, but on day seven, rather than breaking the final egg, bury it in a place where no plants are currently growing.

. . . .

Spell to Remove a Curse or Ill Wishing Using Essential Oil and a Salt Bath

Again we are removing a curse, which is an alternative to reflecting it back. You can choose which method you prefer. In this spell, too, we are using liquid plus cleansing salt to wash it away.

Ingredients and Tools

Lavender or rose essential oil or a Moroccan argan oil bath or shower
  product
A small empty bowl
Some sea salt

Timing

Saturday night at midnight so that the spell tips into Sunday, the day
  of Michael, the archangel of light

The Spell

To a bath of warm water add six to nine drops of essential oil or your usual amount of the oil product, saying,

> *Oil of midnight take from me*
> *The curse that brings captivity,*
> *That cleansed and purified*
> *May I be.*

Add four pinches of salt to the water, saying,

> *Salt of midnight, take from me*
> *The curse that brings captivity,*
> *That cleansed and purified*
> *May I be.*

Swirl the bathwater in both directions alternately nine times, saying nine times,

> *Take from me*
> *This burden of iniquity*
> *And set me free.*

Sit in the bathwater, make crosses on the surface of the water, and
clear each with your hands, saying as a continuous chant,

> *I uncross this iniquity,*
> *That it may flow away*
> *From me*
> *And only blessings stay.*

Take the empty bowl, half fill it with bathwater, and set it on the
side of the bath. Get out of the bath, take out the plug, and afterwards
rinse out the bath with cold water. Put just a pinch of salt under your
tongue and wash the rest away.

Place the bowl of salt and oil bathwater above your head as you lie
in bed (put a small table behind the bed if necessary) to protect you
while you sleep. In the morning pour it away down an outside drain
or out of a window if you are in an apartment. As you do so, say,

> *The curse is gone,*
> *The power is done,*
> *And I have won.*

. . . .

Spell to Remove a Curse or Ill Wishing Using Candles and Garlic

This spell removes the curse or ill wishing whether it was made directly or you have been told of it by a third party. We used garlic and
candles in banishing magic to banish threats and bullying, but here

in this stronger version we will capture the curse in wax and then dispose of it. Candles are especially good for burning away a curse.

Ingredients and Tools
Five beeswax candles of the same size
A jar of garlic salt or dried garlic granules
A small bowl for the garlic
A sharp knife
A paper bag
Strong red thread

Timing
Tuesday evening after dark, the day of Samael, archangel of cleansing fire

The Spell
Set the candles in a small square formation on a metal tray, secured by melting wax from a fifth candle you can leave burning as light. Put them close together so that you will get a pool of wax from all four in the centre. (It does not matter if they melt as well outside the square.)

Place the candles in a row in holders, lighting them counterclockwise round the wax square, saying,

> *I do not accept your vicious curse;*
> *I send it back, so do your worst.*
> *Fire burn, flames rise,*
> *As this wax melts,*
> *So your curse dies.*

As the wax melts in the centre, drop bits of garlic into the warm wax, saying,

> *Your vampire hold burns, melts away.*
> *Into my life you dare no longer stray.*

When all the wax is melted, as it cools, cut a square round the place you sprinkled the garlic and carefully lift it out, saying,

The light fades; you have done your worst.
Now feel the pain of your returned, unwanted curse.

Put the wax square in the paper bag and carefully scrape any other wax off the tray, shred it, and add it to the bag.

Tie the bag with a strong red thread tied in three knots with a loop and hang it early next morning on a bush or tree, well hidden and away from your home.

Throw away the candles and any remaining garlic salt.

The Ring of Fire Spell

This is yet another powerful fire anticurse ritual, and it is especially good if a curse is life-threatening. Water is effective in washing away curses (as with the oil and water ritual), and burying in earth and throwing into the air (as with the egg ritual) are all powerful elemental forces against curses. For the most vicious, fire is the most powerful (and volatile, so do not do if you are angry).

Ingredients and Tools

Nine small red candles

An incense stick in a strong fire fragrance, such as dragon's blood, frankincense, or ginger, in a holder

Timing

Tuesday, the first hour of sunrise, Samael's special hour

The Spell

Set the candles in a circle on a table with plenty of space to walk round the table. Moving round the table, light each of the candles in turn counterclockwise, beginning with the nearest candle to you in the circle as you face the table. Say for each,

I bring alive the ring of fire
To defend me from the malicious desire
Of those who wish me ill or danger,
Whether false friend or hostile stranger.

When you have returned to the place you started, light the incense from the first candle lit and, walking round the table clockwise three times, create circles of incense smoke in the air at waist height as you walk, enclosing yourself and the table in the smoke circles. Repeat the words continuously as you walk. Then reverse direction and walk round the table counterclockwise three times, repeating the words and actions exactly.

Now, start with the first candle you lit and walk round the table once more clockwise, stopping to quickly blow out the candles one after the other. Say,

So remains the ring of fire.
None may fulfil their evil desire.
The light is my shield;
The curser must yield.

Relight the candles and let them burn through.

• • • • • • •

Capturing the Curse

In chapter 5, I described the use of protective bottles to absorb or reflect harm. The same method of using a bottle is remarkably successful for capturing and so removing a curse or ill wishing, especially if it is a hex put on you by a magical practitioner of any persuasion. In chapter 10, I will describe trapping spirits in a bottle, but you can also use the method below for ill-intentioned spirits.

. . . .

Spell to Capture a Curse, Hex, or Malevolent Spirit

Ingredients and Tools

Whole pointed cloves, chopped nettles, or thorns (Natural ingredients seem to work better than the traditional metal nails in this spell.)

A wide-necked sealable bottle or jar, preferably in dark glass

Three pinches of sea salt and six pinches of red (cayenne) pepper dropped into a small jug of white vinegar (All cleansers are swirled six times counterclockwise.)

A beeswax or red fast-melting candle

Timing

10:00 p.m. on a Monday during the waning moon

The Spell

Light the candle and work only by its light. Add the thorns or sharp plants to the jar. Pour in enough vinegar mix to cover the thorns, saying,

Evil curse, enter here,
Where you are trapped
With barbs so fierce
I need no longer fear.
By thorns be pierced,
And pierced stay;
No longer harm by night or day.

Put on the lid and seal it by dripping wax all round, saying,

Now the evil threat is bound.
The curse is trapped and sealed around.
Evil is no longer found.

In my life,
I am freed from strife.

Next morning take the jar in a sealed bag to a garbage site well away from your home or workplace, if the issues were located there.

• • • • • • •

Beware Charlatans

Curse removing is an area where you can sadly all too easily get ripped off. When you are frightened, it is natural to trust someone who promises to help you and tell no one. But unscrupulous practitioners can amplify the problem by telling you it is really serious and then charging you a lot of money. I have even come across cases in which someone had sent off for an ordinary e-mail tarot reading, only to be told that there was a really serious curse round them or a loved one that must be removed for their safety.

If you can't seem to shake off bad feelings, even after doing rituals yourself, talk to a priest, a medium attached to a local Spiritualist church, or someone found through a reputable healing association or by recommendation. Don't pay out huge sums of money to have a curse removed. If you are told that the curses around you will take a lot of expensive work to remove, you have almost certainly found a charlatan. The charlatan will charge you more and more, as it seems there is no end to the problem, and you may end up paying hundreds or, as some people have, thousands of dollars.

May, a woman in her sixties from Chatham in Kent in South East England, paid for an online reading with, according to the website, a very well-qualified medium because she had suffered a lot of illness and several of her relatives had died.

The medium proved very expensive (more than ten times what I charge for a consultation), and after the first consultation, instead of offered comfort, May was told she was in great danger and that it would take several months to remove the curses on her and her family. May paid out several hundred pounds for cheap charms and protective amulets, blessings to various saints and archangels, and the weekly total cleansing of May's aura energy field, all handled remotely by mail. When I met May at a healing festival, she was even sicker and more stressed than when she started and had run through a lot of her savings. She had been told it would take at least another two months of intensive rituals for the curse to finally be removed.

I persuaded May to cut contact and ask for her money back (the woman dealt directly in cash sent by registered post to a mailbox address) and helped her for free, as there never had been a curse—just a run of really bad times. I described earlier in the chapter ways you can tell if you have been cursed or are simply having a run of bad luck. May was in fact suffering from a hereditary illness, and the relatives who died had been very old and all chronically ill.

When I checked the false medium's website, it had disappeared, and her e-mail address bounced back. No doubt, as many charlatans have done, she had simply changed her name, as she may have had other clients chasing her and started afresh. Few victims will tell the police because they are too embarrassed to have been dealing with mediums, and that is what the charlatans rely upon.

This is a far more common problem than is ever openly revealed, as there can be a conspiracy of silence, but I have to rescue a lot of people who have been conned in this most emotive area.

Cursed Objects

If the person cursing you knows a bit about magic, then an object can be cursed and sent to you. Many cursers are amateur practitioners who have picked up information from the Internet or are practitioners paid on behalf of the instigator (and the instigator is as guilty as the person they have paid). Beware of unexpected gifts from someone you know does not like you, especially if the gifts are personal items like jewellery or artefacts. Be particularly wary of old or natural objects, as these can hold a curse quite powerfully.

Generally, even if they are cursed, you do not have to throw the items away if they are beautiful or valuable, though you may wish to do so. However, you do need to cleanse them thoroughly using a herb like hyssop, the ultimate cleansing herb, or by smudging using sagebrush, cedar, or wood, or a sage or cedar incense stick. The power of hyssop,

Hyssopus officinalis, goes back to biblical times: Psalm 51:7 says, "Purify me with hyssop and I shall be clean, wash me and I shall be whiter than snow." I will describe how to do this later in the chapter.

Julia's Cursed Shell

Julia, who lives in Twickenham on the River Thames near London, had a boyfriend called Bill. He came from a very sad family. His mother lived in the West Indies, and his father had been shot in an accident that also left his mother wounded. He never forgave himself for being in London at the time, as he felt he could have saved them, and his mother never forgave him either. After that, she wrecked every love relationship he tried.

Bill went to Australia on business for a couple of months, stopping en route to visit his mother. He phoned Julia upon reaching Australia to say his mother had a marvellous cowrie shell that was also a musical instrument, and she had given it to him to give to Julia. To Julia, it sounded hopeful if Bill's mother was sending her presents. Bill told Julia that it was so beautiful that he didn't want to wait till he came back for her to have it, but it was too delicate to post. Luckily, a friend of his who was coming back to England that week would drop it off at her apartment.

Julia was away when the shell was delivered. On her return, she took it in her hands. It wasn't at all pretty, like Bill had told her, but wide, deep, and ugly. She put it to her left ear to listen for the sea, and a tendril of black smoke rose. The walls and ceiling of the room seemed to close in on her, and it became incredibly hot.

Julia knew instinctively that she had to take it to the water. She threw it into the Thames, and as it landed in the water, she could see flames rising from it. Then it sank without trace. As soon as she'd thrown it, she'd known it was some kind of nasty magic from Bill's mother.

Months later a friend of Bill's from the West Indies told Julia that Bill's mother had gone to a woman in one of the outlying villages and paid her a great deal of money to put a curse on Julia and get rid of her. The relationship broke up anyway, as Bill had changed so much after seeing his mother.

. . . .
Hyssop Infusion Spell for Removing Bad Energies from a Cursed or Unlucky Object

Ingredients and Tools

Dried hyssop (substitute nettle or dandelion if pregnant)

A cup of water

A teacup

A tea strainer

A small bottle

Timing

Friday morning, the day of Anael, archangel of love and beautiful
  things

The Spell

Place one teaspoon of dried hyssop or three teaspoons of the fresh
herb in a cup of water that has just been brought to the boil.

Stir nine times clockwise and then nine times counterclockwise,
saying,

> *Hyssop, hyssop, remove the pain.*
> *Let on this* (name object) *the curse not remain.*

Cover the brew and leave for five to ten minutes, and then strain
off the herbs and discard.

Stir the strained liquid again nine times clockwise and nine times
counterclockwise, saying the words again.

Sprinkle the infusion counterclockwise round the item if it is delicate or would mark the object; otherwise, sprinkle it on top. Say as you
do so,

> *By this hyssop, the evil goes.*
> *From this* (name) *the curse does flow.*
> *Away, darkness; be purified.*
> *Wickedness no longer here abide.*

Wash the remaining infusion away under a running tap, repeating the second set of words.

· · · · · · ·

Items with Bad Energies

Even if an object is not directly cursed, it can carry bad energies from the person who owned it, especially if they dabbled in the occult. So if you buy things from a garage sale or antique dealer, always smudge them. If they are small enough, leave them on a plate on a plant pot containing soil and a small plant for twenty-four hours after the smudging, so the earth can absorb any negative energy. If the item is large, like furniture, set a green, thriving plant pot on it in the centre for twenty-four hours to the same effect, and if possible, set a circle of nine small amethysts around the plant on the furniture item.

Phil's Cursed Wand and Spell Book

Phil, who lives in a remote part of coastal Northwestern United States, told me that there was an old woman, reputedly a witch, who lived in a tumbledown shack and cast curses for high prices to blight rival farmers' lands—and certainly she seemed to have some success because some of the people she cursed did go out of business.

When she died, the witch left no relatives. Her home and magical artefacts were cleared out, and many ended up in a local antique store. Phil was fascinated and bought her spell book and her wand for a very high price because he thought they would be fun to show at parties and pretend to spook people. He never opened the spell book but displayed it in a glass cabinet, and he often fooled around with the wand at barbecues.

Gradually, he noticed that things were going wrong in his life. His dogs would not enter the room where the book was located and would sometimes stand at the door, hackles up and growling. His daughters were complaining about an old woman standing in their bedroom doorway watching them, surrounded by little fiery figures, and the house always seemed dark even though it was summer. Even his precious indoor plants were wilting. Normally, I would suspect soured earth energies (as I describe in chapter 12), but the fact that the problems only came after the wand and book had arrived made me suspicious the witch had either put a djinni spirit in the wand to protect it (the fiery creatures the girls saw), or because it and the spell book had been used for dark purposes, they may have retained the witch's negative energies (and fooling around with such artefacts is guaranteed to cause a bad reaction).

I suggested, since Phil said the witch's cottage remained unsold and was already falling into disrepair, that he bury the spell book in her garden and throw the wand into the nearest running water (she had a stream at the bottom of the garden), saying, "I return what is yours, and I meant no disrespect. Rest in peace."

He did so, and after a few days, the atmosphere in Phil's home dramatically improved, the dogs would go into the room where the spell book and wand had been, and the children saw the old lady no more.

James Ussher and the Latin Book of Anglesey

Phil had encouraged the nasty vibes in his home by making a joke of some pretty dark magic connected with the artefacts. But sometimes there seems no direct cause to trigger the negativity. When I was thirteen, my family rented a cottage in the hills of the small Welsh island Anglesey, once called Mona, where in 61 CE Suetonius Paulinus and his legion had wiped out many of the Druids and Druidesses, the Celtic priesthood, and (it was said) the dark-robed priestesses who may have belonged to an old order of the Morrígu or were raven priestesses.

My mother collected old books, and we started visiting a rather creepy, beamed bookshop in the main town, Beaumaris, where the elderly bookseller persuaded her to buy a leather-bound tome written in Latin by James Ussher, an Irish Archbishop and scholar who died in the mid-1600s.

We took it home to the cottage, which was about two hundred years old, and left it on a small table next to the fireplace. All night were strange howling and groaning sounds that my father insisted were the wind, though it was a relatively calm night. In the morning when I awoke, there was a huge spider crawling over the book, which was covered in deep scratches that went almost through the thick leather.

My mother insisted on keeping the book, but I would never touch it.

. . . .

Spell to Remove Evil from an Object, Yourself, or a Loved One

This spell removes evil through smudging or fragrant smoke burning. Here the element of air is combined with the element of fire to cleanse a cursed object or person, in an even more potent version of the ring of fire and a stronger technique also than the hyssop cleansing. It is especially effective if black magic or a professional practitioner is involved.

Ingredients and Tools

A small sagebrush or cedar smudge stick or a sage or cedar incense
     stick
Nine red candles (the colour of Samael, archangel of cleansing fire)
The cursed item or a photo of you or a loved one under threat in the
     centre

Timing

Tuesday, the day of Samael as well as Camael, archangel of Mars and
     courage

The Spell

Arrange the candles in a circle large enough to safely stand in. Light
each candle in counterclockwise order, saying,

> *I call upon Samael to purge this curse away.*
> *Against his power can no evil stay.*
> *None may stand against his name,*
> *No one resist his cleansing flame.*

Hold the smudge in each candle flame in turn, blowing the tip so that it glows. Say for each,

Samael, by the power of air,
The curse, you command, no longer is there.

Spiral the smudge in counterclockwise smoke round the inside of the candle circle nine times, saying,

Be gone, be done.
Samael triumphs; the battle is won.

Finally, stand in the centre of the candle circle and turn in all four directions counterclockwise (west, east, south, and north). Raise the smoke or incense stick in a counterclockwise spiral in each direction, then raise it above your head, and finally point it to the ground. As you do so, say at each direction,

Above, below, and all around,
No sign of evil may now be found.

Blow out the candles fast counterclockwise, saying,

None may do harm within Samael's guardianship of fire.

Take the smudge outdoors and leave it to burn through. If you don't have the space to make a candle circle large enough for safety, stand outside the candle circle and move and smudge round the outside of it.

· · · · · · ·

The Evil Eye

The evil eye is linked with envy, jealousy, or resentment. It is performed when the perpetrator looks enviously on you, your family, or what you or your family have and often makes a disparaging remark about the unfairness of your good fortune. We say "if looks could kill" or "he looked daggers at me" to describe this.

The first references to the evil eye appear in the cuneiform texts of the Assyro-Babylonians from around 3000 BCE, and it was mentioned in many incantations. Here is an Assyrian chant:

Thou man, son of his god,
The Eye which hath looked upon thee for harm,
The Eye which hath looked upon thee for evil.

This comes from a book by Sir E. A. Wallis Budge called *Amulets and Superstitions*, listed in the recommended reading section, that gives much useful material on Assyrian chants and magic and indeed the ancient Egyptian world.

The ancient Egyptians also feared the eye. Egyptian women used eye shadow made from powdered lapis lazuli and painted their lips for beautification as well as to prevent the evil eye from penetrating their eyes or mouths. I discovered this when I was doing research for my own book on ancient Egyptian magic in Museum of Cairo, working with a group of young and very enthusiastic Egyptologists, but again Budge is a good source. The small Petrie Museum at University College London is also an excellent source of all things Egyptian if you want to know more and want to see fine rare Egyptian artefacts.

Roman men, women, and children so feared the eye that they carried phallus-shaped charms (to counter the oval, female shape of the eye) called *fascini* in gold, silver, and bronze as antidotes. I have seen these on display in the British Museum in London and also in the Ashmolean Museum in Oxford, but any museum throughout the world with a Roman history section will have examples of these. (If you want to know more, the *Dictionary of Greek and Roman Antiquities* is available to read for free online in the Internet Archive and Open Library: visit https://archive.org/details/dictionaryofgree00smituoft.)

According to the late Alan Dundes, formerly a professor of anthropology and folklore at the University of California, Berkeley, evil eye beliefs are Semitic and Indo-European in origin. People from China, Korea, Myanmar, Taiwan, Indonesia, Thailand, Sumatra, Vietnam, Cambodia, Laos, Japan, Aboriginal Australia, Aboriginal (Maori) New Zealand, indigenous North and South America, and south of the Sahara in Africa do not have this belief as part of their indigenous culture. The concept was introduced into the Americas, the Pacific Islands, Asia, sub-Saharan Africa, and Australia by colonists and the trade links from Europe and the Middle East. My own theory is that the evil eye occurred where systems of land and property ownership were or became rigid and where there was a sharp division between rich and poor, often introduced by colonizing peoples. You may enjoy the book edited by Alan Dundes called *The Evil Eye: A Casebook*, which is listed in the recommended reading; it will also give you background to a number of concepts I refer to in this chapter.

The Evil Eye in the Modern World

"Eviling" is generally directly eye-to-eye, and its effects can be both instant and long-lasting. In the modern world, especially with social media, a wedding, family, or birth photograph can also trigger intense envy, and the evil eye can also travel through cyberspace after the perpetrator has looked jealously at the image of the happy couple, family, or new babe. Equally, if you are pictured with your new car or standing in front of your home, this can attract the evil eye over the Internet as well as directly if you are showing a colleague or neighbour a photograph of something new you have. So the use of the Internet for social interactions has actually meant that eviling can now occur across thousands of miles between perpetrator and victim, through photographs online as well as by direct video messaging.

Indeed, the evil eye operates on both a conscious and unconscious level, transmitting negativity to another person through envy, jealousy, or resentment when seeing a person considered fortunate or an artefact belonging to that person that provokes an intense desire to possess it. This desire, whether focused on property, wealth, health, or fertility, was traditionally believed to especially affect infants and children because they were vulnerable and open to psychic influences. The evil eye could also, it was said, be cast upon grazing animals, fruit trees, and crops, with which wealth was frequently bound. Houses might, according to superstition, burst into flames and ploughs (or in more recent times, machinery) break, as a result of covetousness. Ironically, the malicious influence was often believed to be passed by overt *praise*—for example, complimenting a pretty or healthy child, a fine animal, or an orchard with trees in blossom—and so in more superstitious times and places, even a genuine compliment was feared. A bad harvest, a sick child, or a blighted fruit crop might unfairly be blamed on a stranger or someone who appeared different from the community and had tried to be friendly by admiring a newborn infant or a well-tended garden. In the Middle East, Italy, Spain, Central America, and Mexico even today, belief in the evil eye remains strong, especially in remote areas, and blue-eyed people are especially under suspicion.

Because belief in the evil eye was, through the centuries, relatively widespread and its powers did not seem to depend on the perpetrator possessing special psychic powers, fears of psychic attack were quite common—and still are in some locations. Therefore, if a person did genuinely want to admire an infant or animal, he or she would afterwards spit or touch the infant or animal to remove the eye. If this was not done, the mother or owner would either offer a prayer or mediate the praise by pointing out a defect in the infant or coveted object. A child might even be smeared with dirt before being taken out, and bells were hung from cradles and prams for the same reason. Horse brasses were also protective and would be handed down by carters and ostlers from father to son, not only to be attached to bridles but hung in the home. If you see one at an antique fair it is an excellent domestic defensive device against envy and can also be hung in horse stables over the door.

The Hidden Dangers of the Evil Eye

You may not know who is sending you the evil eye, though almost always you will have met the perpetrator and felt a sense of unease even if the encounter was a smiling one.

Bad vibes are transmitted through envy, jealousy, or resentment bubbling inside the ill wisher, whenever this resentful person sees, talks about, or thinks about a person considered to be unfairly fortunate. For example, a jealous mistress can continually obsess about a wife who may be unaware of the affair but sense streams of hatred pouring towards her. These can make the wife feel anxious or even unwell if the attack is particularly vitriolic. You may have no idea that the woman you see daily at the school gate hates you because you have a new car, even though you worked every night on your computer when the children were in bed to pay for it. Having stabbing pains behind the eyes or in your temples can be an indicator of these malicious thoughts winging your way.

However, you may just have a vague sense of unease around the woman, and if she enters your home, perhaps to collect her child who has been playing with yours, you may feel suddenly vulnerable. Sometimes the jealousy is spoken, not as a curse but as bitter or even sugar-sweet words that it is unfair you should be happy when someone else is not.

Ida, a relative of mine, once said when my children were small, it was unfair I had lovely children because her grandchild had serious health problems. Almost immediately afterwards (maybe coincidentally, maybe not), my previously healthy youngest child, still an infant, was rushed to hospital with an unknown virus. I can recall Ida glaring at my baby as she made the remark, then afterwards returning to her smiling self.

If you do have this unease, in this chapter I have suggested ways of making yourself a protective eye charm to carry or wear as a precaution.

Traditional Ways of Detecting the Evil Eye and Mitigating Its Effects

These old remedies can still be used and indeed are, for I have friends in Mexico, Chile, Spain, and France (and among European settlers' families in Australia) whose older relatives swear by their effectiveness in protecting the family from envy.

If a child or animal became sick, frequent household accidents occurred, or crops became blighted, the evil eye was in earlier times, sometimes unfairly, considered a prime suspect, along with deliberately bad witchcraft. Water, oils, or other liquids were used, since it was thought that the evil eye caused the natural fluids that sustained life to dry up, an indication, according to Alan Dundes, that the origin of the evil eye was in desert regions where water was precious.

These beliefs have continued in households where superstition is still prevalent. In Eastern Europe, for example, charcoal, coal, or burnt match heads are dropped into a bowl of water. If they float, it is said that "the evil eye has been cast." A local wise woman who knew the secret words to take away the influence would be sought. These formulae have been passed down through the matriarchs of large families and communities. Holy water would sometimes at the same time be sprinkled on a victim, whether human, animal, or blighted tree.

In Italy olive oil is dripped into water, a single drop at a time, while the matriarch recites her secret mantras. If the drops form an eye, prayers are said over the victim while oil is continuously dripped until a series of shapes appear but the eye formation no longer does. A variation of this involves boiling water, reducing it to simmer, and dripping three drops of oil in the water. If the oil separates, smears, or mixes, the evil eye is considered not present. If the oil drops come together the evil eye has, it is said, been cast. A needle is sterilised in a candle flame and then pierced into the oil so the oil breaks apart with such words as these:

> Holy Mary, Mother of God/Sweet Saviour/Good St. Benedict
> (a saint associated with breaking the evil eye),
> Take away this cursed eye from me (or name).
> That I (or name) may be freed of its thrall.
> That is all.

In Mexico, an egg is traditionally rolled across the supposed victim's body and then cracked to see if an eye shape formed in the yolk. If it does, a cross is drawn on the forehead with the egg while incantations are made. Afterwards the egg is thrown away in a shady place or buried to prevent a second attack. Holy water is also sprinkled over the victim. I have been told all these anecdotally by adults whose older relatives practised them and whom I have met as I have travelled round the world, and I am always glad to hear from readers of their family folk customs.

Traditional Charms against the Evil Eye

Carrying charms, especially eye charms, was regarded as a potent method of repelling attack. One example is a representation of the hieroglyph the Eye of Horus, the ancient Egyptian sky god. From Assyrian times, camels were traditionally protected by wearing a stone with a hole round their necks, and horses in many cultures had blue beads, sometimes specially made of turquoise, attached to their manes and bridles. (See the recommended reading list for a journal article by Marie-Louise Thomsen of Copenhagen University, an excellent source of Assyrian evil eye practises.)

In Greece and Turkey a blue, glass eye charm was said to mirror back the evil eye and thus confound it. In India cord charms from which hangs a blue bead are still worn by newborn babies. Once the cord breaks, the child is thought old enough to resist attack. I was told this by an Indian friend who studied under me for a time.

The most common protective symbol in India, Israel, and Arab lands is an engraved eye within a palm that is covered with magical or religious symbols. It is called the Hamsa (romanised as Khamsa) in the Middle East and the Hand of Fatima in Islam, which in Catholic Christian tradition is called the Hand of God. Also used is *la mano poderosa*, though this does not specifically have the eye in the centre. Spiral ammonites, peacock feathers, and flint arrowheads, as well as shiny witch balls (like big Christmas baubles or glass fishing floats, described in chapter 6), were other traditional protective methods.

Carrying pennyroyal, rosemary, rue, and sage in a little bag or growing them outside your door also offers defense against the evil eye. This I have seen in the West Country of England, where I lived for a number of years, and also in Brittany in France, where again I stayed extensively.

In the case of a vehicle with the evil eye on it (you will experience a number of sudden unexpected breakdowns or minor accidents), keep the crystals in a bag in the glove box. If someone has put the evil eye on your work or home computer and so it is malfunctioning or your e-mails and documents keep disappearing, place four bull's-eye-like green and black malachite, one at each corner of the computer. Malachite is good with any electronic device to protect it from hacking and viruses. If you work successfully from home, envy can be a hazard from other, less successful companies.

Removing the Evil Eye from Juan's Orchards

Juan came to South Australia and established a successful fruit farm. His two sisters were nuns living in a convent near Seville in Spain. I met him when I was doing consultations.

Juan said that on one of their rare visits, he was suddenly aware of his sisters standing side by side and staring at him intently as he was working in the orchard, and he felt the malice flowing towards him "like tongues of fire." Before entering the convent, the sisters, like their mother, had dabbled in bad magic, and Juan suspected they still did.

The sisters approached him, pulled some blossom from the tree, threw it to the ground, and continued to stare contemptuously at him. The older sister said with a smile how beautiful his orchards were and that it was not right he should have success when he had abandoned his faith on leaving Spain. Furthermore, she warned him that God would blight his trees unless he turned back to God and promised to donate a quarter of his profits each year to the convent as penance. Juan laughed this off, but before long his trees were wilting, and there was no logical reason for the sudden downturn in production of healthy fruit while his neighbours' similar trees were flourishing.

Juan came to see me, as he was losing his income and his health was suffering through worry. He was convinced his sisters had put the evil eye on him, as he knew they had done it to neighbours in Spain who had offended them. The family they put the eye on (they had boasted of this) became very sick.

Where land or a home has been affected by the evil eye, eye crystals such as some banded agates (you will need to look carefully for one with an eye in the centre), green tiger's eye, or chrysoberyl (cymophane) are especially effective when buried at the corners of the land. In the case of a relatively large acreage like Juan's or where it is the home that is affected, the four crystals can be buried in a cloth bag near the doorstep of the home. Four is the number of Archangel Cassiel and also mighty Uriel, who defended the earth with his fiery torch, both of whom are linked to Saturn and so the limitation of harm. Juan buried his bag of crystals in the orchard nearest his house.

To speed things and prevent further attacks, I suggested Juan place sun catchers, clear quartz or citrine crystals on chains, at his windows to suffuse rainbows through the rooms when the sun shone and also hang one from a tree in each orchard. You can use wire cradles to support the crystals on lengths of cord, and sun catchers are excellent against the evil eye, especially in children's bedrooms or near pet beds.

It was also necessary to do a spell to remove the evil eye from Juan as well, for Juan was the target of the malice. I carried out for him the olive oil spell that follows.

Two months after the spell and burying of crystals, Juan's trees were slowly coming back to life. It does take time after an attack for things to return to normal, as the damage is not undone overnight, just stopped in its tracks. Juan is also trying new varieties of tree that are proving very popular in the speciality market to replace those that had already died, which he would not have done if the original trees had not been blighted. He has cut off all contact with his sisters, a wise move if at all possible for those who resent you.

Olive Oil Spell to Take Away the Evil Eye

This spell is for removing the evil eye of envy and resentment from any person, land, home, or possessions. For extra power leave the crystals you will bury in the centre of the spell table while you carry out the spell.

In Mediterranean lands, virgin olive oil is used both to detect and remove the evil eye, and this spell is a basic but powerful form that can be adapted against all kinds of ill wishing and envy. It uses the fire and water elements, both powerful in removing the evil eye.

Ingredients and Tools

A white candle
A bag of crystals
A large bowl of cold water
A bottle of virgin olive oil with a pouring lid

Timing

At dawn on a Sunday, the day of Michael, who casts the Eye of Truth over everything
Towards the end of the waning moon cycle if possible

The Spell

Set the bag of crystals in front of the candle. Set the bowl in front of the candle and light the candle. As you do this, say part of Psalm 121 that is especially appropriate for removing the evil eye:

I will lift up mine eyes unto the hills, from whence cometh my help....
The sun shall not smite thee by day, nor the moon by night.
The Lord shall preserve thee from all evil: he shall preserve thy soul.
The Lord shall preserve thy going out and thy coming in from this time
forth, and even for evermore.

Alternatively, use the Lord's Prayer or a special prayer from your own religion, or if you prefer, say,

Turn away the eye of evil with the clear light of truth.

Add the olive oil drop by drop into the water until it makes a ring or circle of oil on the surface of the water. (Practise beforehand if you wish, and use an eyedropper if necessary). Repeat the words once more as you do so. When the ring has formed, swirl the bowl counterclockwise fast until the oil spreads or breaks apart and say,

The eye of evil is dimmed and gone.

Extinguish the candle and say,

Gone and done with the dimming of this light.

Throw the water out the front door, close the door, and wash out the bowl thoroughly. Dispose of the candle; do not relight. Bury the crystals in the bag.

. . . .

Using Mirrors to Reflect and Protect against the Evil Eye

We have already encountered using mirrors defensively when making psychic shields. Mirrors, or indeed any reflective surfaces, are also a remarkably effective way of bouncing back the evil eye if you have had it put on you, your family, your vehicle, your pet, or your property. In addition, they prevent attacks recurring if you have to see the perpetrator at work or socially. Minimise contact if you do, and always avoid eye contact. Later in the chapter I describe a way of secretly empowering jewellery with a defensive evil eye to act as a shield.

Removing the Evil Eye from Jim's Pets

Jim is a professional dog breeder in Florida well known for his rare breeds and excellent pedigrees, and he has won many shows throughout the state with his animals. He has a deadly rival called Veronica who deeply resents his success and in the past has tried to ruin his reputation and cause trouble.

At one dog show recently she turned up with a very strange older woman with piercing eyes who clearly was not connected with the dog world. Unusually, Veronica was very friendly and stood with the person who turned out to be her aunt from England, and both stared intently at the dogs and at Jim. She then said quite calmly and quietly, "I was telling my aunt what beautiful dogs you have and how they are always winning prizes. You have been very lucky with your animals so far— very unfair when people like me work so hard. Be careful though, as there are a lot of nasty canine diseases around at the moment."

They turned away before Jim could reply. A friendly warning? Jim felt uneasy at the way they had been staring so intently, and he could see them across the arena still looking at him and the dogs.

He felt as if a knife had gone into his head, and the dogs became very distressed. He had to take them home without competing. Thereafter, one disaster followed another. One by one, his animals got sick from a rare disease that was very hard to cure. His favourite and most valuable bitch died giving birth, and none of the pups survived. The show dogs became uncooperative in the arena, and he was increasingly coming away from shows empty-handed.

Jim's wife, an acupuncturist and one of my Internet clients who I've worked with extensively, persuaded him to contact me, and there seemed no logical explanation for the bad events that began after the two women stared so intently at him at the show. I felt sure he had experienced the evil eye, and though he was a very sceptical person, he was willing to try anything. I suggested using mirrors to reflect back the nastiness, as this would not only reflect back the eye, but also protect the animals against further attack. The spell involved surrounding a reflective mirror with a circle of reflective metal tags, one for each dog, with their name engraved on one side and the other completely blank, with blank sides uppermost. He defended the animals by fitting their collars with the small polished metal discs, as a repetition of the nastiness seemed likely.

I sent the following spell, and his wife Penny did it on his behalf—Jim was very nervous and a little doubtful of the "mumbo jumbo," as he called it. Penny empowered the protective items, the mirror and discs, during the spell as well as removed the eye.

Gradually, things got on track for Jim: the animals' illnesses were cured, another bitch had successfully given birth, and Jim is successfully competing again with the dogs. Perhaps significantly, Veronica has totally avoided him at shows.

. . . .

Spell to Reflect the Evil Eye and Protect against Future Attacks

Light (the mirror), earth (salt), water (oil), and fire (the candle) are potent against the evil eye.

Ingredients and Tools

A double-sided, small, reflective mirror

A shiny metal medallion, to give to the person under threat to wear or carry in a bag and get out when under threat from the perpetrator

A small white cloth

A gold candle with the mirror directly in front

A small dish of water containing a few grains of salt and a drop of
olive oil (both known removers of the evil eye)

Timing

As the sun is setting

The Spell

Set the medallion in front of the mirror. Light the gold candle and lift
the mirror so that you can see the candle in it, then flip it over so the
candlelight is reflected in the other side as well. Say,

> *You who have put the eye of envy upon me,*
> *In fire your evil desire,*
> *Your glance of jealousy,*
> *Reflected to you back shall be.*

Sprinkle both sides of the mirror with a little salt and oil water,
and as you do so, repeat the words.

Blow three times on the surface of the mirror, look into it, and say,

> *My eye fears not your glance.*
> *Your chance*
> *To harm is past.*
> *On me look your last,*
> *For I return the eye of envy.*
> *No more shall you see or harm me.*

Polish the mirror and then the medallion with the cloth, rubbing
each counterclockwise and saying softly and continuously,

> *Light is stronger than darkness,*
> *Love more powerful than jealousy.*
> *The mirrors reflect back only what you send.*
> *Your eye of envy here must end.*

When you have finished, leave the candle to burn through. Then hang the mirror inside the house so that it faces the front door, and wear or carry the medallion.

If your car is the subject of the evil eye, start the spell with the rubbing of the cloth counterclockwise on the interior and wing mirrors, and say the third set of spell words. You can also do this with computers, tablets, or cell phones. Use a special cloth on your screen, rubbing gently counterclockwise and again repeating the third set of words.

When you meet the envious person, avoid eye contact and say the third set of spell words in your mind three times.

· · · · · · ·

Using an Eye Formation to Repel the Eye of Envy

Even if jealous folk do not directly put the evil eye on you, their resentment and whisperings can make you uneasy and affect you psychologically or even physically. You may fear you are in danger of psychological attack if you work in a very competitive workplace where others resent your success or promotion, if you have had a new baby, or if you just got married and know your partner's ex is furious or your stepchildren are unfairly resentful for your taking their parent's attention. Too many young people are seriously bullied on social media by those who resent them because they have a nice boyfriend, are attractive, are doing well at school, or are in an apprenticeship.

In all these cases wearing a protective eye is helpful, whether visible or unseen, to shield and send back any nastiness. By far the majority of anti–evil eye rituals feature an eye, whether drawn in incense smoke over jewellery, painted on a stone or crystal, or drawn on paper and stuck, for example, on the back of a computer or behind your driving mirror. Crystals that have a natural eye formation within them can also be empowered as psychic shields against jealousy.

Invisible eyes drawn either with the smoke of an incense stick or the index finger of the hand you write with over a crystal pendant or belt buckle imprint the eye's protection on the aether, the spiritual plane where magic takes place.

Spell to Protect from the Eye of Envy Using an Invisible Eye

This spell creates an invisible eye on jewellery or a belt buckle to protect you from the eye of envy and jealousy in your daily life. The fire and air elements used in the spell are a good combination against the eye.

Ingredients and Tools

A white candle
A frankincense or dragon's blood incense stick in a holder
Your favourite piece of jewellery (Blue is the most common colour stone used as an anti–evil eye amulet.)
A dish of sand or soil

Timing

Tuesday evening after sunset, during the waning moon cycle (which is good for removal of the evil eye and for protection)

The Spell

Set the jewellery in front of the candle. Light the candle, saying,

> *Be as a shield for me against envy.*
> *Day and night shine your light*
> *To reflect back jealousy,*
> *Three times three.*
> *So may this be.*

Light the incense from the candle, repeating the words. Using the incense stick like a smoke pen and holding the jewellery in the hand you do not write with, draw an eye shape over the jewellery nine times in incense smoke a few centimetres above it, saying continuously,

> *Turn away the eye from me,*
> *Think not of me, speak not of me,*
> *Act not against me, envy not me,*
> *Three times three.*

Extinguish the incense by putting the lighted end downwards in the sand. Blow out the candle, saying afterwards,

> *Three times three, be gone envy,*
> *Malice, and jealousy,*
> *Returned to all who send thee.*

Wear the jewellery or belt and touch it whenever you feel under threat. Repeat the spell monthly to reempower the crystal, jewellery, or buckle.

. . . .

The Ancient Egyptian Eye of Horus

Blue crystals such as turquoise, blue tiger's eye or falcon's eye (because Horus was depicted as a falcon-headed deity), and gold- and blue-flecked lapis lazuli were considered especially protective against the evil eye in ancient Egypt. They were usually painted or engraved with the Eye of Horus, the young sky warrior god.

Eye of Horus

The original Eye of Horus charm was made of blue glass or faience (a glass and ceramic mix) and a glass bead with the image of the Eye of Horus painted on, or it was a bead painted with a black dot surrounded by a white circle that could be attached to a bracelet.

The protective Horus hieroglyph image made of gold was also worn on a necklace or carried as a charm. You can still buy silver or gold engraved pendants with an Eye of Horus, but you can also make your own Horus pendant on a blue crystal such as turquoise, lapis lazuli, blue howlite, or blue quartz, or by using blue sparkling nail varnish on a plain white stone. Create the image with black acrylic, modelling paint, glass paint, or even a permanent marker, though you may have to renew this regularly as it fades.

If you do not want to paint an image on the crystal, draw it on the surface invisibly with the index finger of the hand you write with, or draw it on sticky paper and attach it to the back.

You can attach the crystal to a wire cradle and wear it on a cord round your neck or use a blue donut stone (a crystal of any of the above kinds with a hole in the middle) threaded on a cord or chain. Wear it inside your clothes so it cannot be seen, or carry the individual crystal in a blue drawstring bag.

Gold is especially good for the chain as it symbolises the sun, and Horus became associated with Ra the sun god in later Egyptian times. If someone is particularly jealous of your new baby, hang an eye crystal or bead near the cradle but high enough and secure enough, of course, so it cannot fall and harm the baby. It is also effective hung near a pet bed if you have a valuable pet that others may try to steal.

. . . .

Spell against the Evil Eye Using a Blue Crystal Eye of Horus

Use a blue crystal Eye of Horus to stop a particular person envying you or casting a jealous eye on you or your possessions.

Ingredients and Tools

A round, flat, blue crystal or a blue glass bead with one flat surface

A small pot of acrylic or modelling paint and a thin brush, or a fine-line permanent marker in a colour that will show clearly on your chosen crystal

Timing

During the waning moon, after sunset

The Spell

Draw or paint the Eye of Horus on the flat surface of the crystal or bead, saying softly and continuously,

Eye bright,
By day and night
Turn away the sight
Of all who glance with evil might,
And on them light
Bright blessings.

When you have finished painting, move your hands nine times over the crystal, palms downwards, fingers together, the left hand circling counterclockwise and the right hand simultaneously circling clockwise. As you move your hands say the same words nine times.

Wear the eye charm or place it between you and the envious person. If you feel under threat, touch or hold your charm in your closed cupped hands and say in either case, nine times softly,

May the eye of malice be turned from me.

When the paint chips or fades, replace the charm. If the crystal suddenly cracks or breaks, don't worry: it just means it has repelled a nasty potential attack. . . . .

Using Salt to Keep Away the Evil Eye

Steve and Hillary live in Dublin and contacted me when they had recently had their first baby. Steve's ex-wife, Sandra, who had not been able to have children with Steve during their marriage, had started a gossip campaign against the couple. Sandra was saying that the child was not Steve's and that Hillary had tricked him into divorcing Sandra and moving in with her, none of which was true since Hillary had not met Steve until he was legally separated from Sandra.

Sandra appeared very nice on the surface, bringing gifts for the baby, which I suggested Hillary cleanse magically before use using a lighted incense stick or chamomile infusion. (You can use a herbal tea bag in a cup of hot water and strain it and sprinkle it round the item. Chamomile protects babies and small children.) Several people had confirmed the rumours Sandra was spreading, and the couple was losing friends. Hillary was really sorry for Sandra because she could not have children, but the gossip was making their lives miserable.

First, I told Hillary to protect the baby with a string of amber, red coral, and blue quartz beads, over which she drew the Eye of Horus in a gentle rose incense stick as we were making it for a baby. Amber and red coral are very defensive against envy and indeed all harm for small babies, as is jade. This string she hung high in the baby's room, away from the cradle.

Then, on a weekly basis Hillary carried out the spell described next and changed the dish of salt that she kept in the kitchen between spells each time. This not only made the couple feel safer, as the salt was protecting the house and so the baby, but after doing it weekly for a month, it actually seemed to slow down the gossip.

We also added as a precaution a binding spell for which we made a featureless doll of pink play clay to represent Sandra and put a gentle rose quartz where her mouth would be and two tiny rose quartzes for the eyes. Hillary, who did the spells (Steve was a bit nervous), wrapped the doll in soft pink cloth, saying,

Be stilled your untrue words.
Be quietened your envious stare.
Let this gossip no more be heard,
Anyhow, anywhere.

Sometimes it is good to combine two methods (in this case a spell similar to those we met in chapter 1, "Binding Magic") when the matter is complex or, as in this case, when emotions are riding high.

The pink cloth was kept in a drawer until the figure crumbled, by which time Sandra had moved away, happily with a new boyfriend. But binding was not enough alone, as it was her envy over the baby that was causing the trouble.

. . . .
Spell to Remove the Evil Eye from Family Members, Pets, or Home

This is a spell to remove the evil eye when your family members, pets, or home are under threat from the evil eye or envy from neighbours or work colleagues.

Ingredients and Tools

Six white candles
A bowl of salt

Timing

Weekly on Tuesday (for Camael, the fierce, protective archangel of
    Mars) or Wednesday (associated with Archangel Raphael, who
    fights against envy)

The Spell

Arrange the six candles in a circle. Moving clockwise round the circle, light each of the white candles in turn, saying,

> *Shield me/*(name others who need protection)/
> *my home from all darkness with the Eye of Truth.*

Draw the Eye of Horus or an ordinary eye shape in the centre of the salt with the index finger of the hand you write with. Sprinkle a pinch of salt into each of the candle flames clockwise in turn and repeat for each,

> *Cleansed be of envy* (specify any particular problems,
> such as gossip, and name the perpetrators if known)
> *with the Eye of Truth.*

Now draw one eye in the air round the outside of the candle circle with the same finger and one eye in the air directly behind each candle. Go round the circle three times and draw the eyes in the same place each time, saying continuously and firmly,

Turn away the eye of envy.
Think not of me/us, speak not of me/us,
Act not against me/us.
Bound by the Eye of Truth shall you be.

Extinguish the candles one at a time, saying for each,

May the Eye of Envy be gone with the dimming of this light.

Place the salt dish in the centre of the kitchen table. Whenever you feel under threat, you can draw the eye in the centre of the salt with your index finger, saying once more,

Turn away the eye of envy.
Think not of me/us, speak not of me/us,
Act not against me/us.
Bound by the Eye of Truth shall you be.

Take your salt to work in a twist of foil to put on your desk if you have jealous colleagues or a resentful manager.

Whenever you repeat the spell, throw out and replace the old salt at work or in the kitchen at home with the new empowered dish of salt in the kitchen.

. . . .

Putting the Evil Eye on Others

Though the evil eye is most associated with envy, pure anger can occasionally, even without a deliberate curse, put the evil eye on someone who has infuriated us. I include the following example here and not in the curse chapter because this contact was transmitted through the eyes. It is one step beyond ill wishing and explains how people can, by feeling negatively, especially but not exclusively enviously, transmit harm through direct eye contact, as well as at a distance.

If you do have a bad temper, then be aware that you may be sending out evil eye vibes, even if you don't utter a curse, especially if you notice your eyes start to hurt or people comment they go black when you are angry. I have known a number of magical practitioners who would never curse anyone but release this power through their eyes when they are angry. So especially if you do have psychic powers, be careful, and if necessary, close your eyes for a minute or two, take deep breaths, and do something physical before allowing angry thoughts to intrude. Then you can respond calmly in earthly terms or, if magically, equally calmly and without malice.

Lisa's Angry Evil Eye

Lisa, who lives in Berkshire in the Home Counties of England, became a gifted clairvoyant later in life and confessed that when she was a little girl, she had the power to put the evil eye on people who upset her, though she didn't know exactly what she was doing. When she thought angrily about someone who had laughed at her, bullied her, or teased her in the playground, her eyes hurt and went black, and invariably something bad would happen to the bullies.

"I knew it was wrong, but I had a rotten temper and would sometimes feel so powerless it all welled up," Lisa told me when we met at a psychic evening in the Home Counties of England. "The power continued till it just became to me an ordinary spontaneous response to people who upset me."

When Lisa was thirty-five, she became furious because a builder hadn't turned up when he promised. She was livid because she'd waited in all day. The next day he phoned very agitated to ask if she'd done something to him. He'd seen her jump out in front of his lorry on the M4 motorway as a tyre blew and narrowly avoided a bad accident. Of course, Lisa denied all knowledge but didn't ask why he hadn't turned up. She couldn't persuade him to come back to fix her house, and she determined to keep her temper under control after that.

Of course, the tyre might have blown anyway and the builder may have been speeding, but the fact he saw Lisa just as his tyre blew out, causing him to swerve, indicates her evil eye had reached him.

Protection against Evil
or Restless Spirits
from the Other Side

Many spontaneous negative psychic phenomena occur especially at night to those who are most vulnerable and open to such experiences. This includes children, teenagers, younger people up to the age of thirty, those who are pregnant, those who have just given birth, and those in times of crisis precisely because those are the times when we are most psychically open. Nighttime is when our conscious defenses are down and the unconscious psychic mind most active.

Demonic Encounters

These accounts of being paranormally attacked, usually sexually and especially by incubi (male sexual entities), have been recorded for hundreds of years and seem to be on the increase, perhaps because of the huge earthly sexual pressures on young people as well as the flood of demonic and vampire material widely available to the young. Thomas Aquinas wrote of sexual demons in his thirteenth-century book *Summa Theologica* and said that "the same demon who acts as a succubus for a man becomes an incubus for a woman." Succubi are female sexual demons that traditionally attacked mature men, especially those sworn to celibacy, as well as adolescents, and were associated with Lilith, first wife of Adam, and her demon daughters, the Lilim. Modern alien abduction accounts, especially of women, tell similar stories of sexual attacks, albeit more clinically carried out.

Here are just a few demonic attacks I have been told of in my travels throughout the world:

- Carol, who lived in Liverpool in North West England, was eight months pregnant. Just before her son was born, one night while she was in bed a black thing sat on her chest: "It was trying to strangle me."

- When Steph from North Queensland was a teenager, for several nights she was "crushed by a black monster with horns, like a bull man with hot breath," as she lay in bed. He only disappeared when she said the Lord's Prayer of her childhood.

- Jessica, who lived on a remote Scottish island, saw her attacker "with a pair of horns, robust ones, too big for a sheep or goat and sort of straight, not curled." She was terrified it was an evil sprite of the island or some ancient animal spirit.

- Jill from the Home Counties of England "had an awful vision of the devil" when she was fourteen. She said, "He had huge horns like a ram and a horrible face. His face was dark and half ram, half human. I think I said a prayer. I felt a physical force. He was trying to crush me. I was absolutely terrified. It lasted ten or fifteen seconds, I suppose, but it was like eternity."

- When she was sixteen, Janet from near London woke "to find a heaving weight on my chest choking the life from my body. The room was freezing. I was fighting to breathe as it grasped me and pressed my neck. At last it went suddenly, leaving me shaking and exhausted. This happened on two occasions. The second time I said the Lord's Prayer, and the fiend, as I thought of it, never came back."

- Diane from Gwent in Wales, a young mother, said, "I felt someone holding me on the bed. I could feel a leg over my leg and an arm pressing my arm. It happened a second time when I was on my own, and the following morning I had finger marks and scratches under the skin on my inner thigh."

- Sylvia was much older and living in the Midlands of Birmingham when she said that suddenly there was a great weight, as if someone had jumped on her bed. Then the whole weight was pressing down on her body and she couldn't move. She thought she would be crushed, though she could see nothing. Then it was gone. She had been ill and was feeling very low psychologically.

Not all demonic attacks are sexual. Here are a few more accounts:

- Sally from North West England was in her early thirties when a "black and very dense, malevolent, squat, little person was standing there in my bedroom and wanting to possess my soul, but I would not let it. At last it went."

- Paul is a sixteen-year-old boy from the Far North of Australia, who has Asperger's, and he confided in me about a hideous demon with distorted female features, huge decaying teeth, and immense strength who did not attack him sexually but crushed and throttled him and left him shaking. Luckily his mother believed him, and she helped him bless his room with water with salt in it, in which they drew a cross and asked Archangel Michael to stand guard.

- Anna, an experienced religious education teacher, told me that a fifteen-year-old boy in her class confided in her that whenever he looked in the mirror, he saw the face of the devil over his shoulder. He was frightened, as he couldn't talk to his parents about it.

Dealing with Demonic Attacks

What is significant is that almost all the attackers described to me have characteristics of the stereotypical demonic form with horns, the traditional way the devil was portrayed from the fourth century CE as half goat or ram with horns and cloven hooves. This of course was an attempt by the Church fathers to demonise the pre-Christian Horned God of the Animals that was and still is a feature of indigenous hunting societies. He was also based on a Graeco-Roman goat god of nature, Pan. This is the image still imprinted in church by some more formal branches of religion and has become the stereotype of evil even among those of no faith.

Of course you should act with caution and listen seriously if a young person of either sex tells you of these paranormal attacks (most keep the experiences secret for years). Some accounts may be ways of expressing actual sexual abuse, especially in a child or younger teenager. However, the majority are definitely paranormal, and many seem to occur to women in adolescence, their teens, their twenties, and their thirties and to mothers. Not surprisingly they occur at night when the woman is half-asleep and are rarely spoken of openly because the women are too often accused of having sexual fantasies or an overactive imagination. Often those who suffer are very sensitive, are usually psychic, and may be under a lot of stress in their lives. It is vital that younger people can talk about these experiences to parents, teachers, carers, and coworkers and not have them dismissed as fantasy, as the fears are very real and magnify with isolation.

Then it is important that they decide what they want you to do to help, such as a ritual, a chat with a priest, making a crystal angel or cross to sleep with, even leaving on the landing light, a change of bedroom, or making sure bedtimes are not preceded by violent computer games or unsuitable TV.

Often you can do a blessing ceremony yourself, especially calling upon the archangels or angels of the night, and I have described a number of rituals you can use or adapt in this and the following chapter. Usually this will be enough to remove the nastiest presence from your life or that of a younger person and protect you and them against psychic attack during sleep, and you can follow this with psychic shielding.

However, if things are really bad and you feel you need support, approach your local Spiritualist church or priest, even if you are not a churchgoer. They will be experienced in dealing with these phenomena, which are magnified by fear, or they will refer you to an expert, as every parish has an exorcist.

But as a society we should perhaps question whether the cult of vampire, demon, and paranormal fiction in films, books, and computer games is not only feeding our young people's minds with material that should only be dealt with by responsible adults trained in the paranormal, but whether they are actually, as I believe, attracting not the blood-dripping demons of the movies but low-life nasty spirits who are taking advantage of what is the deliberate flooding of modern society with evil material. These spirits are masquerading as demons (especially, as we will see in the next chapter, when people play with Ouijas) and, as I know from my own research, they are definitely dramatically increasing. They are all too ready to play ball with those who call them up (see chapter 11).

. . . .

Sacred Fire and Water Spell to Cleanse Demonic Forces and Malevolent Ghosts

Ingredients and Tools

A small bowl of salt

A small bowl of water

A silver-coloured letter opener

A red drawstring bag

Herbs of Mars and the powerful Samael, archangel of cleansing fire: copal resin, dragon's blood powdered incense, dried lavender, cinnamon powder, and spiky whole cloves (If you cannot obtain all these, you can use one or two, and cinnamon powder and whole cloves are, for example, easily obtainable from the culinary section of any supermarket.)

A bowl

A mixing spoon
Four white candles

Timing
An hour before bed

The Spell
Arrange the bowl of salt to the left, the bowl of water to the right, the letter opener in between, and the four candles in a square around them. Light the four candles clockwise and, taking the letter opener in the hand you write with, touch first the surface of the salt and then the surface of the water with the blade, saying for each,

> *Deliver me from evil spirits, poltergeists,*
> *and all the powers of darkness.*

Add nine pinches of salt to the water bowl. Swirl the water bowl clockwise nine times and make a cross on the surface, repeating the words. Pass the water bowl clockwise four times over each candle, repeating the words.

Now mix all the herbs in the bowl and stir them nine times counterclockwise, again saying the same words.

Add sufficient herbs to almost fill the bag, and secure the top with three knots, saying,

> *One binds against evil spirits, two banishes poltergeists,*
> *three shields from the powers of darkness.*

Leave the candles burning till you are ready to go to bed.

Put salt water drops on either side of the bedroom doorframe, along window ledges, on the four corners of the bed, and on the centre of your brow.

Place the bag next to your bed.

. . . .
Four Angels of Quiet Sleep Nighttime Blessing

This is a gentler ritual for sensitive adolescents or those who are very vulnerable. It is helpful if you or a young person are being spooked or are scared at night. If you are doing the ritual on behalf of someone else, you can adapt the words. If the person is present, they can carry out the candle lighting, etc. The ritual should take place in the room where the disturbances occur, and it includes these angels:

- Jeduthan is the angel of the evening and of the twilight heavenly choirs, with an indigo halo and wings. He brings peace into the home in the evening, encourages a quiet transition between sleeping and waking, and protects against paranormal nighttime intruders.

- Memumah is the angel who sends sleep and soothing dreams if you call on him. He is a misty silvery angel and will relieve nightmares or psychic or psychological attacks while you sleep.

- Muriel, a healer angel, brings beautiful dreams to those who are afraid of the dark and of ghosts or evil spirits. She wears pink and lilac and is surrounded by moonbeams.

- Natiel is a lilac-winged angel who keeps away harm and night terrors from younger people and all who are vulnerable to psychic attack.

Ingredients and Tools
Four tall white candles, one for each angel
A small bowl of salt
A large mirror
A small table placed in front of the mirror, to hold the salt and the candles (if possible, in the room where the disturbances occur)

Timing
As darkness falls

The Spell

Place the candles in a row on the table so that you can see them reflected in the mirror, and stand between the candles and the mirror.

Light the candles left to right, naming an angel for each. Sprinkle salt into the first candle flame, saying,

> *Jeduthan, kind angel of the night,*
> *Turn back the phantoms with your light,*
> *That I may sleep till dawn comes bright.*

Sprinkle salt into the second candle flame, saying,

> *Memumah, kind angel of the night,*
> *Turn back the phantoms with your light,*
> *That I may sleep till dawn comes bright.*

Sprinkle salt into the third candle flame, saying,

> *Muriel, kind angel of the night,*
> *Turn back the phantoms with your light,*
> *That I may sleep till dawn comes bright.*

Sprinkle salt into the final candle flame, saying,

> *Natiel, kind angel of the night,*
> *Turn back the phantoms with your light,*
> *That I may sleep till dawn comes bright.*

Blow softly into each candle in turn, left to right, naming the angel to whom you dedicated the candle. Afterwards say,

> *Jeduthan, Memumah, Muriel, Natiel, angels all,*
> *Hold me in sleep, that I may not fall*
> *Prey to the spectres of the night.*
> *Keep me safe till dawn comes bright.*

Leave the candles to burn through. Say before sleep each night and if you wake afraid in the night,

Jeduthan, Memumah, Muriel, Natiel, angels all,
Hold me in sleep, that I may not fall
Prey to the spectres of the night.
Keep me safe till dawn comes bright.

• • • • • • •

Poltergeists

Poltergeist means "noisy ghost" in German, but it has come to signify those spirits with either malevolent intent or disruptive results from their actions. Disturbances typically include strange noises; banging; rapping; or ornaments, furniture, or stones being thrown by an unseen force. Objects may disappear and reappear, sometimes in different locations; beds shake; small fires start spontaneously; or water appears in pools on the floor from no obvious source. There may be a shadowy presence, a feeling of malevolence, and even verbal and physical attacks from the invisible aggressor.

Friendly Noisy Ghosts: Finding an Explanation

However, by no means are all noisy ghosts malevolent, so don't assume your noisy ghost means harm, as very few are actual poltergeists. Indeed, if you understand why a paranormal event is happening, then it loses much of its power to frighten you.

The simplest and most benign explanation for items being moved and bangs and crashes around the home are those of a noisy departed former resident whose psychic imprints or actual presence is activated by the present residents, especially children. These noisy but quite benign hauntings tend to follow a regular and explicable pattern: for example, footsteps from one room to another at a time when the deceased occupant of the house would have been checking on or caring for a sick relative or child. This can sometimes be verified by elderly neighbours. It may also be an elderly, fussy relative of your own who is keeping an eye on things, and you will know if you do not sense evil that you have a noisy, not a malevolent, ghost. However, constant ghostly noise can be disturbing and worry children. The following spell will not banish your ghost but will merely establish a few house rules. Remember, the home is yours and even a former resident or passing relative is a visitor, but you may need to establish the boundaries.

. . . .

Spell to Quieten a Noisy but Friendly Ghost

Ingredients and Tools
A purple candle

Timing
Before bed for seven days

The Spell
Each night in the room where the ghost is heard most strongly, light the candle. If you know the identity of the ghost, name him or her, or if you just sense a benign presence, call the ghost "friend." Say, at normal speaking volume,

> *Friend (or name ghost), welcome you are,*
> *As long as you would stay.*
> *Guardian kind of my home,*
> *I send you not away.*

Reduce the volume of your voice, gradually saying the following words softer and softer till they become a whisper and fade into silence:

> *But quieter be,*
> *That we may live in harmony,*
> *Not noisily,*
> *Nor loudly.*
> *Side by side, we can abide,*
> *Living peacefully.*
> *Guardian, welcome be.*

Blow out the candle, sending blessings to your (hopefully) no longer noisy ghost, and place a bunch of fresh flowers where you hear the ghost most, renewing these regularly. You will find that the ghost becomes cooperative and that household luck increases.

· · · · · · ·

Unfriendly Ghosts

You can tell if you have any negative phantoms even if you have not seen a ghost. Animals will growl in certain rooms, and children may complain of a dark figure that scowls at them or tells them to go away. You may feel you are being watched, or items go missing only to reappear in the place you left them hours or days later.

The negative presence will be felt or seen most clearly at night. In most cases the ghost is not bad, but unhappy. He or she may not be deliberately spooking you, but may have been hurt by people during life or may feel that you are invading his or her home.

Occasionally, when there seems to be malevolence by the ghost, the cause can be attributed to unfinished business. Earthbound spirits who have died may not have yet crossed to the other side, whether this is from the trauma of dying suddenly or with an injustice that is unresolved. While some are just impressions creating negative energy waves, others just want their story to be heard, like the ghost who appeared to Maggie on the Isle of Wight in her sixteenth-century cottage always wringing his hands by the fireplace, weeping and saying over and over, "I was murdered; they lied." After Maggie spoke back and said how sorry she was and how unfair it was, then the spirit no longer appeared.

An imagined injustice can also cause a restless spirit. For example, Jan's elderly mother died swearing revenge for what she saw as her daughter's neglect. Jan, who lives in the Home Counties near London, said this was totally unfair, but whatever she had done for her mother was always wrong. At every family gathering Jan organised after the old lady's death, beginning with the funeral tea, glasses would fly off the sideboard, crockery would smash as though hurled by an invisible hand, and furniture would tip over. Doors and windows rattled even when there was no wind. Ironically, the same old lady would announce her presence to her favourite granddaughter by the scent of roses.

You may, however, be living on a subterranean ley or energy line, and the energies may have soured or may simply be too powerful and attract wandering ghosts who seem to feed on the energy of the lines. It was believed ghosts travel along straight lines. If they died before your dwelling was built and lived on the land, they may get trapped in the house, not realizing it is there. This is especially so on lines such as the ancient Australian Aboriginal song lines, along which the deceased pass as they did in their lifetime on their trail between sacred sites.

I have come across many accounts of Aboriginal spirits, especially mischievous teenagers entering a modern homestead in Australia built on these lines, who have created havoc. (I describe negative energy lines in detail in chapter 12.) Brian, who had a small ranch in New South Wales in Australia, described crashing and banging round his home, especially at night, with ornaments smashing, lights going on and off, and the television and music centre suddenly blaring. His little girl had been frightened by a little boy with dark eyes who hid in the shadows and jumped out when she went to the bathroom.

I suggest a spell for removing these spirits after the next account.

The Suffering Ghost Who Followed Pat Home

We can also unwittingly attract a restless spirit if we visit a haunted place or ancient site, and I suggest you don't bring home stones or wood from these places because there can be a spirit attached, quite apart from the fact that sites can become depleted of their very fabric by souvenir hunters.

Pat, who is in her forties and lives in Bromley near London, explained that she went to Ightham Mote, an historic house, with her sister. In one room, she felt the most terrible sorrow and a strong frightening presence. There was a huge inglenook fireplace in the room, and on impulse she took a piece of loose stone home as a souvenir.

When Pat got up the next morning, all the chairs in her dining room were tipped over, and the back of her watch was smashed in. That was where she'd left the stone. Then she smelled a dreadful odour like rotting flesh—the smell you get when meat has gone off. And then she saw a woman all dressed in black whose hands were torn and bleeding. "Please help me," the woman cried over and over again. "They shut me behind the wall though I did no wrong."

There is an escape route for priests behind a chimney in Ightham Mote, and the skeleton of a woman was found in a cupboard behind a walled-up doorway in the tower. The body was discovered in 1872 by workmen.

"I threw the piece of fireplace away," Pat said, "but it was no use." The next morning, six crystal glasses were smashed, and the stems stood in a row on the table. Each day something was destroyed. On the sixth day, two precious ivory statuettes were destroyed. Her husband was frightened though she didn't tell him about the woman she had seen.

"On the seventh day, I found my amethyst necklace I always wore round my neck was missing and had been ripped in half," Pat explained. Soon afterwards her marriage ended, and she moved out of the house. So far, she said, the woman hasn't followed her. "But her cries still haunt me."

As with many poltergeist cases where a spirit is not only noisy but destructive, it would seem that tension in the home somehow triggers paranormal activity, caused in this case by removing what amounts to a cursed stone, filled with the suffering of the woman, from the place of the tragedy.

The following spell is very effective for getting rid of any negative spirits, especially those who may be trapped in your home for whatever reason.

. . . .

Spell to Remove a Troublesome Trapped Spirit from Your Home

Ingredients and Tools

A white candle

An incense stick in any fragrance, in a holder

A small bowl of salt
A medium-sized bowl of water
A silver-coloured knife

Timing

Sunday morning

The Spell

Light a white candle and set it on a small table in a room as close to the centre of the home as possible, saying,

> *By this bright flame, go now into the light.*
> *No longer stay here by day or by night.*

From the candle, light the incense stick, saying,

> *By the power of air, go where*
> *Your loved ones seek you.*
> *Your time trapped here is through.*

Into the bowl of water drop three pinches of salt, swirl the water three times in each direction, and then draw a cross on the surface with a knife, saying,

> *By water and by earth, no longer remain here.*
> *Go to those waiting to whom you are dear.*

Beginning in the room where you have the table, walk clockwise, starting at the main door, sprinkling water droplets around the floor and along window ledges, saying,

> *May only goodness and light remain here.*
> *Friend, depart in peace to those who wait for you.*

Spiral the incense stick around the walls and over windows clockwise, repeating the same words.

Finally, walk around the room clockwise, holding the candle and repeating the words.

Open any windows and leave any internal doors open. Repeat this in every room and hallway of the home.

Carry the water to the front door, making a water-drop trail. Open it and throw out the water, saying,

Go now to the light.

Carry the candle to the front door, step outside with it, and extinguish it, saying,

Go now to those who wait.

Do the same with the incense, but leave it to burn outside, saying,

Follow the trail to the sky.
With blessings, I bid you goodbye.

Shut the front door, firmly close it, and then close all windows.

Repeat this weekly for two or three weeks if you still sense the presence. But the first time is generally enough.

. . . .

Making the Removal Fit the Scenario

In removing unwelcome spirits, you should carry out a spell no differently from how you would practically remove any unwelcome earthly visitors, politely but very firmly. Devising your own ritual for your circumstances, adapting one of mine if you wish, means it fits exactly your needs.

Indeed, I was asked to help exorcise an historic pub in Central Australia where incredibly noisy disruptive ghosts were harming business, not only by frightening staff and clients in the pub and bottle store, but also by interfering with the electronic tills. They were also picking on the younger staff by jumping out at them, making them spill drinks and drop food.

So the landlady, her daughter, and her staff, including the ones being harassed, sat down with me, and we devised a ritual that they could all share. They went round the whole pub and into each corner with incense and candles, and we banged saucepan lids together and called,

Time gentlemen, please—you may no longer drink here;
on your way and don't come back.

It took two or three circuits, but the problem stopped. Noise, especially that of bells, is very effective in removing unwanted spirits. Because there is often an excess of bad behaviour and people who are addicted to alcohol and spend all their time there, pubs seem to attract low-life spirits who most likely spent much of their lifetime in alehouses and—especially regarding older inns—may return to where they were once happy.

The landlady reclaimed her territory, and the most vociferous ghostbuster was the young Irish girl most terrified by the ghosts. If she even sensed one was back, she would pick up the billiard cue, her choice of weapon in the original cleansing, and chase the phantom out of the door.

Institutions such as prisons and mental hospitals as well as pubs and clubs, especially where there is drug dealing, can also attract malicious spirits who never lived, but they can be dealt with in the same way as ghosts who lived (see the poltergeist ritual later in the chapter).

Poltergeists and Psychokinetic Energy

One theory cites the cause of much poltergeist activity as emanating from a present member of the household, usually a young adolescent. Often they are the focus for family tension, and their psychic energy, at its height at this age, is expressing unconsciously repressed anger if the parental relationship is troubled.

However, from my own albeit anecdotal research talking to victims and their families over more than thirty years, it would seem the psychic energy released, often through a teenager but which reflects collective family tension, fuels or activates a low-level spirit. This may be a spirit thought form, whether created from the family tension that has taken on an independent form or an elemental spirit called up during a magical ritual, perhaps many years ago, who was not dismissed at the end of the ritual and so hangs around the earth waiting to be fuelled by the concentration of family energy. Family tensions are implicated in every case I have studied.

Such creatures that feed on this accumulated family energy never lived, which is why in poltergeist cases I would always do a poltergeist banishing ritual as well as trying to sort out the earthly issues, as both are necessary.

Sophy's Poltergeist

Sophy is now a twenty-one-year-old trainee accountant but recalled for me the bad experiences she had when she was thirteen. She said they are as vivid now as when they occurred, though her family still becomes angry if she tries to discuss them. She grew up in a large house in Perth in Scotland with her mother and father. Sophy's parents had been experiencing problems in their marriage for some time, and there had been many late-night arguments that greatly distressed her. She told me if there was an unhappy atmosphere when she sat down to breakfast, plates and ornaments would start to move and fall off shelves and smash. In the evenings when everyone was in bed, doors would slam and the smoke alarms would go off without reason. Her parents accused her of playing tricks and took her to a psychologist who said she was seeking attention, but Sophy said she was often the target. More than once she was pinched and slapped when she was in bed, even though she locked her bedroom door, and was several times pushed downstairs by invisible hands, once hurting herself quite badly, but again her parents said she did it deliberately.

The paranormal activity stopped when Sophy's father left home.

Jane's Poltergeist

Jane's first poltergeist manifested itself early (childhood is another very psychically active time) when the family moved to a new house in Hampshire, on the south coast of England. When she was four years old, she started to complain about the wardrobe doors opening, books and toys leaping out of her wardrobe and hitting her, and staring eyes piercing from the darkness. Once an unlit light bulb exploded for no apparent reason, and the pieces shattered directly on to her bed, although the bed was not near the light. Jane moved out of the room to share with her older brother. The experiences stopped.

Jane's mother witnessed some of the action.

When Jane was fifteen, the experiences began again, and books were hurled from the top of her wardrobe, although it was a different wardrobe and indeed a house almost two hundred miles away from her former home. A pottery theatre mask would often turn up in the middle of Jane's bed even when no one had been home, the family had been out together, and the mask had been anchored firmly to the fridge downstairs with a magnet when they left.

Strangely, Jane's boyfriend Dave's family also had a poltergeist in their house, which was built on what was formerly priory land. It created many disturbances in the house before Dave met Jane, particularly in Dave's room. When Dave's father was sitting in the bath one night, the shower suddenly exploded, sending glass from the cabinet flying everywhere and cutting him quite badly. The shower was not in use at the time. On another occasion Dave was telephoning Jane when he was alone in the house, and suddenly all the plates flew out of the cupboard and smashed. Dave was terrified.

Often it is hard to isolate the paranormal from the psychic, and it may be that what is a malevolent ghost is activated by the psychic energy emitting from a child or adolescent, because both Jane and Dave had ongoing marital disharmony in their homes. Initially, it is important to remove the spirit and, if there are underlying family tensions, to resolve them if possible. One remedy without the other rarely works, though it did in the case of Sophy. The following worked well for Jane's family, who also had counselling for the marital issues, but Dave's family refused to acknowledge the problem, and so as far as I know it continued.

Spell to Remove a Spiteful Spirit or Poltergeist Causing Trouble

Remember to speak firmly. Low-life spirits are petty bullies.

Ingredients and Tools

A lemon, lavender, or pine-scented candle, all excellent for strong spirit defensive work

A frankincense or sandalwood incense stick

A bowl of garlic salt

Six pointed amethysts (Amethysts are potent against spirits and negative earth energies and bring balance where there has been psychic disturbance.)

A bell or a pair of Tibetan bells or ones hanging on a red cord

Timing

Tuesday around sunset

The Spell

Arrange the points of the amethysts outwards, in a circle around the garlic salt. Inside the circle place the bell or bells. At a table, light the candle and from it the incense, saying,

Burn, candle, burn.
You, spirit, are not welcome here,
Depart; do not return.
Your presence for me/us, holds no fear.

> *Turn,*
> *Turn away.*
> *You cannot stay.*

Write the following round and just above the garlic, the bell or bells, and the amethysts in incense smoke letters in the air, and at the same time say slowly but firmly as you write them,

> *You must depart in peace.*
> *Your presence I release.*
> *Trouble now must cease.*
> *Be gone;*
> *Your time here is done.*

With the incense in the hand you write with, walk through all rooms in a straight line and any passageways and halls, from the back of the house to the front, making counterclockwise spirals so you end at the front door. (Ghosts don't like spirals, as I describe in the spirit traps in chapter 11.)

Return the incense to the spell table and ring the bell throughout the house, again from top to bottom and back to front of the house, including passageways as before, and again ending at the front door, saying the same words as when you spiralled the incense.

Sprinkle just a grain or two of garlic salt (it smells foul but banishes troublesome spirits) in the candle flame, saying,

> *Spirit, you are not welcome here.*
> *Depart; do not return,*
> *Turn,*
> *Turn away.*
> *You cannot stay.*

Holding the garlic in the hand you do not write with and the candle in the other, make a third journey through the house, but this time open the front door, go outside, and blow the candle out over the garlic. Tip the garlic away outside.

When the incense has burned out, place each amethyst on an indoor window ledge inside your home.

Wash them weekly and replace them, saying,

> *May nothing enter here*
> *That is not from the light.*
> *Gone is all fear.*
> *Evil, be banished from my sight.*

· · · · · · ·

Using Angelic Forces against Unwanted and Undesirable Spirits

I believe just as there are angelic forces, even though they may not be winged beings as we visualise them, so there are negative entities who never experienced life and who just want to cause trouble for humans. Therefore, angelic protection is powerful against them as well as any earthbound spirits or evil ghosts. You can also use these invocations against ill-intentioned spirits unwittingly summoned by people as part of a Ouija session or séance.

I have described earlier in the chapter an angel protection for younger people who are afraid to sleep at night because of negative psychic experiences. Here we work with the "big boys and girls" of the cosmos, the archangels.

Whether or not you belong to a religion that believes in angels, in the modern world, as in ancient times, archangels form the ultimate psychic defense against even the most malevolent spirit.

The Archangel Invocation or Calling

In this ritual four archangels are called, representing the four directions, the four elements, and four unique powers for our defense. In magic these four are the most commonly used together in defensive rituals. I have listed more protective archangels throughout the book and in appendix A.

MICHAEL

Archangel of the sun, Michael is the archangel of light and the warrior angel. He appeared to Moses as the fire in the burning bush and saved Daniel from the lion's den. As commander of the heavenly hosts, Michael, usually pictured with a golden sword and wearing red or gold armour, drove Satan and his fallen angels out of the celestial realms.

According to the Koran, the Cherubim were created from Michael's tears. Michael's traditional position is in the south with the noonday sun and signifies the element of fire.

Michael traditionally stands in the south. If you are in the Southern Hemisphere, you have the option of putting Michael in the north and changing the position of the other archangels, but often with angelology, since it is symbolic, you may prefer to keep the traditional Northern Hemisphere associations. Do whatever feels comfortable.

His colour is gold and his crystal is amber, orange carnelian, or pure crystal quartz. His incense or oil is frankincense or orange.

GABRIEL

Gabriel is the archangel of the moon, the messenger archangel, and the heavenly awakener. She is often given a female focus and appears many times in the Bible, visiting the Virgin Mary and her cousin Elizabeth, mother of John the Baptist, to tell them that they were to bear sons who would lead humankind to salvation. She is usually pictured holding a sceptre or lily and wearing silver or deep blue robes covered in stars. To the followers of Islam, Gabriel is the spirit of truth who dictated the Koran to Muhammad. She is very powerful against phantoms of the night.

Gabriel traditionally stands in the west and signifies the element of water. In the Southern Hemisphere you have the option of placing Gabriel in the direction of the largest body of water. You may need to adapt the words of the invocation slightly.

Her colour is silver. Her crystal is the moonstone, pearl, or opal, and her incense and oil is jasmine or myrrh.

RAPHAEL

Raphael is the archangel of medicine, all forms of healing and science, and the planet Mercury. He healed the earth, gave Noah a medical book after the flood receded, and also healed the blind Tobit in the Christian Holy Scriptures. Raphael gave King Solomon a magical ring to help him in building his great temple. He is also archangel of the four winds and travellers, especially the young and vulnerable who are far from home.

Raphael is usually depicted with a pilgrim's stick, a wallet, and a fish, showing the way and offering sustenance to all who ask. He wears the colours of morning sunlight.

He stands in the east and signifies the element of air. In the Southern Hemisphere you have the option of positioning Raphael in the direction of the nearest mountain range or wide plain.

His colour is yellow, his crystal is citrine or amethyst, and his incense is lavender or lemongrass, which protects against human snakes.

URIEL

Uriel, whose name means "fire of God," is associated with earthquakes, storms, and volcanoes but also protection of the earth with his flaming torch that melts the winter snows. He is often associated with the planet Saturn or, alternatively, Mars. He is the archangel of salvation. He warned Noah of the impending flood and led Abraham out of Ur. Believed to have given alchemy to mankind, he also imparted the wisdom of the Kabbalah to Hebrew mystics. He wears dark purple, burnished gold, and indigo robes.

Uriel stands in the north and signifies the element of earth. In the Southern Hemisphere, if you wish, position him in the direction of the Antarctic.

His colour is indigo or deep red, his crystal is garnet or rutilated quartz, and his oil or incense is copal or patchouli.

The Archangel Calling

The directions can be approximate, although you can use a compass if you prefer. You can use this ritual if you have a trapped spirit you wish to send to the light, as the archangels will do it for you.

Stand facing east looking upwards, with your arms wide, chest high, and palms uppermost. Say as you stand motionless,

> *Before me stands Raphael, who never rests and protects me from all harm in this world and from harmful spirits from the other realms.*
>
> *Behind me is enfolding Gabriel, who takes away all fear and protects me from all harm in this world and from harmful spirits from the other realms.*
>
> *On my right hand is the warrior Michael, who crushes dragons beneath his feet and protects me from all harm in this world and from harmful spirits from the other realms.*
>
> *On my left hand Uriel, with his blazing torch of fire, protects me from all harm in this world and from harmful spirits from the other realms.*

Raise your arms and say,

> *And so I fear nothing.*
> *The circle of light encloses me,*
> *And above me is the shining star of the angels.*

As you say each line, picture each archangel joined in a circle of light and, above, a six-rayed star whose light shimmers in all directions.

Feel yourself filled with light as it passes down your body as white starlight, joins with the red light of the earth, and so mingles and becomes pure gold within you.

Now with your hands create a doorway of light above your head and ask the archangels to take through any troublesome spirit to where she or he may be healed.

Then cross your hands above your head to close the doorway and say,

I thank you, wise archangels, for your protection.

During this invocation, if you wish, you can light the appropriate colour candle and burn an incense stick for each archangel in their fragrance: yellow and lavender or lemongrass incense for Raphael, silver and jasmine or myrrh incense for Gabriel, indigo and copal or patchouli incense for Uriel, and gold and frankincense or orange incense for Michael.

Leave all to burn through.

The Archangel Calling Using Pentagrams

If the spirit is particularly vicious or hard to move or if you fear it is trying to enter you, try this alternative version of the invocation.

The pentagram is a five-pointed, protective, and empowering ancient magical symbol. It has none of the weird spooky symbolism you see in B movies and represents the union of the four elements (earth, air, fire, and water), each of which is represented by one of the four lower points of the five-pointed star. The fifth and uppermost point symbolises spirit, the point where the four elements unite and which in magic symbolises the goddess energy.

Spirit

Air   Water

Earth   Fire

The Pentagram and the Elements

The energy of the pentagram, whether protective or empowering, depends on the direction you draw it. Each of the elements has its pair of pentagrams. In this archangel ritual it is the banishing earth pentagram that is used, and this form is the most commonly used in protective magic.

Looking at the diagram on the next page, practise drawing the banishing pentagram on paper and in the air if you are unfamiliar with pentagrams. Drawing one in front of you in any place of danger or even picturing one in white, violet, or gold light will defend you against any paranormal harm. You can draw the shape invisibly on the windows and doors of your home, on property, and on possessions. Practise drawing it in the air with your elbow bent in front of you, using your index and second fingers together, your whole hand, the hand you write with, your fingers together, or a pointed clear quartz crystal.

Start the bottom left-hand point level with your left hip and move your hand or wand upwards in a single stroke to draw the top point level with your head. Now draw the downwards point to level with your right hip.

Then go diagonally halfway across to draw the middle point level with your left elbow, straight across horizontally to the right and down again to join the point where you started. You have now made your banishing earth pentagram.

Picture your pentagrams as made of white, violet, or golden light, or if you need powerful protection, as flames.

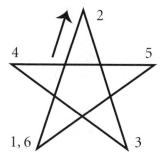

Banishing Earth Pentagram

Pentagram Archangel Calling

Face east and draw a banishing pentagram in the air in front of you with your elbow bent, saying,

> *Archangel Raphael, deliver me from all evil,*
> *both human and from harmful spirits.*

Turn to the south and draw another banishing pentagram in the air in front of you, saying,

> *Archangel Michael, deliver me from all evil,*
> *both human and from harmful spirits.*

Face west and draw another pentagram in front of you as before, saying,

> *Archangel Gabriel, deliver me from all evil,*
> *both human and from harmful spirits.*

Face north to create your final pentagram, saying,

Archangel Uriel, deliver me from all evil,
both human and from harmful spirits.

Face east again and raise your arms, looking upwards and saying,

And above me, Raphael, Michael, Gabriel,
and Uriel is your radiant star. I fear no evil.

Protection against Summoned Evil Spirits

The line between the psychological and psychic is very fine. People of any age, but especially vulnerable teenagers, can seriously mess with their minds if they dabble with amateur séances or call up spirits in Ouija boards. For there is no doubt that low-life spirits, either con men and women during their lifetimes or nasty spirits who never lived on earth, can use these seemingly harmless psychic games to at first lure in and then terrify the unwary.

The communicating spirit may offer information known only to one person present (these spirits specialise in telepathy). They may even in subsequent séances offer accurate tips on winning horse races or lucky numbers, resulting in a minor win. They often claim to be someone famous or a beloved deceased relative. They are good actors and actresses.

Then as the subjects are lured back to the Ouija board or séance table time and time again, the spirit's messages become warnings or give false information to cause trouble in the family or among friends. When you ask the spirit to go, sometimes they remain even after you have put the Ouija board away and follow you home. I could write an entire book on the experiences of those whom I have helped when they get tangled up with evil spirits by dabbling.

As this is such a complex subject, I describe the experiences of being troubled by evil spirits in the first half of the chapter and methods of dealing with these issues in the second half. You will also find the defensive rituals in the previous chapter helpful against evil spirits that have been called up by whatever means.

Ouija Boards

Ouija boards, a letter board, or alphabet cards set in a circle sometimes have answers such as "yes," "no," and "goodbye" added. They are often used informally with an inverted glass on which those present rest their fingers, and as the glass moves, it will spell out words. Séances may also involve table tapping, in which the spirit answers once for yes and twice for no.

Ouija boards became popular in the United States in the late 1880s and were commercially produced, and because of the great interest in Spiritualism, talking to the dead through mediums, and amateur séances, they also became common party games.

In fact, many centuries earlier the Romans used a device similar to the Ouija to get the answers from a *divus* (the Latin origin of the word "divination"), a spirit or god they invoked. In the fourth century CE the chronicler Marcellinus described how a thread with a ring on the end was hung from a small tripod. The tripod was placed in the centre of a circle on which were written the letters of the Roman alphabet. A question would be asked and the ring spontaneously swung towards different letters to spell out answers. Mentions of this resurfaced in the thirteenth century. Ben Hester's *Dowsing* tells of a papal edict issued by Pope John XXII in 1326 that forbade the faithful from the "use of a ring to obtain answers in the manner of the Devil."

We may no longer believe in the devil, but Ouija is far from a harmless party game. Often, as one session follows another, one spirit dominates the board, becoming the antithesis of a spirit guide and revealing a malicious and terrifying side. I have had to help children as young as nine who have made a set of letter cards and experimented in the cloakroom at recess or at home on sleepovers.

Pam's Experience

Pam from Birmingham, England, had tried to talk to her Mom about ghosts because the subject fascinated her, but her mother told her that the psychic was rubbish.

When Pam was fourteen, she started to use the Ouija board at school with her friends. Pam was especially singled out for nice messages, to her friends' annoyance, and they accused her of cheating. The spirit told her she'd meet a new boyfriend called John. This was not unlikely, since John is such a common name, and, as a result of this information, Pam would have been unconsciously giving out positive vibes to every John she met after the séance. The spirit also promised that she'd do well in her end-of-term exams. Pam had worked hard all year, but when her results were good, she was convinced that her success was due to the spirit on the board.

Then the glass told Pam she had a great psychic gift, so she started to play with lexicon letter cards at home alone. But things turned nasty. The spirit said that her best friend Jan was saying nasty things behind her back. Pam caught Jan whispering to another girl in the cloakroom, and after a terrible row, Pam and Jan stopped speaking to each other.

Then the spirit in the glass warned her that if she went dancing, there would be a fire at the disco that would disfigure her face. The spirit refused to say when this would happen, so Pam gave up going to discos even at school. The next week, the spirit told her that the school bus would crash, but again gave no time. Pam was terrified and refused to go to school.

Pam's mother, noticing that Pam was behaving strangely, finally confronted her and asked if she had been taking drugs. Pam confessed to using a Ouija board, and her mother called in the local priest. They destroyed the cards and blessed Pam's bedroom.

Pam's mother felt guilty that she'd not allowed her daughter to talk about psychic matters when she was first interested in them and that she had found it easier to suspect her daughter of taking drugs than of dabbling in the occult.

Teenage psychic experiments are very common, and it's only by bringing the psychic out into the open that a parent can divest the darker aspects of their mystique and glamour and not leave vulnerable youngsters alone with their fears. Even if you do not believe that the experience your teenager is telling you is anything more than fantasy, to your teenager it is frighteningly real (and indeed may be). Helping teenagers rid themselves of the spirit they fear is with them or enlisting the help of a priest will remove the problem.

Franny's Experience

Felicity from the Home Counties of England told me that when her daughter Franny was about twelve, she and some of her friends had been playing with a Ouija board in the school cloakroom at lunchtime after Franny found a book in the school library about it. Franny believes she picked up a spirit because she started to be haunted by an old man soon after she started using the Ouija regularly with her friends.

"My daughter told me he used to sit on her dressing table," said Felicity. "He followed her all the time. He used to just sit there watching her. It was horrifying that she became so distressed."

Things got so bad one night when Felicity's husband was away that Felicity telephoned their local priest, but he was out. She explained, "My daughter was completely hysterical. I talked to her to calm her and we sprinkled holy water round her room. After that, it seemed to quieten down. I made her promise never to fool around with a Ouija board again."

Helen's Experience

Helen went to an exclusive convent school in London and had dabbled with the Ouija board from the age of fourteen during lunchtime break in the classroom with her friends. When Helen was sixteen, she and her best friend, Ally, were playing with the board, and as Helen recalled, "It was a time when school friendships are the centre of your world and you can't imagine it being otherwise. So Ally asked the glass, 'Will Helen and I always be friends?'"

The spirit answered, *No.*

"Why not?"

Dead. Car.

Ally was very upset, and they stopped doing the Ouija after that. But six months later almost to the day, Ally was killed in a car crash. It may well have been a coincidence, but the experience upset Helen for years.

Terry's Experience

Yes, adults dabble with Ouijas, too, and get into difficulties. Others pay dubious practitioners to send demons against their enemies, only to find that the demon also visits them and that the practitioner is demanding a huge amount of money to remove it.

Terry from Auckland, New Zealand, played with a Ouija board in the pub and at first the spirit, a creepy old man called Jack who said he used to be a local farmer, was very helpful and told Terry where a former resident had buried a small pot of money on Terry's land (and sure enough it was where Terry had been told). But then the spirit told Terry his wife was having an affair (totally untrue, though the spirit got the middle name of Terry's mother-in-law right). Spirits, as I suggested earlier, are good at mind reading and also revealing facts not known to the sitters.

Then Jack started to follow Terry home. Terry's young daughter Midge began waking up crying, saying a horrible old man in muddy boots was laughing at her in her bedroom and telling her that her mom was going away because she didn't love her dad anymore.

We got rid of the spirit using the salt and sacred water ritual I describe later in the chapter. However, Terry was a jealous man, so the spirit had played on his weakness, and the suggested infidelity caused a lot of trouble.

Possession

The stuff of bad B movies? Though we no longer live in a mediaeval world racked with superstition, the modern world has created a
popular culture that I am convinced encourages lower-life spirits to
assume the roles of ancient demons whenever people call them up
using an Internet site and reciting old rituals whose significance they
do not understand. My local library has whole shelves in the older
children's section on vampires and demons—and not a single sensible
psychic advice book.

There is fierce debate about whether people can be possessed by
spirits, but with increasingly violent paranormal horror films and
computer games with realistic special effects, people of all ages are
asking me for help for what may be a psychological issue or a nasty
spirit playing mind games—or both. This can lead to panic and over-
reaction. Indeed, when a child who may have a psychological disorder
has been accused of being possessed, less enlightened religious groups
may abuse the child to remove the spirit.

I am uneasy with the concept that evil spirits can possess a child or
adolescent, but I keep an open mind and urge anyone concerned by
a relative's sudden bizarre behaviour to seek medical or psychological advice, as there are psychological conditions that can mimic what
seems like possession. Only when there are no explanations from conventional sources, ask a priest or medium attached to a respectable
Spiritualist church for help. In recent years in conventional religions,
more priests are being trained in exorcism to cope with a greatly increasing demand.

Edmund's Possession and Faith Healing

The strangest story I have ever come across was told to me about fifteen years ago by Louise, a rational businesswoman who described
her son, Edmund, whom she feared had been possessed even before
his birth. She believes this "thing" entered Edmund in Cornwall,
where he was conceived. At the time Louise contacted me, Edmund
was eight. She described, "From the beginning, he was always very dif-

ferent. Sometimes I would look at him and it was as if his face was not his face anymore.

"Somehow, in some strange way, I've always felt Edmund to have a will so strong that any desires of mine or anyone else's were overridden. From the first, he was a very difficult baby. His eyes were peculiar. They seemed unlike a baby's eyes. I remember sitting up in bed with him propped up on my knees, and he gazed around the room very slowly and calmly. Calculating is the way I've always described it, but how can a baby of only a few hours look calculating? Edmund looked like a little old man when he was born. People would say you would not know he was a child."

As he grew up, Louise explained, "Edmund would say, 'I don't know what makes me be like that' when he became malevolent. When Edmund was what we described as 'hyped up,' his skin felt strange, not firm like a child's, and would go yellowy-white in colour. His voice would become loud and strident, and he'd use foul, abusive language. And he would make a hideous face (which always reminded me of a gargoyle), and scrunch his hands up and hold them rigidly beside his ears. His eyes would roll up, and he would leer."

Louise described Edmund as a gifted child with a high IQ but with many problems with conventional schooling. At eight he was asked to leave the private school he had been attending for only a few weeks because of his disruptive behaviour—"an evil feeling or presence which Edmund seems to bring into the class" was how an overwrought teacher had described it.

A friend suggested Louise might take Edmund to Vivien, a psychic healer he knew. Louise talked to the healer and Edmund went to play in the next room. The healer felt that Edmund was possessed by an evil spirit, and suddenly everything fitted together.

"What does it look like? How does it manifest itself?" Louise asked.

"I see it sitting on his shoulder," the healer replied, and made the face Louise had seen on Edmund when he had almost seemed possessed many, many times in the past. "It is quite a malevolent sort of chap who is making Edmund unhappy and doesn't want to go off where he belongs." But Vivien was sure she could get rid of the spirit.

At the faith healing, Louise, her husband, and Vivien made a circle. The healer talked to the spirit, telling it that it was in the wrong place. "The time has come for you to go on," she said.

"I felt tremendous relief and tears rolled down my cheeks. My husband was drained. Since then, we have never seen Edmund's strange face and there has been a dramatic change. The treatment had a profoundly calming effect on him," described Louise. "Edmund had always been a very nervous child and would not go into rooms, saying something would get him. The change in Edmund has been amazing. This holiday, for the first time, he has gone to a holiday club at the local gymnasium with a whole range of activities and seems to be enjoying it and coping fine."

There are many alternative psychological explanations for Edmund's behaviour, but what is remarkable was the lasting change in the boy after the healing.

My Own Mother and the Demon

My own experience of possession in the family occurred when I was about ten, long before I knew anything about the psychic world. My mother was unhappily married and became very fond of a neighbour called Ted, though I don't believe they were having an affair. We went to a fortune-teller in a seaside town called Weston-super-Mare on the western coast of England, and afterwards my mother was very upset, as the fortune-teller had spoken of a man whose name began with *T* who adored her but said they could never be together. Other things that were revealed my mother did not tell me.

Soon afterwards my mother started playing with a set of letter cards and a glass, and a man came through telling her he was George VI and asking her to get a piece of paper and pen. Thereafter he dictated strange, often frightening messages to her, and she started hearing voices that haunted her day and night. At last she went to the parish priest who said he would do an exorcism, as he had come across these matters many times, especially during the war. She knelt down at the front of the church (I was at the back), and the priest blessed her, said prayers, and told the spirit to depart.

Suddenly, a horrible, ugly, dirty old man started running up and down the aisle swearing and shouting. The priest kept praying, and then the man wasn't there anymore.

My mother went back to normal.

In the cases of Edmund and my mother, the priest and healer seem to have removed some evil presence, though in my mother's case it started with the fortune-teller messing with my mother's mind, who I can recall was a very scary woman and who I believe took a lot of money off my mother. Then of course my mother went straight to the Ouija for further information instead of leaving well alone.

Carefully Removing a Spirit from a Person

Possession *is* very rare, and that is why, especially if there are emotional or family issues involved, it is best to consult a priest or experienced Spiritualist church or someone from a recognised healing association. I cannot emphasise this enough. They will be able to identify a true possession and remove it. Never, never try to fix it yourself because evil spirits can transfer themselves to the unwary who are trying an amateur exorcism, or at the very least they can cause physical as well as lasting emotional stress in an untrained exorcist.

However, even an experienced Spiritualist can with a moment's inattention or lack of protection put themselves in the firing line.

Helga from Germany told me a personal exorcism account. She and her husband, Hans, helped with a spirit removal from a teenager who had just reached puberty. The teenager was haunted at night and tortured by what she called her "spirits." The members of the Spiritualist Church had tried so many things to get her back to normal, but nothing worked. At last three very experienced mediums in their 80s from the central church came to help.

Helga explained, "About twelve of us made a circle around the girl, and, following the instructions of the elders, performed the exorcism. Before we started, we were all told to do our personal protection before the ceremony. But my husband did not. We saw the demon fly out of the girl straight through my husband's stomach, around the circle, and out of the door. My husband had a sore stomach for about six weeks afterwards."

Overshadowing

Overshadowing, when a spirit dominates but does not possess a person, is also very frightening. Occasionally, it can happen when a very powerful, negative living person will travel astrally, in their inner spirit body either deliberately or during sleep, and appear in the victim's mirror or even their dreams. Generally, however, it is a deceased person who dominated the victim in life and drew on their energy who refuses to let go (read about energy vampires in chapter 2).

Annette is a mother of two and lives in Victoria, Australia. She still remembers seeing the ghost of her childhood friend Lee, who was killed in a road accident in her late teens. Annette described how after her friend's death, she was terrified by Lee's vision in the mirror. Both Annette and Lee were partially deaf and so they always enjoyed a special form of nonverbal communication that can be more powerful in some ways than words.

Annette wrote to me and explained that Lee died from massive head injuries after she went through the windscreen of a car. She wrote, "One morning not long after her death I looked in my mirror and I could see Lee's face. She was wearing her very sarcastic expression."

When Lee was alive she could be overpowering. Annette explained, "She would look into my eyes, and you could see the determination in hers. To us, eye contact was a different way of talking. About six months before her death I found if you blinked it broke the spell, and she hated that because she always wanted to be top dog."

Annette saw Lee in the mirror several times since she died, her face over Annette's as though she was trying to take her over. "I know it would have been so easy for me to let her spirit in my body, but I knew her too well. I wouldn't be strong enough to control her," she said. She used the paranormal experience to assert her independence from Lee. It was a battle she would have had to fight on the earthly plane had Lee lived.

Spirits in the mirror are quite common, especially at times of stress after bereavement, and if you do not want to see the spirit because you suspect its intentions are bad, cleanse the mirror with an infusion of hyssop, as described in chapter 8, "Overcoming Curses," and afterwards keep the mirror covered with a dark cloth.

The Dangers of Amateur Spirit Rescue through Séances

Spirit rescue of earthbound spirits is a very common duty for experienced mediums. If you have a spirit in your home and you want it to go, you can carry out an effective "go to the light" ceremony or ask the four guiding archangels (Michael, Gabriel, Raphael, and Uriel) for help, as described in the previous chapter. The spirit is in *your* home causing problems, and you have every right to ask it to leave as you would any unwanted visitor.

But some people with very little or no training from a Spiritualist church or reputable training establishment sit down with friends or family, joining hands and asking, "Is there anyone there?"

Calling in any spirits who would like to enter your séance room is no different from leaving your front door open all night. You can attract trapped spirits into your psychic circle who are earthbound for a variety of reasons or, worse still, low-lifers pretending to be earthbound spirits, and in either case it can be very hard to get rid of them afterwards. Why would they want to go to the light when they are having fun scaring you?

Mandy was in her forties and sat in a psychic group she held weekly with her friends in a suburban town in the east of England. She told me, "For a long time, we would engage in spirit rescue and feel really good afterwards. It was heady stuff."

One night in the group while they were calling up spirits who needed help, Mandy drifted off, and it felt light and nice, she explained. Suddenly there was a hospital bed and an old man lying on the bed. It was so cold. The top half of him moved off the bed but the bottom part could not move, and she was inside the old man. "I was trapped between heaven and hell with this old man," she said.

When Mandy came back to consciousness in the group, she couldn't move her feet, and she was so cold. Two of the group placed hands on her shoulders, and soon she could move her feet again. But the old man would not go. All week she felt shattered. She couldn't let him go. She was cold all the time and just couldn't get warm. She didn't go to the group for a couple of weeks because she felt so ill.

When she did go back in the circle, Mandy saw the room was filled with blood, and a fellow was coming with a knife. A woman was trying to back off and screaming, but no one could hear and she was not able to get away. This brought the most horrendous panic in Mandy.

When she came round, she told the others that a woman was dying traumatically. When she got home that night she felt totally unreal. "I could not get rid of this woman. She said she was called Mary, and I knew I must take her where she belonged," she explained.

She was sitting on Mandy's bed, so Mandy took her along a corridor with a light at the end and took her hand. Mandy walked behind her till she was through. Suddenly, she was gone and Mandy went to sleep.

The next morning, Mandy sat up, and the first thing she saw was Mary's blouse, cotton piqué with leg-of-mutton sleeves. So she did it all again, but it was no use. She couldn't get rid of her. She felt so rotten for about a week, too ill even to work, as Mary was draining her strength. At last she went to an experienced medium and healer she knew and admitted what she'd been doing.

The healer told Mandy that Mary had walked into her aura. She explained, "As she healed me, I felt someone pulling a sheet off me like chewing gum and felt washed and clean. I have learned from this that it is important to not just blindly accept every psychic force. That is so dangerous, and anyone working in a circle must understand what they are doing and not play with fire. At the moment I just don't want to know about the psychic."

The greatest form of defense against earthbound spirits who may try and drag you down with them is to not call them up in the first place!

Summoning Demons

Karl, who lives in Stockholm, described how when he was thirteen, he and a group of friends had seen a horror film about demons. As a dare they agreed to call up a demon. Karl had seen pictures of demons with wild eyes and long black hair and tongues of fire on websites taken from old books and thought it would be exciting.

He, an older boy cousin named Christer, and two girls named Sonia and Ingrid went upstairs to the attic while the family were having a party downstairs. They wrote out the alphabet letters on pieces of paper and set them out in a circle with an upturned drinking glass in the middle, as they had seen in the film. His cousin Sonia had downloaded some old magical demon names from a nineteenth-century magical society ritual, and, giggling, they sat in a circle and chose a demon to call.

They chanted, "I invoke thee," followed by a lot of names meaningless to them, and then round the glass they scattered blood from the chicken giblets they had taken from the refrigerator. They had seen blood scattering in another film their older cousin had put on when he was taking care of them one evening. Then Sonia said they had to sprinkle graveyard dirt. So Karl crept down and got some soil from the big plant pot at the bottom of the stairs and scattered the soil on top of the blood. Finally, they lit a red candle and called upon the demon to show himself by writing his name in the letters.

Then it all went wrong. Someone switched off the lights, or maybe they fused. There was a growling sound. Karl kicked over the candle in his haste to get to the lights, and it was only Sonia's swift action in smothering the candle with a metal pot (luckily in the attic) that stopped what could have been a very nasty accident. They all insisted afterwards they saw the hideous demon with blood dripping from his teeth in the flames.

They tried to get out of the attic but the door was jammed and the growling got louder. Their parents heard the commotion, opened the door, and were furious the teenagers had been dabbling.

If your teenager is acting strangely, talk tactfully to them and see if they have frightened themselves playing with Ouija or summoning up dark spirits. So often these are subjects hard to broach, but from about age nine in today's world, your children may be summoning up forces they cannot control.

Sending Demons against Your Enemies

Though a common practise, especially among mediaeval magicians, was to send demons against enemies, the modern danger on a psychological level is that teenagers and indeed older people who are hooked on pseudodemonology use demons as a way of getting at people they don't like.

There is a huge amount of information on demons—most of it inaccurate—in seemingly fun games for consoles or computers that can be downloaded or bought. Indeed, the Internet is full of demonic information, some historically accurate but all relating to past times, and many demons were in fact former pagan gods.

Will was sixteen when he fell victim to Katherine, leader of the in-crowd and her gang at school. They had all been experimenting with what they imagined was high magic, summoning demons and performing strange-sounding rites while their parents weren't around. And Will dived headfirst into it all when they invited him to join them after school. It gave him power and instant popularity, as he had few friends and suddenly was accepted as a high magician by the most popular girls in the class.

But then Katherine turned on Will, at first for a joke, as he was the weakest in the group, and then for a power trip when the girls realised how they were scaring him. She and the other girls told him they were going to send the demons to plague him at night in his bedroom. Will would wake in the middle of the night from disturbed dreams to shadowy demon-like figures in his bedroom and harsh laughing voices, and he refused to sleep unless the light was on. He begged the girls to stop, which of course only encouraged them. Each day Katherine would tell him the name of a demon who was coming, and sure enough he would see it that night taunting him.

His bedroom was always freezing cold, even during the day with the heating full on. Eventually Will was not eating and sleeping, his schoolwork was suffering, and he became terrified to go to school. He tried paying the girls off, but the tormentors were in full swing.

Will performed magic protective rituals he found on the Internet, but they seemed to make matters worse. The demons increased in number and would howl and scream at him, always black with hideous faces and dripping blood.

At last Will confided in his parents, who were sceptical, but when they realised their son was becoming a nervous wreck, they consulted me and even confronted the chief perpetrator, the daughter of a local magistrate, and her parents, all of whom of course said Will was making it up and was crazy.

I reassured Will's parents that even if these demonic figures were purely the result of psychological bullying and Will's own earlier dabbling in high magic he did not understand, Will was actually manifesting these creatures in his bedroom, and so they were real to him. I didn't want to worry his parents further, but as I mentioned earlier in the chapter, malevolent spirits are more than happy, when asked to do so, to take on a scary role, and they feed off the victims' and indeed the perpetrators' energies. The tormentors were also putting themselves in danger.

So I gave Will amulets and protective bags of the kind I described in chapter 5, and I taught him rituals, some of which I describe later in this chapter.

Though Will was disappointed, having got himself well and truly into magic, that I was not prepared to curse the girls who were frightening him or summon up mighty demons to fight back, I did tell him, as with any unwanted sending, he could assert to the demons first that it was his room and they were not welcome, and second that they should return to their sender. Most of these thought forms are minor bullies.

Gradually (sleeping in his brother's room had not worked out), Will took control of the situation, kept out of the girls' way where possible, stopped doing his garbled high magic defensive rituals that were actually stirring up the energies, and blocked the girls on social media. (Amazingly, he hadn't blocked them earlier, thus leaving himself open to another modern-day channel for negative energy, as with nonparanormal cyberbullying.)

Before long the girls realised their threats weren't working anymore, and Will was no longer begging them to stop. After a final assault from them—which we blocked with defensive crystals, specially empowered smoky quartz, turquoise, and malachite—they stopped or most likely found another victim. But it actually took several months of e-mailing Will and countless rituals he could do nightly before he felt totally safe. His life is now back to normal.

Whether demons are psychological, psychic, or, as I suspect in many cases, a mixture of both (a thought form created by dabbling that nasty energies will fill), it is important to deal with what the victim perceives as the issue and remove it.

The Protection of Salt

Salt has in all ages and cultures offered protection against paranormal attack. Indeed, salt rituals have always been central to religious and magical practises because salt is an absolutely pure substance. Salt and water mixed together and empowered or blessed to make sacred water are potent in the exorcism of evil spirits. In the previous chapter and throughout the book, I have described salt water banishing. Salt is traditionally scattered around thresholds and in protective circles against all evil influences.

. . . .
Banishing Salt and Sacred Water Spell

This can be used either for a particular room or a whole apartment or house and is an even stronger version of similar spells mentioned in the book. This was a ritual used to help Will clear the demonic energies from his bedroom, and it will help if you or a family member has been playing with Ouija boards or been involved in demonology.

Ingredients and Tools

A white candle

A dish of sea salt

A bowl of sacred water (You can buy holy water from some churches or from sacred springs online, but make sure it comes from a genuine sacred well or spring site.)

A totally clear, round quartz crystal you have soaked in the water overnight

A clear pointed quartz crystal (Archangel Michael's crystal, to infuse the water with light)

Timing

Sunday morning as it gets light, the time of Michael, archangel of the sun, who traditionally drives away demons and all evil

The Spell

Place the candle in the centre of the home or affected room. Carefully remove the crystal from the water and touch the water surface, making a cross using the crystal point, either diagonal with equal-length arms for the Earth Mother or the Latin or Christianised cross shown below.

The Latin Cross

The four arms of the cross represent the four directions and the ancient elements (earth, air, fire, and water). They also symbolise the vertical line of spirit and infinity integrated with the horizontal limits of time and the material world. Therefore, all are united in the centre of the cross to create something greater than the separate parts, and the cross will empower the sacred water to repeal even the worst of harm.

Say as you make the cross,

Light in the darkness;
Good over evil.
None may withstand thee,
Bad spirit or devil.

Now draw the same cross formation in the salt with the pointed crystal, repeating the words.

Tip salt into the water and stir it nine times in each direction, starting with counterclockwise, saying,

Spirits from the darkest recesses
Now into the Michael light must fall.
This salt water banishes you
And brings protection on us all.

Keep adding salt, saying the words softly and swirling until the water is cloudy.

Leave the bowl of salt and the bowl of salt water (to the right of the salt) as near to the centre of the house as you can or in the affected room, angling the pointed crystal as you hold it in your dominant hand at 45 degrees towards the bowls.

Drawing the cross with the pointed crystal above first the salt then the salt water bowl, say for each,

Begone all you who have no place here.
Return to your realms; I have no fear.
You are bound, barred, banished,
Forbidden to enter my home/room anymore.
Around my territory, my boundaries I draw.
Trouble me (or name person affected) *no more.*

If you know who is sending demons, you can substitute the second line with this if you wish:

Return to she/he who sent you; I have no fear.

Leave the salt and the salt water for twenty-four hours in the centre of the house or affected room to absorb any dark powers and fears. Then tip them away under a faucet, saying,

I pour away the evil.
Thought form, demon, dark spirit, or devil,
Your power ebbs away.
Enter no more my heart, soul, or mind.
To you I say,
By the power of Michael, I do you bind.

Only now light the white candle and say,

Flame of fire, Michael flame,
Purge all evil in his name.
Powers of darkness,
Before his might,
By his sacred light,
You never may return again.

Blow out the candle, sending the light to every corner of the room or house.

Relight each evening for five minutes before bed, repeating,

Flame of fire, Michael flame,
Purge all evil in his name.
Powers of darkness,
Before his might,
By his sacred light,
You never may return again.

Continue nightly until the candle is finished.

• • • • • • •

Creating Spirit Traps

Because spirits travel in straight lines, it is traditionally said, using spiral shapes is a good way of tangling spirits. Some people will make a protective amulet and leave it where a spider will walk over it or cover it with an old spiderweb for twenty-four hours to create a trap.

A mediaeval tradition in England and Scandinavia was to have a labyrinth in the west end of the church by the door, west being the direction of death and spirits. This was said to be so that if the devil tried to come into the church he'd run into the labyrinth, get confused, and run out again. One such labyrinth, though not the original, can still be seen in Ely Cathedral in Cambridgeshire, England, in the Fenlands.

The Triple Spiral

The triple spiral shown below is easier to draw than a labyrinth but operates on precisely the same principle, so it is an excellent form of spirit trap. One of the most striking examples of the triple spiral, when three spirals run together, is found at Newgrange passage grave in Ireland, originally built about 3100 BCE.

The Triple Spiral

The Triskele

The triskele, my favourite, is the Celtic form of the triple spiral, used today by modern Druids and Druidesses, and it is even easier to draw than the conventional triple spiral.

The Triskele

You can create your own triple spiral or the triskele version as an amulet to drive away any malevolent spirits, either to wear as a pendant or carry in a small bag or purse. You can also draw either form invisibly in the air in front of you with the index finger of the hand you write with or with incense stick smoke, or you can visualise it made of golden light to protect yourself from and banish any demonic forces or troublesome spirits that may have been called up. This can be good to seal your bedroom door before sleep if you are plagued at night.

Spell to Protect Your Home from Demons or Evil Spirits

Before making the amulet, create a triskele or triple spiral spirit or demon trap to keep in your home, not much different from a psychic mouse trap, if you are worried about dark presences in your home or who may be affecting you or family members, however they may have been summoned.

Ingredients and Tools

A red candle

A large piece of paper

A thick black pen

A spool of red thread

A wide-necked, sealable bottle or jar

Nine blackberry leaves, nine sharp cloves, or a thorn twig

Three pinches of sea salt and six pinches of red (cayenne) pepper
   dropped into a small jug of vinegar and swirled six times counterclockwise (Pepper and vinegar are also anti–evil spirit substances.)

Timing
10:00 p.m.

The Spell
Light the red candle and say,

> *Deliver us from all evil by this flame.*
> *Like moths to light,*
> *May all that is not right*
> *Trapped and bound remain*
> *Locked within*
> *Till purged of sin.*

Draw your triple spiral or triskele on the paper and repeat the words. Open the bottle and add the nine blackberry leaves or cloves, saying,

> *Evil spirits enter here,*
> *Where you are trapped and pierced*
> *With barbs so fierce,*
> *I need no longer fear.*

Now start to break off lengths of thread and tie each in a knot, saying for each,

> *Now the evil threat is bound,*
> *Evil forces trapped and wrapped around.*

Add enough knots to half fill the jar, afterwards pouring in enough vinegar mix to cover the twig or leaves and knots and fill the jar. Put on the lid and drip candle wax all around the top to seal it, repeating,

> *Now the evil threat is bound,*
> *The spirits trapped and sealed around.*

Place the jar in the centre of the triple spiral or triskele.

The next morning, take the jar in a sealed bag to a garbage site or hide it in a dark place till the refuse is collected. Cut out the spiral and put it behind a piece of furniture or on a wall where it cannot be seen.

Creating Your Triskele or Triple Spiral Amulet

Practise drawing your triskele or triple spiral on paper until you can complete it in sweeping counterclockwise movements from the centre. Then draw a circle round it to enclose the protection.

The upper left coil represents sky, the upper right coil water, and the bottom coil earth, and the same applies if you are drawing the more complex triple spiral instead.

To create your amulet, you can use almost any natural substance. It may be a metal or wooden disc on which you etch the triskele. If you want to wear it, make a hole in the top of the disc for a chain. Paint one on a crystal (using a wire cradle if you want to wear it), or draw one on thin paper or papyrus and roll it into a tiny gold or silver tube that you wear around your neck. You can also make one in clay. Alternatively, draw one in incense stick smoke over a favourite pendant or trace it with the index finger of your dominant hand.

My own favourite method is to melt a small beeswax candle on a metal tray and etch the symbol in the melted wax. Carefully lift it out when cool and keep it in white silk or a tiny purse you carry with you.

Empowering Your Triskele or Triple Spiral

To empower your triskele amulet before wearing or carrying it, place it on a white cloth and sprinkle it with a few dried rose petals or potpourri to represent the power of the earth. As you do so, say,

> *Earth, sky, and sea,*
> *Let evil not come near me.*

Next, make a clockwise circle of water or, if you prefer, lavender or rose water round the triskele, saying,

Sea, sky, and earth,
Let evil not come near me.

Finally, using a pine or fennel incense stick for the power of the sky, make an equal-armed triangle in the air enclosing the amulet, saying,

Sky, earth, and sea,
By triple decree,
By the power of sky,
From low to high,
Let evil not come near me.
· · · · · · ·

The Power of Free Will and Burning Away Evil in a Beeswax Candle

Throughout the book we have called on the angels and our personal source of light and goodness for protection. Now we are adding the most powerful force of all: our own free will to assert our own boundaries and to refuse to admit evil spirits into our life. Taking control is an essential element in becoming and remaining free of malevolent spirits from whatever source.

Again we ask for help from higher powers, and I have left this very open, whether you want to call more generally on the source of ultimate goodness or choose a specific angelic or deity focus. But though we ask for assistance from higher powers, the following spell is essentially, by making our own candle (an act of creation and therefore of power) and inscribing it with what we wish to remove, a statement of intent, and then burning the evil away is a final banishing. Because you make the candle yourself, it is endowed with your unique essence and therefore is very powerful to shut out spirits you do not wish around you.

In fact, candles are remarkably simple to make, and there are many sites online that share even more details or alternative methods. The following is a ritual I have used many times with people who are very afraid of being taken over by negatively intentioned spirits. In fact, I first saw this candle-burning ceremony in a home in the wild countryside of Brittany in South West France when it was believed Ankou the Breton's death spirit was haunting the area and rattling windows at night to seek admission. Because Brittany is very remote and the land has remained unchanged for many centuries, there is still a great deal of belief in spirits, good and bad.

Candle Making and Burning Spell to Reclaim Your Own Power against Evil

Be careful, as lighted beeswax candles can spit. Burn your candle well away from anything flammable, carpets, or curtains, and embed the candle in a deep, nonflammable pot of soil before lighting.

Ingredients and Tools

A sheet of beeswax (approximately sixteen by eight inches) from
    craft stores or online
A square braided wick
A palette or paper knife
A pot of soil for the protection of Mother Earth

Timing

Friday

The Spell

Spread out the beeswax on a flat surface. Score a ditch towards the horizontal end of the beeswax sheet, about an eighth of an inch from the edge of the wax.

Raise your arms high over the wax and ask for the protection of light and goodness to enter the wax in the way that is right for you. Say,

> *I ask the angels* (name one or more who are special to you)/
> *the ultimate source of goodness and light/God/the Goddess*
> *to help me drive away all evil with the burning of this flame.*

Lay the wick in the wax so the end of the wick is level with the bottom of the candle and the wick extends about a thumb length at the top, which you can cut when finished to a thumbnail height. Gently warm but do not melt the wax (use a hair dryer if you wish).

Now write invisibly along the wax, using the index finger of your dominant hand,

> *Deliver me from all evil. May all that is not pure,*
> *all that terrifies me or threatens me from the spirit world,*
> *be burned away as this candle melts and never return.*

Crease the edge of the beeswax sheet over the wick and press firmly so that it is well sealed, making the first roll very tight. When you have finished rolling, press the outer edge of the candle gently but firmly to seal the candle, again warming it gently if necessary, and do the same with the bottom.

As you seal the candle, say,

> *So is the power to overcome all evil sealed within the wax.*

Press the candle so it is well embedded in the soil and will not tip over, and touch the soil lightly, saying,

> *Mother Earth, bring transformation*
> *and your loving protection to surround me.*

Light the candle, saying,

> *As this candle burns,*
> *So turns and melts away*
> *All harm, peril, and evil,*
> *No more to stay.*
> *Return to the world beyond,*
> *Gone from me;*
> *So shall I be free.*

When the candle goes out, even if not completely burned through, sprinkle soil from the pot over the melted wax and any remaining wick and candle stump, and bury the remains beneath a thriving plant.

· · · · · · ·

Protection against
Negative Earth Energies

Even if the people in your home or workplace are naturally harmonious and well balanced, the place can still feel dark and cold even in summer or if it's recently been decorated; plants do not thrive and animals and children are restless or fight for no reason, especially in certain rooms. There always seems some lingering illness, constant breakages, even minor accidents, and the strange sense of being watched. At work there may be frequent absenteeism for trivial reasons; a lot of in-fighting; carelessness with property; malfunctioning computers, photocopiers, and fax machines; missing e-mails; and broken phone calls in which you are cut off midway through conversations.

If you consistently experience more than one or two of these symptoms in particular areas of a building, you can be reasonably certain there are negative earth energies beneath it. Negative earth energies can either be too fierce or be blocked or soured. I describe in this chapter ways of detecting and overcoming these different kinds of negative energies, as they are one of the main causes of domestic and workplace unease.

Even if you work or live in a tall block, both fierce and blocked or soured energies will rise, and in offices they are sometimes called sick building syndrome, though logical souls may give other physical reasons for this syndrome.

What Are Negative Earth Energies?

Some pieces of land have unpleasant atmospheres that are sensed by almost all who visit them. Over the centuries they often acquire legends and a name to explain their spookiness: tales of giants, the devil, or, in Scandinavia and Germany, trolls. Some become the reputed haunts of ghosts, and indeed as I said in the previous chapter, nasty spirits do seem to be attracted to locations where powerful negative energies are strong.

Two main causes have been identified for unpleasant energies on land that seep into any structures on it.

Malevolent Energies from Past Dark Deeds

One explanation of the cause of these energies relates to residual human feelings and actions etched or imprinted into the land by strong traumatic emotions, and any house or workplace subsequently built there will experience these negative feelings. The cause may relate to a specific dramatic past event, such as a battle or murder, or a sorrow built up over time on the site, such as a former prison, mental hospital, converted warehouse, or Victorian factory where there was much suffering.

A number of these old buildings have recently been converted into apartments, workshops, offices, or studios, but some residents say their homes or workplaces never feel right. Actual ghosts may be seen, though these may be imprints or impressions of the past rather than actual presences, and these hauntings are especially prevalent on the anniversary of a bad or sad event on the site. In chapter 3, I describe how Joanna was affected during the Second World War in London by working on the site of the old Bedlam mental hospital, where in the 1600s people would pay to torment those who had psychiatric illnesses.

Evil Rituals

Naturally occurring negative earth energies in a building or complex can be magnified or even caused if black magic took place on the site. Evil rituals, even performed hundreds of years before, attract hostile spirits who once took part. They will attack anyone in the building on the old site and may be earthbound there. The following account was given to me by a security guard who worked on an industrial estate near Glasgow in a factory unit where the security firm had problems persuading even experienced guards to work on the site for more than two nights because of apparent nightly paranormal activity.

David, a former security guard at the site, explained that guards often rang the control room and the police complaining of strange noises. However, searches revealed nothing untoward. After talking to a couple of guards when he started working there, David discovered that one guard had been terrified when he saw a dark face and bright eyes staring at him from the gloom of the corridors. Another guard insisted that he saw, sitting on top of the metal rafters in the main corridor, two ugly, grotesque, gargoyle-type creatures watching his every movement.

Once David saw from outside a room full of swirling mist that lasted several hours into the night before finally disappearing. He knew it was not smoke and so did not bother to call out the fire brigade. Other guards complained of doors opening and shutting of their own accord, lights switching on and off, and a strange phosphorescent glow in the darkness about the size of a football. David first noticed objects being moved from their original positions when he returned from his patrols. They would then turn up a few hours later in the original position. One night after returning to the small security room after the completion of an outside patrol, he saw that the light, closed-circuit television, and fire had all been switched off and unplugged. No one else was present.

However, David was determined to stick the job out. On other occasions, he witnessed fleeting dark shadows all around the building, but when he focused on them, they disappeared completely. "From the security room I heard the bangs and crashes that the factory made even on the most windless of nights," he said.

In one particular area stood a workshop where most of the noises originate. The door to the workshop would never remain locked. David said that he put the bolt across on two occasions, and each time he moved a couple of steps away, it would slam back with force. It was not a spring lock, so from then on he decided to leave the bolt alone.

One Sunday morning, David walked into the building and headed for the security room. "Standing outside the door was a small man with a bald head dressed in a brown robe staring at me with black piercing evil eyes. In an instant he disappeared," he explained.

David could stand working there no longer. A medium, who was at last called in, said that the ground was covered in occult markings and was surrounded by a mass of people dressed in dark brown robes from 300 years earlier. The group was chanting rhythmically in a trance-like state, involved in some kind of dark magical ritual. In the centre stood a roughly made stone altar. On top of it were lighted candles.

The medium described a man standing to the side of her, staring at the wall in front of him. He wore a brown robe and had a sallow complexion. He then turned to stare angrily at the medium with black piercing eyes before fading away.

Becoming a Psychic Detective

If you do suffer from a general feeling of spookiness in your home or workplace and can't identify a specific ghost, such as a former resident who died there, study local history, especially place names. See if there are any local legends connected with negative energies, an indigenous sacred burial site that has been disturbed by building works, or a path leading to a cemetery along which the deceased would have been carried to burial and along which the corpse lights, the spirits of the deceased, travelled to collect them.

The following ritual will clear the ghostly energies. It will also prevent further spirits that are attracted to the negative energies imprinted on the land from entering. Then you can use some of the methods in this chapter to counterbalance what may be soured energies, caused by past events. The ritual also works well if you are living on an invisible subterranean energy line that is too powerful for domestic buildings or workplaces (covered later in the chapter), though it is not necessarily unpleasant energies—just where the underground invisible energy streams are flowing very fast.

. . . .
Ritual for Removing Paranormal Presences

This is a ritual to remove paranormal presences that are caused by previous negative events on the land from your home or workplace. It will also prevent ghosts entering your home if you live in a haunted area or near a known ghost path or powerful earth energy line.

Ingredients and Tools

Four large, single-pointed, deep-coloured crystals, such as amethyst
    (the ultimate antispook crystal), smoky quartz, obsidian, onyx, or
    jet (They can be all the same kind.)
A bowl of water
Nine pinches of salt (dissolved in the water before the ritual)

Timing

The last day of the month

The Ritual

Stir the water four times with the pointed end of each of the crystals in turn, saying for each,

> *Salt and water, four by four,*
> *Against restless spirits bar the door.*
> *All negative presences stay away,*
> *Forbidden to enter by night or by day.*

Immerse each crystal in the water four times, repeating the words four times for each dip. Four is the number of the Archangel Cassiel, who will act as a gatekeeper against wandering spirits that, even if they are not harmful, can be disturbing, especially if you have children.

In the home, set one crystal on each side of the front door just inside it, points facing outwards, and the same for any back door. If you have no back door, set the second two just outside the front door, one on either side, again points outwards.

Throw the water out of the front door, repeating the words.

Wash the crystals under running water monthly and repeat the ritual.

If protecting a workplace, set the empowered crystals in a square in your workspace or put them on a window ledge in a square near where you sit or work.

· · · · · · ·

Natural Causes of Negative Earth Energies

Subterranean earth energies, which are often pictured as streams though they are not physical ones, may become blocked and soured because of a new road, a phone mast, old mine workings, or major industrial development in the area. If, conversely, the energies are too overpowering this is because they are built on or near a powerful earth energy line that is not suitable for domestic or workplace structures. These problematic energies are often called geopathic stress.

Accounts of energy lines, helpful or harmful, exist in almost every culture from China to the Americas. The Chinese believe that adverse or bad energy, *sha chi*, travels in a straight line, accumulating in what are called poisoned arrows that can be created by the sharp corners and diagonals from adjoining buildings or badly positioned furniture. Negative energy, or sha chi, is sometimes called "tiger energy."

In Western traditions, the most common name for these energy lines are ley lines, and the negative effects of their running beneath properties of all kinds are great, with the exception of sacred buildings or structures such as ancient stone circles that draw power from the subterranean forces as well as from the sky.

Ley Lines

Ley lines are one way of describing the psychic energies that span and energise the land and converge or are amplified at places marked by sacred places. The power of such places has for thousands of years attracted people to build a temple, stone circle, or, in more recent times, a church there, often on the site of a former temple. Its ritual use increases the sanctity of the place, and such sites are ideal for connecting with the divine. Indeed, until the 1400s many monks and nuns knew how to identify ley energies. Benedictine monasteries across Europe were routinely aligned with one another along energy lines, extending hundreds of miles.

Ley energies are found worldwide connecting sacred sites. Most are invisible to the physical eye, but some, like those in Chaco Canyon in New Mexico set down by the Ancestral Puebloans, are marked by actual pathways.

Subterranean straight psychic energy paths, or leys, are not negative in themselves. However, though ideal for siting places of worship, their energies are too powerful for humans to live or work over. This becomes especially problematic where energy lines intersect or if a sacred site has been built over by housing, though luckily in the modern world this is increasingly rare. Until the 1800s, stones from sacred circles were often used for local buildings. For example, the Avebury Rings, Neolithic stone circles in Wiltshire, United Kingdom, were constructed during the third millennium BCE. Historian and antiquarian William Stukeley, who died in 1765, witnessed in 1719 stones being torn down from the Avebury circles and broken up for construction purposes. Houses and even a pub (through which a major ley line runs) have been built within the original circles. (During the fourteenth century, the pious locals had also torn down and buried some of the stones for religious reasons).

However, the modern tendency of converting small churches and chapels into housing can make for restless sleep, as I found when I recently stayed at a converted chapel near Cairns in the Australian tropics, where I was plagued all night by paranormal mutterings and utterings.

These invisible ley energies are believed also to be spirit tracks to the other world. While travelling through Australia, I have come across a number of homes built on the indigenous song lines that run between Australian Aboriginal sacred sites and rock paintings. In these homes there are constant hauntings, inexplicable breakages, lights fusing, electrical equipment malfunctioning, computers breaking down, and accidents, seemingly caused by the psychokinetic power of the energy lines that manifest as psychic electricity. Song lines are traditionally travelled both by living and deceased spirits and are marked by particular distinguishing features, such as a rock in the shape of an animal, where indigenous people will retell the story on their journeys and hold a sacred ceremony.

In Ireland invisible fairy paths run between ancient earth works, believed to be the home of the Little People. It was and still is considered bad luck to build on these fairy hills and pathways, while in Iceland even roads will be diverted round land or a special rock sacred to the land wights or guardians. These straight tracks in different lands are also called ghost paths. Along them are a remarkable number of legends about ghosts and spirit beings, and invariably you can trace a straight line between the sites of such legends.

If your home is built on or close to a ley line or especially where they cross, then you may well experience a sense of being spooked or watched by an invisible presence and the wandering spirits that are attracted to these lines. Often in Australia mischievous young indigenous spirits can be drawn into such a homestead or house out of curiosity and then become confused when they try to continue on their journey along the spirit path or song line because the house simply wasn't there in their day. This can cause a lot of banging and crashing.

You can find ley line path maps for your area online or in your local library, when an earth energy expert or dowser has taken an interest in them and recorded his or her findings.

The previous ritual and ones in the previous two chapters will also remove these spirits and prevent others entering.

Identifying Too-Powerful Negative Earth Energies

Even if you are not subject to hauntings, you will know the energies are flowing too intensely if you or family members manifest frequent restlessness, hyperactivity, and irritability apparently without reason; a lot of breakages, especially of glasses and mirrors; and quarrels, misfortune, and constantly unstable finances. Around the building there is often an absence of birds, but rodents may be drawn into your home and outbuildings.

You can detect these over-intense energies by walking round your home or workplace with an amethyst or rose or smoky quartz pendulum swinging freely in the hand you write with. Clear quartz pendulums are best for detecting blocked energies. If you prefer or need to be subtle if testing the workplace, use your hands, with fingertips pointing downwards, and the sensitive soles of your feet, if practical, barefoot or in thin socks, to sense the location of very jarring, discordant feelings. The same basic pendulum method will work whether you are detecting paranormal or ley energies or testing for blocked energy streams.

A ley line is about seven feet wide, and if one flows through your home or workplace, its effects will permeate the whole home or workplace as a straight corridor of energy, though it will be felt most powerfully in certain spots or rooms. Your pendulum may vibrate like a road drill when you hit one of these very powerful places.

If either excessive straight ley power or negative spirit energies are present, they tend to become concentrated in particular circular spots in a room. In the case of a ley, this can make the circle six or seven feet or even wider in diameter, though when you draw the spots on a map, you will see in fact they are in a straight line, even though this may be a diagonal (for example, a northeast to southwest direction), and some of it may be outside the house.

Using Your Pendulum

A pendulum is a weight on a chain or cord held in the hand we write with by whose differing movements we can detect the course of negative earth energies within the home or workplace by accessing the intuitive powers we all possess but may find hard to trust without external evidence.

To discover the different responses, you can specifically direct your pendulum by holding it loosely. You can program your pendulum in advance by deliberately making a counterclockwise swing with it and saying,

Make this response when you encounter a place of powerful negative earth energy.

The pendulum will swing positively, usually clockwise, as you walk with it until encountering a negative energy. Again, before you begin, you can make a clockwise circle with it and say,

Let this be the positive response when the earth energies are good.

Begin to walk from the front door at home and through each room swinging the pendulum in large circles so you cover the whole room until your pendulum feels suddenly unpleasantly cold and heavy or swings out of control in a counterclockwise spiralling. This is a negative place. At these places you may feel nauseous or slightly dizzy.

If using your fingers and feet, walk also in circles (you may be able to do this when the workplace is empty), and you will feel a grating of your teeth, like biting on a cold ice cream with a sensitive tooth. Walk in decreasing circles round the negative spot till you find the centre, where the negative swing will be strong and your teeth feel totally on edge. You may feel cold till you move outwards again. Through your hands, the most powerful centre will feel like holding your hands over an emptying bath plughole, and through your feet, like standing in knee-deep swirling water.

Plot each place where you experience the negative swing of the pendulum on a small chart of your home or workplace, using different-sized circles to indicate the size and intensity of each negative area. There may be a series of larger circles of negativity or one main one, perhaps caused by the intersection of energy lines.

Work downstairs at the lowest level of your home, as the energies will rise and have the same pattern on upper storeys. Now go along the outside walls inside the home and ask the pendulum to indicate by its negative swing the entry and exit points of any earth lines. These points once known can be used on the physical walls to divert the energy field's path. For leys, these points will link with the row of circles indoors.

If you can't get access to the workplace, draw a map of the lowest floor of the workplace and pass your pendulum over that.

. . . .
Spell for Removing Over-Intense Energies Using Crystals

The following spell is one you can do at home whether the problem is in the home or workplace, and then you can follow up with the ongoing remedies I suggest later in the chapter.

Ingredients and Tools

Four of any of the following deep-coloured crystals: amethyst, brown jasper, dark banded agate, obsidian, or tiger's eye. You need only use small ones. If you can obtain unpolished stones, so much the better, especially if they are embedded in rock.
A large, unpolished clear quartz point
A glass of water

Timing

Wednesday, the day of healing, at home in daylight, repeating it weekly till you sense the energies becoming softer

The Spell

Set a square of the deep-coloured crystals, with the clear quartz in the middle of the square, in the centre of your home whether you are cleansing workplace or home. Specify in the spell the place you are clearing.

Hold each of the deeper-coloured crystals in cupped hands in turn. Then open your hands, raising each stone to the daylight, and say,

May all fierce energies flow away;
Be absorbed into the light of day.
Leave my home/workplace completely free,
That harmony only shall there be.

Return each crystal to the square, and then hold the clear quartz with its point upwards to the daylight before holding the point downwards a few inches above each deeper-coloured crystal in turn, saying,

Light from darkness,
Calm from stress.
Misfortune shall no longer be.
Gone be irritability.
My home/workplace shall only good energies see.
Cleansed, cleared, washed away
By the glorious light of day.

Put the deep-coloured crystals in the four corners of your home indoors or hide them in different parts of the workplace, perhaps in plant pots.

Keep the clear quartz in the centre of your home or your personal workspace.

· · · · · · ·

The Effects of Soured or Blocked Energy Lines

Other, less powerful earth energy lines that normally run under homes and workplaces without harm can become blocked or soured because they have been disturbed by nearby major construction work, such as by creating a freeway or housing estate or by earlier quarrying or mining of nearby land. Mobile telephone masts or badly sited electricity pylons can also adversely affect the flow of subterranean energies.

The building will always seem dark and cold, even if there is plenty of natural light; plants will not thrive; family members may constantly have colds or minor illnesses and allergies; and plans and money will be slow to materialise. The energies also make it hard to lose weight or to give up alcohol or cigarettes, and they contribute to the intensity of fears and phobias. Even expected opportunities do not come. If your bed is over a blocked energy stream, you may find it hard to sleep or may suffer from nightmares.

These subterranean psychic energy streams are more undulating, serpent-like energy paths and may even be part of a vast network of underground veins of water that have become soured or polluted psychically—and sometime physically—for reasons I have suggested above.

Dwellings or workplaces built on what are often called black streams may seem dark and damp, even on a summer's day or with heating blasting away in the house or office.

Finding Blocked Energies

If the energies beneath your home or workplace are blocked or soured, as you walk round using a pendulum, you will find that the pendulum becomes heavy and draws downwards with very slow negative movement as you encounter a place where the energy is blocked. If using your hands and feet as before, you may suddenly feel exhausted and as if your limbs can hardly move. At the centre of the blockage, the pendulum will just stop moving and feel unbelievably heavy.

As I suggested for detecting overactive energies, continue to walk inwards and outwards in circles through every ground floor room until you feel the effects of the deadness increasing as you hit the centre and then decreasing as you move outwards.

Again plot this on a plan, and you may find the dead places follow a definite undulating pattern through your home. Detect where the stream enters and leaves your home, as there will again be a wide channel on an outside wall inside the home at entry and exit points.

For your workplace, you can draw a plan and use the pendulum on it to detect blocked workplace energies if you can't do it physically.

. . . .

Spell to Clear Your Home
of Blocked Energies Beneath It

This spell is for clearing blocked energies flowing beneath your home that may cause lethargy or misfortune.

Ingredients and Tools

Two large incense sticks in patchouli, pine, or lavender
A bowl of sand or soil

Timing

Wednesday around 10:00 p.m., the healing hour of the air archangel, Raphael, who rules the winds

The Spell

Light the incense sticks. Hold one in each hand and move your hands away from your body and back towards your body in a circular motion, making sure the incense sticks temporarily overlap each other when bringing them back towards your body.

Say softly and continuously as you move the incense,

May the winds stagnation blow away,
The blocked, the stagnant, sour,
That from this hour
They may no longer stay.

Walk around each ground floor room, if you live in a house, or every room in an apartment, crossing and uncrossing the incenses and saying the same words again softly and continuously.

In each room or passage start in the left-hand corner nearest the door, and move in a counterclockwise direction, pausing in front of the windows, again circling and chanting.

Leave each room or area by facing inwards through the door and crossing and uncrossing the incenses once, saying,

Flow free, harmoniously.

When you have finished, stand as close to the centre of the house or apartment as possible and plunge the incense sticks' lighted ends down together in the sand, saying,

Flow free,
Harmoniously, you energies below.
With the dimming of this incense,
Your stagnant powers shall go,
And new life flow.

For a workplace, draw a map of the workplace and spiral lighted incense as above over related areas, saying the same words.

• • • • • • •

Ongoing Remedies for Neutralising Negative Energies

Having carried out the relevant ritual for either overactive or blocked energies, the following ongoing remedies will neutralise both too-intense and too-slow energies in the home and workplace.

- Amethyst crystals are perhaps the most effective stones for neutralising all forms of negative earth energies. Small amethyst inclusions, still in the rock, are not expensive and make excellent paperweights or ornaments. Position these near the centre of the larger spots of negative energy whether overactive or blocked, on tables, desks, printers, photocopiers, or any other office equipment you deem needs neutralising. Wash the amethysts weekly. Set small amethyst crystals under the carpet or in plant pots, following the line from where the energy enters the home to where it leaves. Hide them in plants. Aloe vera or African violets are best for plants at home and work for counteracting any negative earth energies.

- If your desk, your bed, or the chair you usually relax in is over a major negative energy centre, move it to a more congenial spot in the room.

- Phone calls and personal interviews at work should be carried out from a place of positive energies.

- If you cannot make major rearrangements at work, ensure you always have fresh flowers or a plant pot above a major spot of negative power to absorb any bad feelings. You may need to replace these frequently, as it is not a conducive place for growth, so try to rotate plants. Keep them fresh with water in which you have soaked a clear quartz overnight. You can take this to work in a small clear bottle.

- A dish of rose quartz crystals at home or work takes the edges off too-sharp energies, and yellow citrine adds vitality to energies.

- At home place a large stone, containing quartz if possible, next to the spots on the external wall through which the negative energies are entering. Place a large rock at any entry or exit points against the wall outdoors, or, if you have a shared internal wall with a neighbour, set a small rock in a plant pot next to the wall where the lines enter and leave your property.

- At home you can also block the flow outdoors from entering your home with a dobbie stone at the entrance and exit. The dobbie stone has a small hollowed indent. The stones come from the Anglo-Saxon and Viking traditions of East Anglia and Scandinavia and are also placed near entrances to farms and where tracks intersect. They are traditionally filled with honey or milk as offerings to the earth spirits. Make your own dobbie stones using small stone urns, and plant flowers or herbs in them to ensure the flow of positive energies. Set these on either side of the front door just outside. This is in addition to anything you use at entry or exit points.

- At home hammer protective iron staves into soil outside the four corners of your home and also at gateposts and boundaries, to divert any underground dark waters. You can do this with strategically placed plants in the workplace.

- Smudge the home with a sage, pine, or cedar smudge stick or incense stick by lighting it and spiralling the smoke in alternating clockwise and counterclockwise circles in the air on a Sunday morning monthly. Do the same on the workplace map.

Conclusion

In this book I have shared with you rituals and experiences I have collected over almost forty years. I belong to the tradition of hands-on magical practitioners who travel through many places, collecting first-hand accounts of those who have suffered from encounters with malicious people or negative paranormal forces.

As technology has transformed my life more and more, I am able not only to visit personally those with psychic problems, but also to counsel and send rituals via the Internet as well, directly through consultations in the United Kingdom, Australia, New Zealand, Scandinavia, and France and on visits to America.

I have no doubt that evil exists both in this world and beyond it, but I am equally convinced that good can and will overcome evil, that blessings are stronger than curses. What is more, we all have the power and right to protect ourselves and vulnerable loved ones using defensive techniques, such as binding and banishing.

I have suggested many methods, rituals, and empowerments that you can use exactly as they are written in these pages. However, you have the option to use them as a template and adapt them to your own circumstances and according to your own magical level of development. Everything here can be used by total beginners, is safe, and will harm no one.

Psychic attacks occur frequently to real people in the everyday world, though many are reluctant to talk about them for fear of ridicule or being considered unbalanced. So I have shared in these pages their stories and the ways we have worked to overcome malice and deliberate evil both here and hereafter. And if you would like to share your stories with me or seek advice, you can contact me via the publisher or my website, www.cassandraeason.com.

The world is basically a good place and most people are well intentioned. The power of love is the greatest gift and weapon we have to deliver us from evil.

Appendix A:
The Archangels

You can call on the archangel whose protection you most need during the day ahead by lighting their candle, burning their incense, or holding their crystal.

The Seven Protective Archangels

Michael

Role: Supreme archangel and archangel of the sun who oversees the natural world, the weather; leader of all the great warrior angels; traditional dragon slayer

Image: Golden wings in red and gold armour with sword, shield, and a green date branch; carrying the scales of justice or a white banner with a red cross

Day: Sunday

Colours: Gold, orange

Fragrances: Copal, frankincense, orange, rosemary

Crystals: Amber, carnelian, diamond and clear crystal quartz, tiger's eye, topaz

Metal: Gold

Messages: Gold or orange ink on white paper

Rules: Abundance and prosperity where there has been a lack of it, new beginnings after endings, the restoration of hope and energy, problems relating to middle age, male and fathering issues, overcoming lack of self-confidence caused by unfair criticism or undermining, overcoming evil spirits

Globally: Revival of barren land, overcoming drought, slowing down global warming

Gabriel

Role: Archangel of the moon, carrying divine messages, regarded as having female energies

Image: Clothed in silver or dark blue with a mantle of stars and a crescent moon for her halo, a golden horn, and white lily; alternatively, with a lantern in her right hand and with a mirror made of jasper in her left

Day: Monday

Time of Day: Sunset

Colour: Silver

Fragrances: Jasmine, myrrh, rose

Crystals: Moonstone, mother of pearl, pearl, selenite, opal

Metal: Silver

Rules: Protection against inclement weather and natural disasters, safe travel across water; matters concerning women, infants, and children; mothering, pregnancy, childbirth, and fertility; diminishing self-destructive tendencies; peace in the home and at work; defense against hauntings at night

Samael/Sammael

Role: Archangel of personal integrity, cleansing fire, and overcoming all obstacles in the way of truth

Image: In midnight blue and red, with blue and red flames in his halo and midnight blue wings, with a huge, gleaming, dark gold sword

Day: Tuesday

Time of Day: Midnight (or late evening)

Colours: Red, indigo

Fragrances: All spices, acacia, cinnamon, cypress, dragon's blood, ginger

Rules: Physical courage and strength; protection of the home, workplace, vehicles, and personal possessions; bullying; road rage or accidents while commuting; malice; mind games and psychic attack; overcoming addictions and destructive habits or bad influences; protection for all in the armed forces or security services; defense against demons

Globally: Overcoming dictators, bad prisons, and terrorism; protecting those in war zones or former war zones

Raphael

Role: Archangel of healing, the four winds, and travellers

Image: Carrying a golden vial of medicine, with a traveller's staff, dressed in the colours of early morning sunlight, a green healing ray emanating from his halo

Day: Wednesday

Time of Day: Dawn

Colours: Lemon yellow, grey, green

Fragrances: Lavender, lemongrass, lemon balm

Crystals: Ametrine, any agate, citrine, falcon's eye, yellow jasper, malachite, onyx, serpentine, white sapphire, green and lemon chrysoprase

Metals: Aluminium, platinum

Messages: Black ink on yellow paper

Rules: Restoration of health; safety on short-distance travel and relocation; protection against road or travel accidents; defense against liars, tricksters, and those with vicious tongues

Globally: Community matters, free media everywhere, and the dissemination of unbiased information

Sachiel

Role: The Divine Benefactor, archangel of charity and of good harvests

Image: Deep blue and purple, carrying sheaves of corn, with a rich purple and golden halo and blue and purple wings

Day: Thursday

Time of Day: Afternoon

Colours: Deep blue, purple

Fragrances: Honeysuckle, sandalwood, sage, sagebrush

Crystals: Azurite, blue sapphire, blue topaz, chrysocolla, lapis lazuli, sodalite, turquoise

Messages: Dark blue ink on white paper or blue ink on light purple paper

Rules: Justice and truth, long-distance travel and house moves, restoration after financial loss, redundancy, emotional breakdown, or illness

Globally: Good harvests, relieving lands where there is famine or disease, alleviating world poverty

Anael/Hanael

Role: Archangel of love and marriage who guards the gates of the west wind, usually regarded with female energies

Image: Surrounded by rose and green light, with silver wings, delicate features, and hands full of roses

Day: Friday

Time of Day: Twilight

Colours: Pink, green

Fragrance: Apple blossom, lemon verbena, rose, strawberry

Trees and Plants: Coconut, magnolia, all fruit trees

Crystals: Amethyst, emerald, jade, pink or mangano calcite, moss agate, pearl, rose quartz

Metal: Copper

Rules: Love and marriage, protection against abusive or overpossessive love or cruel lovers, loving when all hope is gone, the arts, and works for reconciliation when there is coldness or undue family pressures

Globally: Reforestation, preservation of mineral resources and earth's natural fuels

Cassiel

Role: Archangel of stillness, compassion, great thinkers, and all ancient traditions, indigenous and developed

Image: Bearded, riding a dragon, wearing dark robes with indigo flames sparking from his halo

Day: Saturday

Time of Day: Midnight (but any time after dark is fine)

Colours: Indigo, burgundy, dark purple; also brown, black, grey

Fragrances: Patchouli, sage, ivy, mimosa, tea tree

Crystals: Fossils, hematite, jet, obsidian, onyx, black tourmaline, green aventurine, Turritella agate, smoky quartz, snowflake obsidian

Metal: Pewter, lead

Rules: Restoring light in the darkness, bringing balance, patience, all slow-moving matters, practical or financial worries, problems and opportunities concerning older or disabled people, healing or alleviating chronic illnesses and overwhelming sorrow or grief, inheritance disputes, debt worries or problems with officialdom, the restoration of good luck

Globally: Conservation of ancient sites and beautiful buildings, restoration of the knowledge and homelands of indigenous peoples

Angelic Script

In the ancient magical writings there is an angelic script used for writing messages to angels and archangels and used in other forms of magical ritual. What follows are the four glyphs associated with the four main protective archangels, who are described in detail in chapter 10.

Archangel Glyphs of Uriel, Gabriel, Michael, and Raphael

You can etch these glyphs on candles to be burned or draw them in incense smoke over a protective amulet or jewellery you wear. You can also make amulets of them in melted wax or clay.

Draw them on paper or your computer screen at work for instant protection, and conceal them facing the four directions inside your home (Michael in the south, Raphael in the east, Gabriel in the west, and Uriel in the north).

Paint the sign on or draw it in incense smoke above a crystal (clear quartz for Michael, citrine for Raphael, moonstone for Gabriel, and red garnet for Uriel) and carry it in a small purse to take with you the power and protection of a particular archangel strength you need in your life.

Appendix B: Colours

You can wear the appropriate colour or carry a coloured crystal and burn candles for background protection. Make amulet bags in the colour closest to your need.

Red

Use red for all urgent or dire domestic protective needs and overcoming obstacles. Use it also for a massive surge of strength to reverse bad luck and against physical attacks, theft, fire, bullying, or threats.

Blue

Use blue for defending yourself legally or against massive injustices or attacks by officialdom. It is also for changing the balance of power when there is threat of intimidation or someone using their higher status to intimidate you. Blue helps with protection against accidents, high winds, and floods, whether natural or due to faulty plumbing.

Green

Green is the main luck-changing colour and the one for all ongoing protective needs. Use it also for protection against jealous ex-lovers, love rivals, and predators who may be trying to break up your relationship; protection against land subsidence and earth tremors; and protection while travelling.

Orange

Orange is for establishing defensive boundaries of all kinds, especially at work and against people who intrude, interfere, or attempt to control you or your life or stop you from enjoying it.

Yellow

Yellow is for all workplace defensive bags, especially against dishonesty, gossip, spite, and intrigue. Use this colour if you work from home to prevent Internet fraud and for protection from customers, people, or suppliers who try to con you or not pay you. It is also for protection against storms.

Brown

Use brown to protect against nasty neighbours, unpleasant relatives, or those connected with people whose families you have married into. Use it to guard land, property, or animals against attack of all kinds; for protection against loss of home or security by whatever means; and for safety against financial threats, whether from ex-partners or debt collectors.

Pink

Pink is for protecting the young and vulnerable and also anyone who is old or sick, as well as for prevention of illness of all kinds. Use for the protection of young animals, newborn babies, and children's rooms, to keep away all harm. Pink is good as a defense against nightmares or fears of the dark.

Purple

Use purple for defense against all forms of paranormal harm, whether unfriendly ghosts, curses, ill wishing, or other forms of mind games, psychic and psychological attack, and bullying.

Grey

Grey is for matters you need to keep hidden and for protection against intrigues, secrets, and false friends or colleagues who are openly friendly to you but who you suspect are gossiping behind your back or spreading rumours.

Appendix C: Protective Crystals

Wash crystals under running water after use and leave them to dry naturally. If they are delicate stones, spiral incense or smudge sticks over them or leave them on a plate for twenty-four hours on greenery.

Orange, Yellow, or Brown Amber

These crystals protect against negative outside influences and interference to you or family members. Amber, stone of the sun, contains the power of many suns and the souls of many tigers, and so it brings confidence and quiet courage to make your unique mark on life and to love yourself as you are, if you have been made to feel inadequate or unfairly guilty. It removes obstacles caused by others or those you put in your own way through fear, improves short-term memory, melts rigid or confrontational attitudes in the workplace.

Green and Red Bloodstone or Heliotrope

This tone represents courage to stand against individuals and organisations who seek to intimidate you. It is useful in an overcompetitive workplace or if you are pressured to achieve unrealistic targets (families can do this too).

Orange Carnelian

Orange carnelian is excellent for giving women the courage to stand up for themselves in the workplace and if unduly burdened by selfish relatives. It deters physical abuse by either sex and protects against accidents during DIY or if you work in the construction trade or have a physically hazardous job.

Red Garnet

Red garnet brings victory in the way most desired if you have faced prejudice or opposition. It melts emotional coldness and unfriendliness in a new neighbourhood or workplace, guards against emotional parasites and those who drain you of money and time, and stops pets from fretting when owners are at work.

Metallic, Shiny Grey Hematite

This crystal protects you from all harm and those at home or work who emotionally drain you. Called the lawyer's stone, hematite brings justice in legal, official, and personal matters. As a magnetic stone, hematite will repel all who wish you harm, so carry when you travel in dark or hazardous places.

Iron Pyrite

Use iron pyrite if the odds are stacked against you financially or careerwise and to guard against paranormal harm.

Red Jasper

This crystal offers strength and stamina for busy times when you cannot rest. If anything is stagnant or moving backwards, red jasper unblocks the obstruction and sets you back on the path to achievement. Use it for taking centre stage, overcoming bullies, tackling prejudice or hostility head on, and protection against physical, psychological, and paranormal attack.

Yellow Jasper

Yellow jasper protects pets and children from nasty neighbours; brings freshness to urban living; and guards against envy, spite, gossip, lies, con merchants, and false friends, as well as unfaithful partners.

Lava or Pumice (Lava with Holes)

Lava helps with protecting the home from natural disasters and intruders and attracting good luck after a spate of misfortune or illness. It also guards against accidents.

Black Onyx

Black onyx is the ultimate antipanic crystal, defusing dramas at home or in the workplace. It's good for clearing your mind if you've got to make a decision and there are lots of conflicting opinions or pressures on you. It also reduces overdependency on or by you; brings order to chaos; calms hyperactivity, perfectionism, and pressure to do ten things at once; and reduces the effects of bad influences and mind games on you or loved ones.

Cream, Yellow, and Blue Shimmering Moonstones

These prevent nightmares and negative paranormal experiences, especially at night; protect night shift workers, travellers, and commuters; and guard against those who promise much and deliver little or who lie about their identity or achievements.

Appendix D:
Protective Herbs, Roots, Incense, and Oils

You can place dried herbs you use for cooking in rooms in small bowls that you replace when the herbs are no longer fragrant. You can also buy pots of the growing herbs or burn essential oils, incense, or scented candles. Roots can be carried as part of a protection bag.

Adam and Eve Roots

The male root is pointed and the female root is round. These are for overcoming jealousy, lovers who have another secret partner, and love rivals.

Archangel Root (Angelica/Masterwort) or Dried Angelica

Try these for protection of the home and for healing sicknesses that seem to linger or pass from one family member to another. Angelica, together with olive leaves, will stop sniping and spite in the home and workplace.

Basil

Basil defends against intruders, accidents, and physical, psychological, and psychic attack. It also conquers fear of flying and is good against road rage.

Bistort

Bistort guards against spirit attack and hauntings in the home when kept in bowls or sprinkled around the home as an infusion. Put a small spoon of the dried herbs into a cup of boiling water. Stir and cover, and leave for five minutes. Strain the liquid off and use this to sprinkle round your rooms. Use it also to purify items with sad memories and artefacts from garage sales. This is an alternative to the traditional hyssop cleanser (see the hyssop infusion spell in chapter 8).

Black Snakeroot (Black Cohosh)

Black snakeroot is for courage when the odds against you are great and for overcoming human snakes.

Clover or Trefoil (Shamrock)

Clover is for banishing evil spirits and attracting good luck, especially as the four-leafed clover.

Coriander or Cumin Seeds

These protect equipment, vehicles, premises, and luggage.

Devil's Shoestring

This herb is for fighting against unfair dismissal and workplace discrimination and attracting the right employment when there is a shortage of jobs.

Dill

Dill is the ultimate anti–evil spirit herb. It guards against mind control and attempted possession by humans or spirits and is good against unfair officialdom, especially in taxation matters.

Garlic

Hang a string of bulbs in the kitchen to drive away negative ghosts and nasty humans. Every three or four months bury the garlic on the waning moon and buy some more.

Ginger

Ginger overcomes business troubles or unemployment.

Hawthorn Berries or Thorns

Use hawthorn for fierce defense against physical attack, mind games, emotional blackmail, and also fertility.

Lemongrass

This herb protects against gossip, spite, venom, and human snakes.

Lemon Peel or Oil

Lemon peel or oil prevents rumours, lies, intrigues, and dishonest actions.

High John the Conqueror

This herb (poisonous) is for overcoming poverty, debt, and constantly missed opportunities and for bringing money and major success in their place.

Low John the Conqueror

This herb (galangal) is for justice, especially in legal or custody or divorce suits and in all official matters, especially where there has been corruption; it's good for obtaining compensation.

Lucky Hand Root

Lucky hand root is for overcoming unemployment, the constant outflow of money and resources, and offering success in speculation and games of chance. Good luck.

Peppermint

Peppermint can be burned as incense at home or used as a floor wash to drive away all negativity, evil spirits, and poltergeists. Make the infusion as for bistort and add the strained liquid to warm water for a floor wash; alternatively, use a peppermint tea bag dropped in the warm water for a minute or two; squeeze and remove. Peppermint tea can be drunk to keep away bad dreams and night phantoms.

Sage or Sagebrush

These offer protection against all evil when burned as incense, smudge, or fragrance oil or when the dried herb is kept in a dish in a room till it loses its fragrance. Sage guards the home and family from nasty house ghosts. Traditionally, the herb can also be thrown on an open fire to remove sickness, sorrow, and misfortune from the home, while you say nine times, "Sorrows away."

Tarragon

Tarragon is associated with the courage and fierceness of the dragon and repeals physical attack and threats.

Appendix E:
Defensive Metals

Metal amulets are either engraved or invisibly empowered with a spoken spell or by writing over them in incense stick smoke. Charm bracelets with different charms (such as a boat for safe travel, a horseshoe for good luck and keeping away bad luck, a miniature dollar for restoring and preserving prosperity, and a heart for lasting love) linked together on the chain are among the most common and effective forms of transforming misfortune and unhappiness into good luck and joy.

Copper, the Metal of Venus

Copper protects against infidelity, jealous love rivals, destructive love, and the inability to let an abusive, cruel, or inconstant lover go; against sickness of all kinds; against infertility; and during pregnancy and childbirth, especially when there are difficulties.

Gold, the Metal of the Sun

Gold represents success, wealth, lasting love, and good fortune, so it is a powerful amulet against the loss of any of these and will bring their restoration. It is good if others challenge your authority or try to rule your life and interfere in your relationships.

Iron or Steel, the Metal of Mars

The most powerful defensive metal can be hammered into a door or furniture in the form of a metal nail or stave or stake buried in the earth, in order to protect your home and family against any kind of attack and negative earth energies. It is also used as nails in protective witch bottles (see chapter 5).

Pewter or Lead, the Metal of Saturn

Use pewter for restoring security and stability, for protection of home and property, and for regaining what has been stolen. It also works for anticruelty for animals and children. In Roman times lead was used for curse tablets, but because it is toxic, it is not used so frequently in modern banishing and binding amulets.

Silver, the Metal of the Moon

Silver protects against secrets and lies, excesses of any kind, psychic attack (both here and from the afterlife), fears and phobias, and against illusionists and those who manipulate or try to control others' minds. It guards mothers, babies, and children.

Tin, the Metal of Jupiter

Tin is for wise leadership; protection against dictators and all who abuse their power; justice, especially against large corporations or organisations or when you fight alone; and the restoration of career after redundancy or unfair treatment. It is also good for compensation.

Appendix F: Astrological Signs

Each astrological sign offers defense in different areas of life, and in protective magic they are drawn as amulets or etched or drawn invisibly on the side of the appropriately coloured candles, which are then burned to release the protection you need. You can use any of them regardless of your own personal sign. When the full moon is in a particular sign, which happens for about two and a half days each month, that is also potent for defensive work where there are obstacles to remove.

Aries, the Ram

Dates: 21 March–20 April
Symbol: ♈
Colour: Red
Uses: Antibullying, handling aggression, fears of confrontation and
   physical attack

Taurus, the Bull

Dates: 21 April–21 May
Symbol: ♉
Colour: Pink
Uses: Protecting the home from theft or vandalism, keeping possessions safe, avoiding breakages or domestic accidents, antidebt

Gemini, the Heavenly Twins

Dates: 22 May–21 June
Symbol: ♊
Colour: Yellow
Uses: Seeing through deception and con merchants, protection of computer and personal data, avoiding unwise speculation and gambling addiction

Cancer, the Crab

Dates: 22 June–22 July
Symbol: ♋
Colour: Silver
Uses: For protection of family, especially new mothers and all who are vulnerable; problems with eating, alcohol, drug, and cigarette-related disorders or excesses; protecting your physical privacy; avoiding mind manipulation by those who would intrude on your thoughts

Leo, the Lion

Dates: 23 July–23 August
Symbol: ♌
Colour: Gold
Uses: Avoiding being dominated by strong personalities, drama kings and queens, and those who use anger as a weapon to intimidate you; stopping others stealing credit for your ideas or work; stopping family members or work colleagues using you as a scapegoat or butt of their humour

Virgo, the Maiden

Dates: 24 August–22 September

Symbol: ♍

Colour: Green

Uses: Stopping pressuring yourself to be perfect and do more than your fair share of work, reducing stress and moving away from people you can never please, resisting the guilt others may try to load on you to cover their inadequacies

Libra, the Scales

Dates: 23 September–23 October

Symbol: ♎

Colour: Blue

Uses: Trying to keep the peace at the expense of yourself; overcoming injustice and unfair practise; preventing a flirtatious partner from straying; making a partner who is sitting on the fence commit, set you free, or stop trying to run two love affairs and selling you short

Scorpio, the Scorpion

Dates: 24 October–22 November

Symbol: ♏

Colour: Indigo or burgundy

Uses: Protecting yourself from the evil eye and black magic, overcoming a person who uses sex as a weapon to keep you in thrall, driving off anyone who is trying to steal your partner

Sagittarius, the Archer

Dates: 23 November–21 December

Symbol: ♐

Colour: Orange or turquoise

Uses: Safety while travelling, especially long distance or overseas; overcoming obstacles in the way of learning new things; dealing with those who pretend to be friendly but you know are waiting

to stab you in the back; curbing overspending and those who ex-
pect you to pay for everything

Capricorn, the Goat

Dates: 22 December–20 January
Symbol: ♑
Colour: Brown
Uses: Overcoming debt; succeeding in career when it is an uphill
struggle; keeping your home if you are threatened with eviction;
removing stubbornness, meanness, or prejudice in a relative or
partner who is ruining your life or a boss who refuses to pay you
what you are worth

Aquarius, the Water Carrier

Dates: 21 January–18 February
Symbol: ♒
Colour: Purple
Uses: Overcoming excesses of all kinds in self or others; protecting
yourself from hurt with a cold or detached partner who is always
too busy for you (or maybe walking away); dealing with friends
of your partner or family members who are leading them into bad
ways or a partner who is taking a family member or children away
from the family, maybe after a divorce

Pisces, the Fish

Dates: 19 February–20 March
Symbol: ♓
Colour: Soft white
Uses: Seeing through illusions and impossible dreams in others that
get in the way of reality, avoiding being swept away by the emotional demands of others or their constant life crises, avoiding the
temptation to take the shortcut or cheat and hope you will not be
found out

Appendix G:
Defensive Egyptian Amulets and Symbols

The ancient Egyptians were the first to use amulets and charms in formal magic, and so they have exerted great influence over modern usage. They empowered symbols like crystals or clay figures with magical words and substances like incense and carried the amulet with them and invoked from the deities and ancestors power and protection from the cradle to grave and then into the afterlife.

We have already met the hieroglyph of the Eye of Horus that deflects the evil eye (see chapter 9). A hieroglyph releases the power of its meaning when written or etched magically and carried or worn. You can draw your own hieroglyph charms on parchment, linen, or good-quality white or dark paper with fine coloured-ink pens, acrylic paint, or glass paint and hide these around your home or workplace.

If made very small, your chosen hieroglyph can be rolled into a scroll to wear in a metal tube round your neck or kept in a clear bottle, half-filled with dried rose petals or lavender heads. Alternatively, empower crystals or jewellery by drawing the hieroglyph in incense smoke over the symbol or with the index finger of the hand you write with.

The Ba or Spirit

Ba Hieroglyph

Ba, a hawk with a human head, represented the part of the spirit of the deceased that flew out of the mummified body and gave life to the spirit body that dwelled with the blessed dead. The hawk image linked it to Horus, the falcon-headed god.

Use Ba for freedom from restrictions, oppression, destructive relationships, and fears and phobias, as well as protection against criticism and those that unfairly block your path.

Djed, Tet, or Backbone of Osiris

Djed Hieroglyph

The Djed represented the trunk of the plant that grew round the wooden chest containing the murdered body of Osiris, the Father God and husband of Isis, which, empowered with his strength, grew into a mighty tree.

Djed is for physical and emotional strength and endurance, protection against all harm and fears, resistance to pressure or coercion, antibullying and all matters of justice, prevention of deceit or betrayal, and defending the home from intruders and the family from ill wishers.

The Scarab

Scarab Hieroglyph

Sacred to Khepri, the god of the sun at dawn, who was depicted as scarab headed, this amulet was a profound symbol of rebirth to the Egyptians. *Khepri* means "he who is coming into being," and Khepri was likewise said to roll the ball of the sun across the sky, bringing each new day.

Khepri is for restoration of what has been lost or taken unfairly from you, especially careerwise or financially; protection against all harm and fighting illness or depression; and transformation of a seemingly hopeless situation.

Shen

Shen Hieroglyph

Shen represents the orbit of the sun around the earth and so was a symbol of endless time. As an amulet placed upon the dead, it promised eternal life so long as the sun endured.

Use Shen for career and business security if under threat, safety within the home and from external attack, better days ahead, protection against sudden loss of any kind, and relationships under stress through a third party or jealousy by exes and relatives.

Tjet or Buckle of Isis

Tjet Hieroglyph

This amulet represents the buckle of the girdle of Isis and is associated with the fertilising blood of Isis. There are numerous ancient chants that have passed from the funerary texts into popular folk tradition that can be woven into a protective chant to empower this amulet; one such chant begins, "The blood of Isis and the power of Isis and the words of Isis make me strong."

This is the ultimate female power hieroglyph for all matters of loss or lack of female power; protection against abuse, inequality, and discrimination of all kinds; the restoration of lost love; and defending women against jealousy, spite, and slander.

The Vulture

Vulture Hieroglyph

The Vulture hieroglyph represents the protection and power of the Divine Mother Isis and was used as protection for the deceased with the ankh, the hieroglyph for life, engraved on each talon.

Isis demonstrated the power of maternal protection when she cared for her son Horus in the marshes, guarding him against his evil uncle Set, who would have destroyed him. Her wings were also outstretched, shielding Osiris and the pharaohs.

This Vulture is for protection against all harm from whatever source, freedom from illusion, starting again under difficulty, successful major life changes, banishing what is destructive, and overcoming addictions. It is good for travel, especially by air or long distance, and for safe pregnancy, childbirth, mothers, and children of any age.

Appendix H:
Protective Pentagrams

Use the eight elemental pentagrams for protection from earthly and paranormal harm and for power. Create a pentagram shape drawn from the point shown for the required element in the eight pentagrams that follow according to whether you want to banish or protect or to attract the power of a particular element into your working, social, family, or love life. You can draw it in the air or invisibly over artefacts or jewellery using incense sticks or the index finger of the hand you write with.

For total power and protection, use the banishing aspect of the chosen element to remove sorrow and misfortune, and afterwards trace the attracting or invoking elemental form over it, to replace negative with positive, an often forgotten aspect of defensive magic.

Earth

The banishing earth pentagram protects you from all harm, whether paranormal or earthly, and from physical attack. It offers you stability if you feel insecure, reduces financial worries, and slows you down if you are getting too hyped up. Some people find it helpful for chronic pain relief.

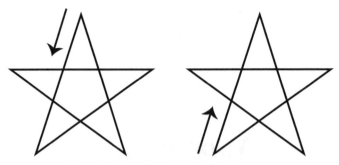

Invoking Earth and Banishing Earth Pentagrams

An invoking earth pentagram brings your practical abilities to the fore, attracts money, helps you to care for others if you are tired, and offers tangible results for ventures. It is good if you are seeking improvement in domestic or property matters or finance.

Air

The banishing air pentagram repels gossip, spite, sarcasm, and lies and brings you back in touch with your true feelings, your instincts, and life if you feel detached or alone.

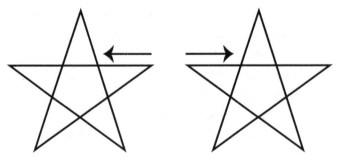

Invoking Air and Banishing Air Pentagrams

The invoking air pentagram brings logic; helps you to remember facts, figures, and where you should be; and helps you communicate clearly. It also helps conventional medicine or surgery be more effective.

Fire

The banishing fire pentagram guards against anger, your own and that of others, and is protective if you have to deal with a bully or abuse in your life or workplace. It is a good survival pentagram.

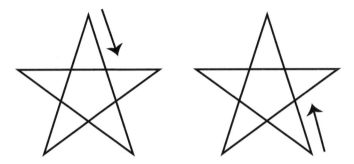

Invoking Fire and Banishing Fire Pentagrams

The invoking fire pentagram brings inspiration, illumination, courage, passion, and creativity and assists you to make changes.

Water

The banishing water pentagram is excellent defense if you are emotionally blackmailed, manipulated, made to feel guilty, or swamped by your own or the emotions of others. It is good to counteract possessiveness.

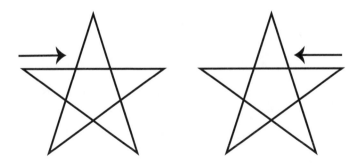

Invoking Water and Banishing Water Pentagrams

The invoking water pentagram attracts love and friendship; opens your spiritual gifts, imagination, and intuition; brings healing, especially using alternative, spiritual methods; and encourages growth.

Appendix I:
Protective Runes

Like hieroglyphs, runic symbols, beloved of the Vikings, release their power when drawn, etched, or worn. Traditionally, they were made of wood (a sliced-up broom handle is ideal), or you can scrape the bark off twigs. They are also drawn on smooth, small, oval or round stones in red (originally blood, but not recommended).

You can etch your chosen rune on wood using an electric wood-burning tool or scrape out the shape with an awl and paint the indentation red. On stone you can paint or draw runes with a permanent red marker.

If you wish, you can buy a ready-made set painted on crystal to use as amulets. I have listed several runes here, in the order they appear in the rune sets. These are the Viking (Elder Futhark) runes, but the Anglo-Saxon and Icelandic versions are slightly different.

ᚢ Uruz: Wild Cattle, Primal Strength

The horns of these huge, untameable, fierce oxen that galloped across the plains of Scandinavia till the mid-1600s were, according to myth, worn on Viking helmets to transfer the strength of the creature to warriors.

Uruz is for successful business risks and speculation when it is an all-or-nothing situation; improving health when the prognosis is not good; making a huge effort to overcome obstacles; and strength and courage in the face of adversity or a major force of opposition.

Þ Thurisaz: The Hammer of Thor

The hammer of Thor, the thunder god, defended the deities against the frost giants and became a sacred symbol at marriages, births, and funerals.

Thurisaz is for fierce protection against human nastiness and physical threats as well as evil spirits in the home; escaping the fall-out of conflicts; overcoming infertility and impotency; defeating love rivals, especially after you have been married for some years; and uncovering secrets or deceptions that affect your well-being.

R Raidho: The Wheel, the Wagon, Riding

Raidho is the long and dangerous but exciting ride after the inaction of winter and also the sun moving through the year.

Use it for safety while travelling, especially to places of potential danger; success in legal matters when the odds seem against you; the need to seize opportunity, even in less than ideal circumstances; preventing accidents and road rage attacks, especially for long-distance drivers, if kept in a vehicle; life after losing your home.

H Hagalaz, Hail

Hagalaz is the rune of the cosmic seed, the ice that met the fire in creation, the frozen seed within that melts to bring life-giving water. Use it for embracing and surviving necessary change or disruption by natural events, and, within a few months, transformation and rewards will result. It is also for overcoming unfair exclusion from the family or socially because of your beliefs, chosen lifestyle, or being made the scapegoat for family ills, perhaps from early childhood. Use it also to quit a bad habit or overcome a fear or phobia.

ᚾ Naudhiz: The Need or Ritual Fire

Naudhiz is the wooden spindle that generates the festival fire by friction to release, it was believed, the fire within the wood, and it is therefore represents both self-generation and the passion of fire.

Naudhiz is for overcoming love issues where love is complicated through other relationships or the need for secrecy; resisting temptation to stray from an established relationship; starting your own business in a difficult climate or oversubscribed field; and freedom and independence if you are being stifled at work or home.

ᛁ Isa: Ice

Isa is the rune of ice, the fifth element in the Norse tradition, and is associated with an ice bridge between dimensions that needs to be negotiated with care but must be crossed before the ice melts.

Use isa for overcoming family estrangements and coldness; protecting yourself in a situation where all you can do is wait for the right time to leave; surviving against seemingly impossible odds; and the release of hostages, prisoners of conscience, and those imprisoned in abusive situations who cannot free themselves.

◇ Ingwaz: The Protective God of the Land

Ing or Frey drove his wagon over the fields after the winter to release the creative potential of the soil. He was also protective god of the hearth. His symbol was often fixed in iron in the side of a house in Northern Europe and Scandinavia for protection from bad weather.

Ingwaz is for protection of the home and all within from fire, storms, earthquake, floods, intruders, nasty neighbours, and malevolent ghosts; antidote to infertility and impotency; preventing the draining of money and resources and the inflow of new sources of revenue; and calling missing animals home.

Recommended Reading

Buckland, Raymond. *Advanced Candle Magic: More Spells and Rituals for Every Purpose.* St. Paul, MN: Llewellyn Worldwide, 1996.

Budge, E. A. Wallis. *Amulets and Superstitions, the Original Texts with Translations and Descriptions of a Long Series of Egyptian, Sumerian, Assyrian, Hebrew, Christian, Gnostic and Muslim Amulets and Talismans and Magical Figures...* New York: Dover Publications, 1978.

———. *Egyptian Magic: A History of Ancient Egyptian Magical Practices Including Amulets, Names, Enchantments, Figures, Formulae, Supernatural Ceremonies, and Words of Power.* New York: Random House Value Publications, 1991.

Canard, John. *Defences Against the Witches' Craft.* Glastonbury, UK: Avalonia Press, 2008.

Collins, Derek. *Magic in the Ancient Greek World.* Malden, MA: Wiley-Blackwell, 2008.

Connolly, S. *Curses, Hexes & Crossing: A Magician's Guide to Execration Magick.* CreateSpace Independent Publishing Platform, 2011.

Cunningham, Scott. *The Complete Book of Incense, Oils & Brews.* St. Paul, MN: Llewellyn Publications, 2002.

———. *Cunningham's Encyclopedia of Magical Herbs*. St. Paul, MN: Llewellyn Publications, 1985.

Dundes, Alan, ed. *The Evil Eye: A Casebook*. Madison: University of Wisconsin Press, 1992.

Eason, Cassandra. *Alchemy at Work: Using the Ancient Arts to Enhance Your Work Life*. Berkeley, CA: The Crossing Press, 2004.

———. *Ancient Egyptian Magic: Classic Healing and Ritual for the 21st Century*. London: Vega, 2003.

———. *Angel Magic: A Hands-On Guide to Inviting Divine Help into Your Everyday Life*. Woodbury, MN: Llewellyn Publications, 2010.

———. *The Art of the Pendulum: Simple Techniques to Help You Make Decisions, Find Lost Objects, and Channel Healing Energies*. Boston, MA: Weiser Books, 2006.

———. *Becoming Clairvoyant: Develop Your Psychic Abilities to See into the Future*. London: Piatkus Books, 2008.

———. *The Illustrated Directory of Healing Crystals: A Comprehensive Guide to 150 Crystals and Gemstones*. London: Collins and Brown, 2015.

———. *The Modern-Day Druidess: Discover Ancient Wisdom, Prophetic Power, and Healing Arts*. London: Piatkus Books, 2003.

Fortune, Dion. *Psychic Self-Defense*. San Francisco, CA: Weiser Books, 2011.

Hester, Ben G. *Dowsing: An Exposé of Hidden Occult Forces*. Self-published, 1984. At Issue. http://www.sdanet.org/atissue/books/dowsing/d01.htm#12.

Matthews, Caitlín. *Psychic Shield: The Personal Handbook of Psychic Protection*. Berkeley, CA: Ulysses Press, 2008.

Penczak, Christopher. *The Witch's Shield: Protection Magick & Psychic Self-Defense*. St. Paul, MN: Llewellyn Worldwide, 2004.

Penry, Tylluan. *Knot Magic*. Tonypandy, Cardiff, Wales: Wolfenhowle Press, 2015.

Sullivan, Danny. *Ley Lines: The Greatest Landscape Mystery*. Somerset, UK: Green Magic, 2004.

Thomsen, Marie-Louise. "The Evil Eye in Mesopotamia." *Journal of Near Eastern Studies* 51, no. 1 (1992): 19–32. http://www.academicroom.com/article/evil-eye-mesopotamia.

Thorsson, Edred. *Futhark: A Handbook of Rune Magic.* York Beach, ME: Weiser Books, 1984.

Thurnell-Read, Jane. *Geopathic Stress & Subtle Energy.* Penzance, Cornwall, UK: Life-Work Potential, 2006.

To Write to the Author

If you wish to contact the author or would like more information about this book, please write to the author in care of Llewellyn Worldwide Ltd. and we will forward your request. Both the author and publisher appreciate hearing from you and learning of your enjoyment of this book and how it has helped you. Llewellyn Worldwide Ltd. cannot guarantee that every letter written to the author can be answered, but all will be forwarded. Please write to:

Cassandra Eason
℅ Llewellyn Worldwide
2143 Wooddale Drive
Woodbury, MN 55125-2989

Please enclose a self-addressed stamped envelope for reply,
or $1.00 to cover costs. If outside the U.S.A., enclose
an international postal reply coupon.

Many of Llewellyn's authors have websites with additional information and resources. For more information, please visit our website at http://www.llewellyn.com.